The Struggle for Equal Adulthood

THE STRUGGLE FOR
Equal Adulthood

*Gender, Race, Age, and the Fight for
Citizenship in Antebellum America*

Corinne T. Field

The University of North Carolina Press / Chapel Hill

This volume was published with the assistance of the
Greensboro Women's Fund of the University of North Carolina Press.
Founding Contributors:
Linda Arnold Carlisle, Sally Schindel Cone, Anne Faircloth, Bonnie McElveen Hunter,
Linda Bullard Jennings, Janice J. Kerley (in honor of Margaret Supplee Smith),
Nancy Rouzer May, and Betty Hughes Nichols.

Set in Miller by codeMantra
Manufactured in the United States of America

The University of North Carolina Press has been a member
of the Green Press Initiative since 2003.

Library of Congress Cataloging-in-Publication Data
Field, Corinne T.
The struggle for equal adulthood : gender, race, age, and the fight for citizenship in the
antebellum United States / Corinne T. Field.
pages cm. — (Gender and American culture)
Includes bibliographical references and index.
ISBN 978-1-4696-1814-2 (pbk   ) — ISBN 978-1-4696-1815-9 (ebook)
1. Citizenship—United States—History—19th century. 2. Adulthood—United States—
History—19th century. 3. Equality before the law—United States—History—19th century.
4. United States—Politics and government—History—19th century. I. Title.
JK1759.F43 2014
323.0973'09034—dc23
2014008430
18 17 16 15 14   5 4 3 2 1

Portions of this book were previously published in the following articles:
"'Are Women . . . All Minors?': Woman's Rights and the Politics of Aging in the
Antebellum United States," *Journal of Women's History* 12 (2001): 113–37;
© 2001 *Journal of Women's History*. "'Made Women of When They Are Mere Children':
Mary Wollstonecraft's Critique of Eighteenth-Century Girlhood,"
Journal of the History of Childhood and Youth 4 (Spring 2011): 197–222;
© 2011 by The Johns Hopkins University Press. Both used with
permission from The Johns Hopkins University Press.

For Lynne, Thea, Phoebe, and Elliot

CONTENTS

FIGURES

ACKNOWLEDGMENTS

This project began at Columbia University, where I was lucky to work with Elizabeth Blackmar, who has remained the most encouraging, intellectually challenging, and insightful of colleagues over these many years. Rosalind Rosenberg, Alice Kessler-Harris, Eric Foner, and Farah Jasmine Griffin fundamentally shaped this project. Members of the Black Women's Intellectual and Cultural History Collective, organized by Farah Griffin, Barbara Savage, Martha Jones, and Mia Bay, met my ideal of a scholarly community and sustained this work.

I am most grateful for the support of the Schlesinger Library, Radcliffe Institute, Harvard University; the Virginia Foundation for the Humanities; and the Institute for Advanced Studies in Culture, University of Virginia. Working at the Schlesinger was an intellectual delight thanks to the marvelous staff, especially Diane Hamer and Ellen Shea. At the VFH, Robert Vaughan, Hilary Holladay, Paula Marie Seniors, Jerome Handler, and William Freehling, among many others, sustained this work at a crucial juncture. The vibrant community at IASC—including James Davison Hunter, Talbot Brewer, and Murray Milner—encouraged me to consider the interdisciplinary implications of this research.

This book was vastly improved by the excellent advice of Barbara Savage and the anonymous reviewer for the University of North Carolina Press, series editors Thadious Davis and Mary Kelley, and my editor Charles Grench. I thank Paul Betz and Lucas Church for their editorial assistance and Julie Bush for her excellent copyediting. While completing this project, I began editing a book on chronological age with Nicholas Syrett. His willingness to discuss the complexities and contradictions of nineteenth-century age qualifications has greatly improved this book, as has the opportunity to read the scholarship of the contributors to that volume, especially the work of Sharon Sundue, Jon Grinspan, James Schmidt, Shane Landrum, William Graebner, Andrew Achenbaum, Timothy Cole, and Rebecca de Schweinitz.

At conferences, I received advice and insight from Matthew Gallman, Kathi Kern, Paula Fass, Patrick Ryan, Jesse Ballenger, Stephen Katz, John Gillis, Kristin Hoganson, Allison Sneider, Lisa Tetrault, Elsa

Barkley Brown, Michele Mitchell, Rosemarie Zagarri, Anya Jabour, Karen Sanchez-Eppler, Leslie Paris, and Lakisha Michelle Simmons. Margaret Morganroth Gullette, Sally Schwager, Sally Roesch Wagner, Eileen Boris, and Cindy Aron generously commented on various parts of this project. Patricia Sullivan helped immeasurably. Ann Gordon clarified my understanding of Elizabeth Cady Stanton and pointed me to valuable sources. The editors and anonymous readers of the *Journal of Women's History* and the *Journal of the History of Childhood and Youth* greatly improved my argument. Becky Thomas, Jane Barnes, and Alec Hickmott provided wonderful editing.

Friends and colleagues at Columbia helped frame my ideas, especially Lara Vapnek, Francesca Morgan, Hampton Carey, Eliza Byard, Margaret Garb, Michael Sappol, and Jeffrey Sklansky. I am most grateful to Ann Lane, Paul Halliday, and Charlotte Patterson for opportunities to teach at the University of Virginia, where Denise Walsh, Jennifer Petersen, and Jennifer Rubenstein welcomed me into their writing group. Faculty in the Corcoran Department of History and the Women, Gender, Sexuality Program have encouraged my teaching and research, most especially Farzaneh Milani, Brian Balogh, Alon Confino, John Mason, Brian Owensby, Elizabeth Thompson, and Olivier Zunz, as have graduate students and undergraduates, including Willa Brown, Emily Senefeld, and Bayly Buck. Jeanne Amster, Anthony Rotundo, and Kathleen Dalton long ago inspired me to pursue this course of study.

The greatest joy of living in Charlottesville is the sustaining network of great scholars who are also great friends. Grace Hale, Lawrie Balfour, Anna Brickhouse, Bonnie Gordon, and Elizabeth Wittner are all able to talk feminist theory while running fast, uphill, in the rain. Without them and their partners—William Wylie, Chad Dodson, Bruce Holsinger, Manuel Lerdau, and John Pepper—I never would have crossed this finish line. Sophia Rosenfeld and Matthew Affron improved my scholarship and sustained my spirit. Maurie McInnis, Martien Halvorson-Taylor, and Allison Pugh shared citations and good fun in equal measure, for which thanks also go to Dean Johnson, Neal Halvorson-Taylor, and Steve Sellers.

My family and I are supported by a wonderful community, including Kevin and Elizabeth O'Halloran, Jeffrey and Janet Legro, John and Barbara Ciambotti, Francesca Fiorani, Deborah Cohn, and Saphira Baker. I am grateful to the friends who have kept in touch over many years, urged me on, and, most important, taught me the value of deep and lasting connections. My thanks go especially to Brigid Doherty, Paolo Morante, Gregory Fukutomi, Phoebe Barnard, Hilary Krane, Kelly Bulkeley, Alisa

Dworsky, Danny Sagan, Anja Hanson, Derek Pierce, Electa Sevier, Phoebe Brown, Elizabeth McHenry, Christina McHenry, Rachel Simons, Phoebe Roosevelt, Catherine and Jay Fields, Svetlana Prudnikova, Celia Imrey, Claire Ganz, Lauren Taylor, Amira Thoron, Daphne Cunningham, Linsey Lee, and Brendan O'Neill.

I have been able to write this book and raise three children thanks to the people who provided loving, reliable, and fun care for my children. On the deepest level, my thanks go to Molly Joseph, Elizabeth Horgan, Corinne Dugan, Sergei Sergeev, and Alla Potemkina.

It is my great good fortune to have fallen in love with Philippe Sommer, to build a life with him, and to be welcomed into his family, most especially by his sons Daniel and Alex and daughter-in-law Jill. I am grateful to my stepfather, Richard Brickley, for always encouraging me and my work.

My mother, Lynne Brickley, a historian of female education, framed my understanding of women's history and generational relations, influencing both the questions I asked and the answers I found. My children, Thea, Phoebe, and Elliot, challenged me to think more deeply about the issues in this book and why they matter. In the spirit of intergenerational alliance, for which the activists studied here fought so hard, I dedicate this book to them.

The Struggle for Equal Adulthood

INTRODUCTION

In her influential 1845 book *Woman in the Nineteenth Century*, Margaret Fuller surveyed the condition of women in the United States and northern Europe and concluded, "There is no woman, only an overgrown child."[1] Fuller focused on the difference between childhood and adulthood because doing so enabled her to demand profound changes in both public and private forms of power. For example, she critiqued laws that treated the wife "as if she were a child, or ward only," and black people as if they were property but insisted that such laws would not change so long as "there exists in the minds of men a tone of feeling toward women as toward slaves, such as is expressed in the common phrase, 'Tell that to women and children.'"[2] This connection between law and feeling was, for Fuller, the crux of the problem facing the disenfranchised and the reason she focused on maturity. By pointing to the ways in which white men infantilized women and enslaved people, Fuller related politics, law, and economics to sexual desire, family dynamics, and personal aspirations. Much as a later generation of white feminists in the 1960s would deploy the slogan "the personal is political," Fuller urged her readers to connect their individual lives to larger issues, but she did so in a particular way: by urging black men and all women to demand recognition as adults.

Fuller was one of the most articulate champions of what can be called equal adulthood—that is, the idea that all human beings, regardless of race or sex, should be able to claim the same rights, opportunities, and respect as they age. But she was not alone. From the first tentative claims to independence made by black people and white women during the late eighteenth century to the campaign for equal citizenship during Reconstruction, the demand that women should be recognized as adults, rather than classed with children, shaped both the successes and failures of the women's rights movement, particularly the potential for interracial and cross-class alliances.[3] At certain moments—such as during the women's rights conventions of the late 1840s and at the founding of the American Equal Rights Association in 1866—activists unified around the demand that state governments apply age qualifications equally to all citizens regardless of sex, race, or class. At other times, most notably during the later years of Reconstruction but earlier as well, activists relied upon comparative hierarchies of wealth, education, or cultural refinement that construed some adults as more mature than others, thus infantilizing rather than cooperating with potential allies. As Reconstruction drew to a close, women's rights activists failed to achieve equal adulthood for all American citizens in large part because many white men continued to treat black men and all women like children, but also because activists themselves adopted hierarchical measures of individual development that did more to divide than to unite the majority of American citizens who lacked the rights, opportunities, and respect claimed by adult white men.

This book offers a fresh interpretation of familiar feminist thinkers such as Mary Wollstonecraft, Maria Stewart, Elizabeth Cady Stanton, Frederick Douglass, and Frances Harper by focusing on their claims to equal adulthood. Why these activists were so concerned with adulthood becomes clear through an investigation of chronological age, maturity, and generational relations as represented in state constitutional conventions, popular art, literature, advice books, and the writings of leading political theorists such as John Locke, Thomas Jefferson, and Auguste Comte.

From the 1770s to the 1870s, advocates for women's rights fought the persistent association of women with children, protested the praise lavished on girlish beauty rather than on female wisdom, and demanded the right to develop their talents as they aged.[4] Their ideas about adulthood are complex, controversial, and sometimes shocking. They fought for what Wollstonecraft called women's need to "unfold their faculties," what Harper described in terms of achieving moral maturity, and what Stanton succinctly stated as a woman's "right to grow old."[5] Their struggle for equal adulthood encompassed political and economic rights but also reached into the most private parts of the human soul where our erotic desires, individual aspirations, and sense of ourselves are formed.

What united these thinkers was a shared set of questions: if all human beings grew up and grew old, why couldn't they claim the same rights and opportunities as they aged?[6] Why did maturity differ for white men, black men, and all women? In particular, why was women's beauty thought to fade early in life while men often gained sexual allure? Was this difference natural, or was female development distorted to please men?[7] As white boys matured, why did they gain not only rights to themselves but also rights to other people—rights to the labor and person of their wives, rights to children they sired, rights to represent their wives and children in politics and in law?[8] Why did the children of slave owners grow up to own the children of slaves?[9] In short, why did law and public opinion assume that white boys would outgrow their childish dependence to become independent citizens while their sisters and enslaved peers would remain dependent throughout their lives? Women's rights activists gave markedly different answers to these questions, but all agreed that there were fundamental links between maturity, liberty, and equality.

Recovering women's rights activists' struggle for equal adulthood accomplishes three things. First, by examining adulthood rather than gender or race per se, this book returns African American activists and intellectuals to their central place within the mainstream of the American women's rights movement. As other scholars have noted, racial prejudice and segregation often divided white and black reformers from each other. But this does not mean, as others have sometimes suggested, that black people stood on the margins of a philosophical tradition dominated by whites. Rather, white and black activists developed their ideas through spirited debate and mutual influence. While not ignoring racial, class, or regional difference, a diverse range of activists nonetheless conceptualized themselves as linked together through a shared infantilization perpetuated by adult white men in public and private life. From the Revolution to Reconstruction—and beyond—black and white women's rights activists together debated how best to counter the widespread classification of adults with children.[10]

Second, where other scholars employ a conceptual divide between public and private spheres to explain the construction of democratic citizenship, I argue that the political significance of adulthood was precisely that it conferred status in both public and private. Historians analyzing gender in the eighteenth- and nineteenth-century Atlantic world have effectively employed spatial metaphors to describe the separation of politics from family life and the home from the market and, most recently, to demarcate civil society as an arena in which private individuals influenced public opinion. Their research demonstrates how women achieved increased influence in families and civil society over the course of the eighteenth and nineteenth centuries, even as they failed to win equal rights or economic parity.[11]

In sharp contrast to modern scholars, however, the activist intellectuals we will meet in this book were less concerned with spheres of activity than with individual development over the course of life. They argued that as long as men infantilized women and women obliged by behaving like overgrown children, most women would make poor wives and mothers as well as inferior citizens. These advocates for equal adulthood also contended that black people could not exercise a positive influence in public or private life as long as they were confined by slavery and racial prejudice to perpetual servitude. Only by gaining the freedom to develop as fully realized adults, these activists argued, could women or black people build strong families, cultivate civic virtue, pursue prosperity, or ensure the progress of democracy. In short, every individual needed to grow up before he or she could exercise a positive influence in any sphere of activity.

Perhaps most important, analyzing the struggle for equal adulthood helps explain the collaborations and conflicts between various factions within the organized women's rights movement. The third argument of this book is that when leaders focused on claiming equal rights for all adults, they were able to unify a diverse range of reformers, but when they turned to hierarchical measures of maturity, they exacerbated divisions within the movement by infantilizing each other.[12] Their focus on maturity was a double-edged sword that could unify women with their male peers but also divide privileged women from those who could be construed as more childlike. Because of these divisions within the women's rights movement and, more important, because of the tenacity with which white men clung to their monopoly on adult citizenship, the struggle for equal adulthood failed. Black and white women made tremendous gains in education, employment, and political influence; free black communities flourished; and the federal government ended slavery, but white men nonetheless retained laws and cultural practices that classified all women and men of color with children. At the end of this period as at the beginning, white boys grew up to claim rights and respect denied to the majority of their peers. But the question of who counted as an adult was always contested and never fully resolved. By listening carefully to debates about what it meant to be a mature person, we can better appreciate how understandings of adulthood shaped claims for democratic rights and freedoms and, perhaps more surprisingly, how democratic ideals have shaped what it means to grow up and grow old.[13]

The early women's rights movement was not *about* adulthood, any more than it was about the vote, jobs, sexuality, or marriage. Women's rights activists were a diverse lot who championed a myriad of causes, from socialism to vegetarianism.[14] Amid these wide-ranging debates, however, they kept returning to what I have called the struggle for equal adulthood because paying attention to individual maturation allowed them to connect otherwise disparate demands for political rights, control of their own labor, sexual autonomy, cultural power, and familial authority—all of which were things adult white men claimed for themselves but regularly denied to children, men who were not white, and all women. In other words, women's rights activists employed ideas about equal adulthood instrumentally as a means to draw connections between public and private relations.

The activists and intellectuals who figure in this story were those who responded most vocally to ideas about the political significance of maturity first articulated in the late seventeenth century. They lived in the Northeast and Midwest. Most were born into the middle ranks of society, with successful farmers, merchants, or professionals in their families. Many suffered financial reversals and economic privation. A few were wealthy. Most of the black people who joined the women's rights movement were freeborn members of the northern black elite, but a few were former slaves. The vast majority of these activists were Protestant, though many hailed from the more egalitarian wings of Quakerism and Unitarianism or joined new movements such as spiritualism. What they had in common, more than anything, was a self-defined identity as public advocates of African American and women's rights and a keen interest in the question of who counted as a mature citizen.[15]

A central problem for these nineteenth-century activists, as for scholars today, is that there is no English word to denote a life stage for women equivalent to manhood.[16] English writers from the early medieval period onward translated the Latin term *juventus* (mature adulthood, the prime of life) as "manhood."[17] The gender-neutral term "adult" entered the English language in the sixteenth century, when Protestant debates over who could assent to church membership led to a distinction between infant and adult baptism. When discussing a person's right to give consent to government, however, seventeenth- and eighteenth-century political theorists did not use the term "adult." Rather, they discussed the transition from childhood to manhood.[18] Significantly, this was also the period when "manhood" became a euphemism for the male genitals.[19] By the time Mary Wollstonecraft wrote her *Vindication of the Rights of Woman* in 1792, "manhood" had a sex-specific meaning that drew attention to both the legal standing and sexual potency of mature males. The establishment of "manhood suffrage" in the United States further narrowed the meaning of the term to apply only to white males over the age of twenty-one. Nineteenth-century women's rights activists' struggle to conceptualize a stage of life for women and people of color that would bring the same rights, privileges, and respect accorded adult white men is the subject of this book. As I will show, different activists employed a variety of words, metaphors, and descriptions to convey their particular visions of black and female maturity. I have chosen the rubric of equal adulthood, my own phrase, as a label that can contain the full variety of these visions without privileging any particular terminology.[20]

For the purposes of analysis, it is useful to disaggregate three distinct but interrelated ways women's rights activists talked about equal adulthood. First, they contended that age qualifications in law should apply equally to all citizens regardless of sex or race. Second, they employed temporal metaphors of individual development over the course of life to challenge the spatial metaphors of separate spheres for the sexes and segregation for races. Third, they invoked the language of generational relations to insist that all children—not just white sons—should grow up to become the equals of white fathers.

Of these three ways of talking about equal adulthood, the argument that state governments should apply age qualifications equally to all citizens was the most straightforward. State governments relied on age qualifications to determine who had the right to vote, serve on juries, sign contracts, and marry, as well as who had the obligation to register for militia duty and pay poll taxes. State governments applied these age qualifications differently to male and female, black and white, enslaved and free people—for example, allowing white girls to marry at younger ages than white boys while barring enslaved citizens from marrying at all.[21] Black and white women's rights activists argued that age qualifications should apply in the same way to everyone, focusing particular attention on the age of marriage and contract. It was in debates over suffrage, however, that the political significance of chronological age became most salient.

In the first decades of the nineteenth century, delegates to state constitutional conventions eliminated property qualifications for suffrage while retaining the requirement that electors be twenty-one years of age or older.[22] As a result, voting at age twenty-one became both a political right and a rite of passage for white men but not for most black men or any women. Free black men immediately organized to demand recognition as "men" entitled to vote along with their white male peers.[23] Black and white women's rights activists went even further, arguing that age should trump both race and sex in the distribution of political rights. As Susan B. Anthony told delegates to the New York state constitutional convention of 1867, "If you have the right to vote at 21 years, then I have. All we ask is that you should let down the bars, and let us women and negroes in."[24]

The salience of chronological age in suffrage debates is surprising given that social and cultural historians have persuasively argued that age had little relevance in daily life. In the nineteenth century, freeborn Americans left home, completed school, started paid work, and married at widely varying ages, ranging from their early teens to late twenties. Indeed, until well into the twentieth century, significant numbers of people, enslaved and free, did not know how old they were.[25] In this book, I argue that age twenty-one took on political significance because even though people understood chronological age to be arbitrary and often unknowable, they nonetheless regarded it as a necessary boundary to full citizenship: arbitrary because there was no real or even perceptible difference between young white men in their late teens and those over twenty-one; necessary because without some age qualification, young children would have to be admitted to the polls, a contingency that even the most radical champions of universal suffrage did not support. This shared understanding of age as an arbitrary but necessary distinction led women's rights activists and their opponents to very different conclusions. Advocates for women's rights argued that if something as arbitrary as turning twenty-one qualified white males to vote, then it should qualify black males and all females as well. Conservatives seeking to block or limit the expansion of voting rights countered that the acceptance of age twenty-one as a requirement for electors proved that state governments could constitutionally and morally impose other qualifications as well—even if those might prove to be equally arbitrary. This conservative view had far greater traction throughout this period as politicians and jurists insisted that voting was not a natural right that all adults could claim but a privilege that states could regulate as they saw fit.[26]

Women's rights activists did not always conceptualize adulthood in terms of chronological age, however. They also deployed metaphors of individual development over the course of life, metaphors that stressed maturity as an ongoing process from birth to death. It was quite common for

Americans in the nineteenth century to conceive of human life both as a series of distinct stages and as an ongoing journey.[27] What made women's rights activists unique was their insistence that black men and all women could not develop their full potential over the course of life as long as white men imposed restrictions based on race and sex. As Margaret Fuller explained: "We would have every arbitrary barrier thrown down. We would have every path laid open to Woman as freely as to Man."[28] Or, as activist Lucy Stone announced in 1851, "Laying her hand upon the helm, let woman steer straight onward to the fulfillment of her own destiny."[29] By invoking temporal metaphors of life as a path or voyage, women's rights activists challenged the spatial metaphors embedded in the twin ideologies of separate spheres for the sexes and segregation of the races. These activists argued that no human being could develop over the course of life if forced by law and public opinion to remain within a confined sphere.[30]

The measures of individual development employed by women's rights activists and their opponents changed over time. In the eighteenth century, people tended to emphasize the development of reason as a prerequisite for individual autonomy. In the nineteenth century, Americans shifted their attention to political rights as a cornerstone of white manhood citizenship. As these measures of adult autonomy shifted, so did the rhetoric and strategies of women's rights activists. What did not change was the proposition that women as well as men, black as well as white, should be able to gain recognition as mature citizens, whatever the measure of maturity might be.

By stressing the need for individual development from birth to death, black and white women's rights activists critiqued Americans who defined youth as the peak of a woman's life, particularly those who praised dewy beauty and girlish dependence as the ideal of true womanhood. They urged women to realize that physical beauty would inevitably fade and that lasting fulfillment depended upon the development of inner talents. As the black abolitionist Frances Harper mused, once "the bloom of her girlhood had given way to a higher type of spiritual beauty," a woman who dedicated her life to serving humanity would find that "true happiness" consisted not in "vainly striving to keep up her appearance of girlishness" but in "the full development and right culture of our whole natures."[31] Further, activists like Harper argued that women would never succeed in claiming political rights or economic opportunities until they strove to be loved and respected not only when they were young but also when they were middle-aged and old.[32]

Another way in which women's rights activists conceptualized maturity turned neither on age nor on individual development but on familial relations. These activists rightly recognized that democratic political rhetoric—from the high theory of John Locke to the hackneyed speeches of state legislators—relied upon a narrative of male maturation in which white sons outgrew their dependence on mothers and servants or slaves to become the equals of their white fathers. Champions of equal adulthood argued that this narrative did not simply leave out black males and all females but rather relied on the perpetual subordination of black men and all women as the very mechanism by which white men assured themselves that they were independent adults, not dependent children.[33] The activists and intellectuals in this book struggled to conceptualize a path to maturity that would make daughters, servants, and slaves the equals of their white male peers. This would require, advocates of equal adulthood acknowledged, not only an extension of political rights and economic opportunity but also a profound reorganization of household labor, romantic love, and family bonds. White men would need to acknowledge that not only in childhood but throughout their lives they depended on black people and women.[34] Further, white men would need to understand that growing up did not give them a right to their dependents—whether wives, children, servants, or slaves—but rather required constant negotiation with independent black people and women. The far-reaching nature of these proposed reforms helps explain, in turn, why so many Americans argued so persistently that black people and women were more like overgrown children than autonomous adults.

Further, the more white men celebrated their independence in terms of outgrowing mothers, slaves, and servants, the more advocates for equal adulthood had to confront a painful set of conundrums. How, these activist intellectuals wondered, could children be taught to respect the mature capacity of mothers, servants, and slaves while also outgrowing their dependence upon these very people? Did daughters need to reject their mothers if they ever hoped to become the equals of their fathers? Did educated and upwardly mobile free black people need to cast off their association with enslaved ancestors to win rights and respect? Could economically advantaged women of any race become the equals of their male peers without exploiting other women as poorly paid or bound domestic workers? These were questions that the activists and intellectuals in this book repeatedly confronted but never fully resolved. Indeed, I would suggest that these issues remain unresolved—and too often unexplored—in the United States today.

In the nineteenth century, the U.S. population was predominantly young, but significant numbers of people lived to be quite old. What we call life expectancy, the average number of years that an individual could expect to live based on aggregate statistics, was much lower—approximately 36.5 years for men and 38.5 years for women in 1850—largely because so many children died under age five. Life span—that is, the age at which the longest-lived people died—was similar to today. If a woman lived through her childbearing years, she was quite likely to survive into her seventies.[35] Life expectancy was profoundly affected by racial inequalities. A black infant born in the South during the same period had a life expectancy at birth of only thirty-three years; a black woman who had reached age twenty could expect only to live to around fifty-four.[36] It is important to remember, however, that aggregate statistics are misleading. Significant numbers of both black and white women lived into middle and old age, and many of these assumed prominent positions in women's organizations.[37]

During the period under study, American women dramatically reduced their number of children. The total fertility rate for white women fell from 7.04 children in 1800 to 3.56 children in 1900. While no figures for black women are available early in the century, their fertility rate fell from 7.9 in 1850 to 5.61 in 1900.[38] A white woman, and to a lesser extent a black woman, who reached middle age in the nineteenth century could expect a stage of life after her children had grown.

Many scholars have documented that the timing and physical symptoms of menarche, menopause, and old age differ in different cultures, and they have debated whether this is due to genetics, diet, or cultural beliefs.[39] Meanwhile, scholars and pundits continue to debate whether or not gender and racial differences are rooted in culture or biology and, if the latter, whether in genes, hormones, or brain chemistry.[40] This study sidesteps these debates over causality in order to demonstrate the way in which aging, gender, and race have been given meaning through political debates over the nature and limits of democracy.[41] Whether or not women and racial minorities are allowed to attain the status of full maturity has always been a battleground, the response to which has depended not on biology but upon the shifting understandings of political authority, economic opportunity, religion, and science. When I speak of adulthood or maturity, therefore, I refer to a social, not a biological, category.[42]

This book begins with a prologue that explains how Enlightenment political theorists linked individual liberty to white male maturity. During the American and French Revolutions, as I show in chapter 1, female intellectuals on both sides of the Atlantic began to ask why, if women grew old alongside men, they could not also claim the right to govern themselves.

In chapter 2, I argue that the elimination of property requirements for suffrage redefined full citizenship as a normative stage of life for white men, and I analyze how advocates for a more expansive definition of adult citizenship responded to this change.

In chapters 3 and 4, I explore the ideas and strategies of the organized women's rights and antislavery movements in the 1840s and 1850s. First, I show that activists allied around the argument that state governments should apply age qualifications equally to all citizens, regardless of race or sex. Second, I consider activists' contention that every individual should be given an equal opportunity to navigate his or her own voyage of life.

As I explain in chapters 5 and 6, the alliance for equal adulthood reached a peak during the early years of Reconstruction when activists pushed state and federal governments to guarantee equal rights to all adults, a movement that failed as leaders adopted competing and irreconcilable measures of maturity. By the late 1870s, advocates for equal adulthood recognized that black men and all women still shared a common problem—the vulnerability to being treated like perpetual minors—but could not come up with a shared solution.

In the epilogue, I suggest that although the struggle for equal adulthood failed, those who advocated it raised important questions about the connections between public and private forms of power, questions that remain relevant and worth pondering today.

LIBERTY AND MATURITY
IN ENLIGHTENMENT THOUGHT

In the late eighteenth century, highly educated women in Britain and America became profoundly troubled by ideas, customs, and laws that denied women the status of independent adults whatever their age, intellectual accomplishments, marital status, or personal wealth. American patriots like Mercy Otis Warren, British evangelicals such as Hannah Moore, and professional educators including Susanna Rowson spoke out against what writer Mary Hays referred to as women's "PERPETUAL BABY-ISM."[1] Most of these women did not contend for political or legal equality, but they did argue for recognition as mature beings capable of relying on their own reason and moral judgment.

To understand why they did so, it is necessary to appreciate how deeply ideas about white male maturity and liberty were entwined in Enlightenment debates about the nature of just authority. Beginning in the seventeenth century, Puritan, Whig, and Enlightenment reformers in England and America argued that legitimate authority must be based on consent, that children could not provide meaningful consent, and that women and Africans resembled children throughout their lives.[2] This argument placed a new emphasis on white male maturation as the fundamental distinction between those capable of governing themselves and those naturally subject to the will of others, both in households and in the state.

The link between white male maturity and liberty spread through the Atlantic world in a variety of ways, including through religious sermons, political debates, novels, and educational treatises.[3] Amid this general debate, however, the most specific and potent arguments for why mature white men, and only mature white men, developed the capacity to govern themselves were provided by John Locke, the great English promoter of social contract theory; William Blackstone, the most influential commentator on English common law; and Jean-Jacques Rousseau, the French/ Swiss champion of the rights of man. Each of these men struggled to explain how white sons born in a state of natural subjection grew to become free and, just as important, why daughters and nonwhites did not.[4] The fundamental issue for these advocates of self-government was not the validity of any particular age qualification but the political salience of maturity itself. Indeed, each simplified complicated precedents that conferred legal standing at different ages for different purposes into a single age of majority—twenty-one for Locke and Blackstone, twenty-five for Rousseau, the final point at which the guardianship of minors ended in England and France, respectively.[5] Their theories of mature consent influenced lawyers and judges who campaigned to raise specific age qualifications in criminal, statutory, and ecclesiastical law, but this was not Locke's, Rousseau's, or Blackstone's central concern.[6] Rather, each sought to prove that mature white men had the right to govern themselves in sexual relations, families, the market, civil society, and the state, while all other people should remain in subjection throughout their lives. These thinkers each based this argument on the underlying claim that white sons outgrew childish dependence on mothers, servants, and slaves and with age became the equals of their fathers.

As Locke influentially explained in his *Two Treatises of Government* (1690), "We are born free, as we are born rational: not that we have actually the exercise of either; age that brings the one, brings with it the other too."[7] By "we," he meant men. Locke sought to prove that "age" made men reasonable and therefore entitled to govern themselves. He acknowledged that individuals developed the capacity to reason at variable rates and that any particular age of majority was arbitrary, a point fixed by human law rather than by natural law.[8] Under English law, Locke wrote, this age was "one and twenty years, and in some cases sooner."[9] Locke thus acknowledged that English law conferred particular freedoms at early ages, but he nonetheless quite clearly and influentially highlighted age twenty-one as the most important transition between boyhood subjection and manhood freedom.[10] Locke was not concerned with debating the validity of age twenty-one per se but rather with establishing the more fundamental premise that if "such an age of discretion . . . made the father free, it shall make the son free too."[11] Locke sought to prove that age mattered for fathers and sons because defenders of absolute monarchy claimed that it did not.

Locke's emphasis on chronological age as a clear line between boyhood subjection and manhood freedom was innovative and controversial. Chronological age had little relevance in feudal law because a person's legal standing was largely determined by birth. Under primogeniture, rank, land, and political power flowed from fathers to adult sons, but, in the absence of such an heir, nothing prevented young children or women from legitimate succession. As a result, infants and females assumed the throne, teenage boys succeeded their fathers in Parliament, and noble women occasionally voted. Rights, obligations, and crimes differed for masters and servants, nobility and commoners. With no unified law of contracts, children as young as four placed their marks on indentures, wills, and deeds. Criminal defendants, "young in years, yet old in sin," faced brandings, whippings, and even death. In daily life, most adults owed obedience to a lord or master, answering to the call of "boy" or "girl" throughout their lives, not because they were young but because of their subordinate rank.[12] In short, neither maturity nor manhood was as relevant as inherited status.

In the seventeenth century, as Puritans and Whigs argued that just authority was based on consent, conservatives defended the inherited divine right of English kings to govern their dependent subjects. The theory of patriarchalism, most influentially articulated by Robert Filmer, established an analogy between the God-ordained authority of fathers and kings.[13] For Filmer, all human beings were born dependent and should remain so throughout their lives because interlocking dependencies bound society together according to God's plan. English subjects owed obedience to their king as the father of his people, and this relation was not fundamentally altered by either party developing the capacity to reason over the course of life. Indeed, the king could be an infant or a woman, and still English subjects owed their obedience to his or her authority, which derived not from personal capacity but from God. As Filmer explained, "Many a child, by succeeding a king, hath the right of a father over many a grey-headed multitude."[14] White male maturity had nothing to do with patriarchal right.

It was to counter patriarchalism that Locke drew such a sharp distinction between "the freedom of a man at years of discretion, and the subjection of a child to his parents, whilst yet short of that age." Political and parental authority were so distinct, Locke argued, "that the most blinded contenders for monarchy by right of fatherhood cannot miss this difference."[15] The difference was maturity. Because human beings were "born infants, weak and helpless, without knowledge or understanding," they necessarily depended on the will of others—not only fathers but also mothers, servants, and guardians.[16] Locke argued that the natural inca-pacity of children proved Filmer wrong, for even "were the right heir of Adam now known, and by that title settled on the monarch in his throne," should the crown pass to minor child, "must not that child . . . be in subjec-tion to his mother and nurse, to tutors and governors, till age and educa-tion brought him reason and the ability to govern himself, and others?"[17] For Locke, a child clinging to his mother or nurse could not rule himself, much less others.

Further, and most important, Locke argued that once white males ma-tured, they could not justly be subordinated to others against their will. Natural subjection was "temporary."[18] In an evocative metaphor, Locke compared the "bonds of this subjection" under which children were born to "swaddling cloths": "Age and reason, as they grow up, loosen [these bonds] till at length they drop quite off, and leave a man at his own free disposal."[19] From that point forward, a mature white man could not justly be ruled without his rational consent, and this was true in private life as much as in public. Indeed, the young man's liberation may have been more profound in private life, where, at least according to Locke's theory, a youth of twenty-one no longer had to obey his father, mother, nurse, tutor, or guardian unless his reason told him he should. This was a practi-cal freedom likely more salient than the rather abstract right Locke gave a man to consent to the laws by which he was governed.[20]

For Locke, age rather than rank made a man free. A grown man could "make himself a servant to another" by contract and thus owe obedi-ence to his master, but he was still "a free man" as much as his master.[21] There were some exceptional cases in which male maturity did not con-fer liberty—"lunatics and idiots are never set free from the government of their parents" because they lacked reason; criminals lost the freedom they had gained—but as a general principal a white man of twenty-one was at liberty to determine his own destiny.[22]

Locke thus countered Filmer's patriarchal theory by insisting that pa-rental power came to an end as each generation of white sons matured into free white men equal to their fathers. But what of daughters? For Locke, children were undifferentiated by sex, but when the "swaddling cloths" of natural subjection dropped off, a woman clearly lacked what it took to prove that she was "a man at his own free disposal."[23] It was as though the maturation being measured shifted from the mind to the body, from the reasoning faculty to the penis.[24]

This shift from mind to body was not accidental. Locke acknowledged that daughters developed the capacity to reason along with their brothers but argued that adult men should rule over women because men were "the abler and the stronger" sex.[25] Locke treated heterosexual relations leading to parenthood as the first form of "political or civil society." Assuming that mothers and fathers were both necessary for effective childrearing, Locke defined "conjugal society" as the first form of contract, "a voluntary compact between man and woman."[26] For Locke, marriage was historically and conceptually the primary form of human association based on contract, but it was not a contract between equals. Locke explained that always and everywhere women were destined to be subject to men in marriage, not because women consented to their own subjection but because women never developed the strength or ability to rule over men. In cases where the wife's will conflicted with that of her husband, Locke argued, it "being necessary that the last determination, i.e., the rule, should be placed somewhere, it naturally falls to the man's share, as the abler and the stronger."[27] In other words, the wife's subordination to her husband resulted from her imperfect degree of development relative to his.[28]

Locke's recourse to ability and strength as a justification for men's rule over women appears out of place in an argument seeking to base just authority on consent. But, it was logically necessary: Locke's emphasis on white male maturation as the transition from subjection to freedom made sense only if it was a one-way street. Once the "swaddling cloths" of subjection dropped off, a man could not be expected to subject himself to women, for to do so would be to once again resemble an infant dependent on mothers and nurses. Locke therefore shored up white males' transition from subjection to freedom by arguing that their female peers did not develop the same capacities with age. Locke's claim that the husband was the "abler and the stronger" thus made perfect sense insofar as it explained how and why males, and only males, gained liberty along with maturity.[29] According to Locke, boys grew up to become the equals of their fathers because they learned to regard all women, including the mothers and nurses who had raised them, as less mature beings.

Locke also addressed the maturity of Indians and Africans, arguing that under current conditions they resembled children. He contended that environment and education rather than inherent limitations determined differences among men.[30] He justified slavery as the result of war, a captive having forfeited his life to a "lawful conqueror."[31] Locke thus held open the possibility that nonwhite men might someday attain the same liberty as their English peers while also justifying white supremacy as the result of Europeans' superior development.[32] In practice, Locke helped to draft the constitution of Carolina and invested in the Royal Africa Company, the profits of which derived from the slave trade.[33]

Locke's emphasis on white male maturity as a qualification for liberty shaped Anglo-American debates over the nature of just authority in families and in the state. Nearly a century later, William Blackstone, the first professor of law at Oxford, found precedents for Locke's theory in English common law. In the process, he added a stronger emphasis on property ownership as a requirement for independence by claiming that the common law placed servants, wives, children, and wards in equivalent positions of subordination to adult male heads of household.[34]

Blackstone offered his *Commentaries on the Law of England* (1765–69) as a grand summation of established legal precedent.[35] In fact, his commentaries reformed the law, particularly the law of domestic relations. Blackstone ignored feudal precedents that treated inherited status as the fundamental legal category, precedents that granted greater rights to masters than to husbands or fathers and accorded significant legal standing to high-ranking women and children. Instead, Blackstone innovatively argued that adult male heads of household were free to govern themselves while others were not because common law recognized four parallel and equivalent relations in domestic life, those of masters and servants, husbands and wives, fathers and children, and, in the case where fathers died, guardians and wards. In each of these relations, Blackstone claimed, the inferior party lacked an independent legal will, was subject to moderate beating as a form of correction, and was entitled to material support.[36]

Blackstone first discussed the relation of master and servant, identifying three types of servants: domestics, apprentices, and "labourers, who are only hired by the day or the week, and do not live . . . as part of the family." By including this last category Blackstone extended the law of master and servant to employees and thus provided a rationale by which propertied men could continue to control workers even as they signed shorter-term contracts and shifted from household to industrial production.[37]

For Blackstone, servitude was based on contract, as for Locke. But Blackstone differed from Locke in that he did not regard servants and masters as equally capable of exercising liberty. When discussing the qualifications of electors, Blackstone clarified that men without property could not be trusted to exercise mature judgment. "If it were probable that every man would give his vote freely, without influence of any kind," Blackstone mused, "then, upon the true theory and genuine principle of liberty, every member of the community, however poor, should have a vote." But, Blackstone continued, because the common law was concerned with practicalities rather than with abstract theories, legal precedent rightly recognized that free will "can hardly be expected in persons of indigent fortunes, or such as are under the immediate dominion of others." Property qualifications for electors thus served "to exclude such persons as are in so mean a situation that they are esteemed to have no will of their own."[38] In short, before a man could develop the capacity for self-government, he had to not only be of full age but also attain material independence. Until that time, he remained, like a child or ward, subject to others in both private and public life.

Men could always aspire to become self-governing individuals, however, a possibility that Blackstone denied to women, whatever their age or property. Marriage, he claimed, "suspended" the legal identity of the wife, who became "in our law-french a *femme-covert*."[39] Following the logic of Blackstone's *Commentaries*, propertied adult women not under coverture should have been full citizens. Blackstone did acknowledge that unmarried heiresses and propertied widows had legal standing, but he did not grant them political rights. Treating their cases as rare exceptions, he assumed that women were subordinate to either a father or a husband. Only men, as a matter of course, left behind the legal subordination of childhood to enjoy the liberties of English men.

Blackstone echoed Locke in arguing that the subjection of children to parents was a temporary stage but limited familial power to the father: "The legal power of a father (for a mother, as such, is entitled to no power, but only to reverence and respect) the power of a father, I say, over the persons of his children ceases at the age of twenty one: for they are then enfranchised by arriving at years of discretion, or that point which the law has established (as some must necessarily be established) when the empire of the father, or other guardian, gives place to the empire of reason."[40] By the late eighteenth century, the idea that children remained subject to parents until they developed reason had become a commonplace. Blackstone's innovation was to argue that wives, servants, and employees occupied a legal position exactly equivalent to children not yet of full age.

Blackstone treated the significance of chronological age in his discussion of guardians and wards, for age was most relevant to the disposition of property. He detailed how the legal "ages of male and female are different for different purposes." At twelve, a male could "take the oath of allegiance"; at fourteen, he could chose his own guardian, contract to marry, or, "if his discretion be actually proved," make a will; at seventeen, he could become an executor; and at twenty-one he was finally "at his own disposal, and may aliene his lands, good, and chattels." In the case of a female, at seven years of age, she could be "given in marriage"; at nine, she was entitled to dower; at twelve, she could consent or disagree to a marriage, and, "if proved to have sufficient discretion, may bequeath her personal estate"; at fourteen, she could choose a guardian; at seventeen, she could be an executrix; and at twenty-one, she could "dispose of herself and her lands." Having reviewed all these specifics, Blackstone then offered a simple rule: "Full age in male or female, is twenty one years." Until that point, an individual was "an infant, and so stiled in law."[41] Blackstone thus became an important source for understanding twenty-one as the key transition to legal personhood, even as he undercut the significance of chronological age by treating adults without property like minors.

With regard to enslaved Africans, Blackstone condemned perpetual servitude without offering any practical hope of freedom. He claimed that "the spirit of liberty is so deeply implanted in our constitution, and rooted even in our very soil, that a slave or a negro, the moment he lands in England . . . [becomes] a freeman."[42] In fact, the status of enslaved Africans brought to England remained in question until the 1772 *Somerset* decision affirmed Blackstone's logic by ruling that common law did not support slavery and that a slave brought to England could not be forcibly taken and sold elsewhere. By refusing to acknowledge England's complicity in New World slavery, however, Blackstone effectively limited his discussion of rights and duties to white people.

Throughout his *Commentaries*, Blackstone drew a sharp distinction between the "rights and duties of persons, as standing in the *public* relations of magistrates and people," and "their rights and duties in *private* oeconomical relations."[43] In both public and private, however, only adult white men with property left the "empire of the father" for the "empire of reason." All others remained in a state of childlike dependence, whatever their age.[44]

It would be hard to overstate Blackstone's influence in America. The first American edition of the *Commentaries* appeared in 1772, with a list of six hundred subscribers. By the 1790s, Blackstone was the author most frequently cited in American newspapers. Every major nineteenth-century commentator on American law drew upon his work. Finally, his stark formulation of an equivalency among servants, children, and wives became the bête noire of later generations of Anglo-American women's rights activists, particularly those from propertied families who regarded themselves as far superior to either children or servants and deeply resented common-law traditions that denied the privileged both rights and respect.[45]

In addition to social contract theory and common-law precedent, women seeking to prove their capacity as equal adults would have to wrestle with the legacy of Jean-Jacques Rousseau, who dared to say openly what others had only hinted at, which was that women should remain childlike throughout their lives because men found this pleasing. For Rousseau, men could become both free and virtuous only if they learned to desire that which benefited the common good. Loving a woman who remained dependent taught a man to care for others. Women's childishness was not inherent nature, according to Rousseau, but it was something to be cultivated, for female dependence was precisely what gave women power over the hearts of men.[46]

Rousseau coined the phrase "rights of man" in the *Social Contract* (1762), but the only concrete definition he gave was the right to use reason to discover simple principles.[47] In his pedagogical novel *Emile, or On Education* (1762), Rousseau explained how best to cultivate reason and desire so that a boy experienced no conflict between inclination and duty and thus became an adult citizen who was both free and virtuous.[48] Rousseau's educational plan for Emile was graded by age. Where Locke and Blackstone treated particular age qualifications as artifacts of human law, Rousseau claimed that nature set an ideal schedule for human growth through distinct stages that a careful observer could accurately measure.[49] To ensure optimum individual development and social progress, each stage of a man's life needed to begin and end "at the time prescribed by nature."[50] Rousseau thus specified exactly how to treat a pupil "according to his age."[51] Emile's education began at birth and ended at age twenty-four, when he was about to become an adult citizen and a father. The story of his education ended with the words "It is time."[52]

In striking contrast to the age-based schedule of development prescribed for Emile, Rousseau argued that a female's duty was essentially the same throughout her life: "to please men."[53] Indeed, Rousseau found this ideal, which he called natural coquetry, not in grown women but in "little girls [who] love adornment almost from birth."[54] The education of Emile's future wife, Sophie, did not teach her to rely on her own independent judgment but to inspire a man to protect and guide her. Through her youthful beauty, girlish charm, and utter dependence, Sophie inspired Emile to care for another person as much as himself and thereby opened the door to his more general love of all humanity.[55]

Rousseau's attitudes toward nonwhites were complex but largely abstract. His glorification of the "noble savage" placed Native people in a more flattering light than Locke's. Further, Rousseau harshly condemned slavery, but rather than discussing the particulars of chattel slavery in the New World, he treated slavery as a metaphor for mankind's general lack of freedom.[56] For example, one of Emile's last lessons was about slavery. He learned that a man cannot alienate himself, which led immediately to the conclusion that "a people" cannot "alienate itself without reserve to its chief."[57] For Rousseau, virtue entailed resisting all forms of tyranny but did not require one to resist the particulars of France's involvement in perpetuating chattel slavery in the New World.[58]

Many educated white women in France, Britain, and America claimed Rousseau as their champion because he so clearly stressed the power of female influence.[59] Others, such as Mary Hays and Mary Wollstonecraft, argued that women could never exert a moral influence as long as men treated them like overgrown children.[60] All who followed political and philosophical debates had to confront the persistent focus on white male maturity as a qualification for liberty.

Indeed, by the late eighteenth century, maturity had become such a central concept that in 1784, in answer to the question "What is enlightenment?," the German philosopher Immanuel Kant asserted that *"enlightenment is man's emergence from his self-incurred immaturity. Immaturity is the inability to use one's own understanding without the guidance of another."* That Kant believed most people would "gladly remain immature for life" only underlined his view that the Enlightenment was an ongoing process whose ends had yet to be achieved.[61] Further, his denial of equal reasoning powers to the female sex and his commitment to teaching the science of racial difference in his lectures on anthropology were in the mainstream of Enlightenment efforts to define white men, and only white men, as capable of mature freedom.[62] While Kant worked out the details of his moral philosophy, leaders of the American Revolution had already turned to much more practical questions about who, exactly, could achieve mature independence and on what terms.

CHAPTER ONE

ADULT INDEPENDENCE AND THE LIMITS OF REVOLUTION

The crisis of the American Revolution irrevocably altered the rhetorical, legal, and social significance of white male maturation by turning dependent subjects into republican citizens and in the process raising new issues about who could claim liberty and on what terms.[1] Patriot leaders generally agreed that only propertied adult men were fully capable of governing themselves, but public officials could not impose this view without struggle as the disruptions of war enabled young people, women, servants, and slaves to assert both practical and ideological claims to individual freedom.[2]

The argument that females could also become adult citizens stood out most clearly in the writings of three very different women: Abigail Adams, wife and mother of American presidents; Phillis Wheatley, renowned slave poet; and Mary Wollstonecraft, London radical and champion of women's rights. What united these women across class, racial, and national divides was not a shared political movement but a shared insight—that women needed to gain greater recognition as mature adults. Separately and from their very different vantage points, they argued that white men used their status as independent adults to claim political rights, economic opportunities, family authority, and sexual power while classifying women and black people as perpetual minors. Further, though each woman chose a very different method of promoting claims for female maturity—Adams wrote private letters, Wheatley published poems, and Wollstonecraft intervened in a pamphlet war over the significance of the French Revolution—all faced a very similar reaction from conservative critics who trivialized them by comparing women to children or by arguing that females could not make a transition to adulthood on the same terms as white males.[3]

Adams, Wheatley, and Wollstonecraft believed that a fundamental barrier to sexual equality was the lack of any clear transition between dependent girlhood and independent womanhood. "Females," Wollstonecraft wrote, "are made women of when they are mere children, and brought back to childhood when they ought to leave the go-cart for ever."[4] Wollstonecraft agreed with eighteenth-century moralists who argued that women should exert their influence in families, churches, and civil society, but she insisted that they could not do so as long as they retained a childlike dependence on the authority of husbands, ministers, and public opinion. "If women be ever allowed to walk without leading-strings," Wollstonecraft contended, they must be "taught to respect themselves as rational creatures."[5] Adams agreed that women had to develop the mature ability to reason for themselves and expressed outrage at those who would class adult women with children.[6] Wheatley, meanwhile, urged patriots to recognize that human beings held in perpetual slavery were also rational creatures with a desire for liberty. She reminded her readers that all human beings were "lovely copies of the Maker's plan" and that those who grew up in slavery also developed "love of *Freedom*."[7]

This focus on individual maturation is striking, given that historians investigating the significance of gender in eighteenth-century Europe and America have employed spatial metaphors to analyze the separation of politics, family, and civil society. Historians have noted that though women did not gain political rights during this period, they substantially increased their influence in families and civil society.[8] Adams's, Wheatley's, and Wollstonecraft's main concern was not with spheres, however, but with individual development over the course of life. Only by teaching females to develop mature virtue, they argued, could women claim a positive influence on families, religion, commercial relations, politics, and civil society. Further, each saw distinctions between childhood and adulthood as a political issue. Adams sought to reform the laws of marriage. Wheatley hoped that the abolition of slavery would enable Africans to develop their full potential. Wollstonecraft explicitly defined female maturity as a problem of "rights."[9] These women challenged the underlying logic of a democratic political theory that linked liberty to white male maturity while categorizing women and nonwhites as perpetual minors. Their arguments were important to the history of feminism because their focus on maturation linked white men's political and economic opportunities to their private authority and sexual power. By treating females and non-whites as perpetual children, these women argued, white men trivialized black men and all women's aspirations for freedom in public as well as in private life.

ABIGAIL ADAMS AND THE MATURITY OF LADIES

To justify American independence, patriots promoted an analogy between the maturation of sons and the growth of Britain's colonies.[10] These propagandists asserted that just as sons naturally outgrew parental authority, so the colonies had outgrown dependence on the Crown. Thomas Paine, the greatest master of this rhetoric, wrote in his best-selling pamphlet *Common Sense* (1776) that just because America had prospered under the Crown did not mean the colonies should remain perpetually dependent: "We may as well assert that because a child has thrived upon milk, that it is never to have meat, or that the first twenty years of our lives is to become a precedent for the next twenty."[11] In 1777 he compared the attitude of Britain to that of "a covetous guardian" who "for twenty years" had been enriching himself on the estate of a ward about to turn twenty-one. Paine reduced the entire debate over independence to one question: "To know whether it be the interest of this continent to be independent, we need only to ask this easy, simple question: Is it the interest of a man to be a boy all his life?"[12] This question worked as political propaganda because the answer was obvious to so many Americans who had come to believe that adult white men with property could not be justly subject to others without their consent. The colonies were prosperous, no longer relying on Britain for material support, so to subject them further was a form of tyranny. That Britain was commonly referred to as the "mother country" only intensified this argument, for if grown sons might consult their fathers, they certainly did not obey their mothers.[13]

Watching the revolutionary crisis unfold, Abigail Adams and Phillis Wheatley both realized, each in her own way, that the struggle for American independence raised new questions about the link between maturity and liberty. Each was concerned with private as well as public aspirations, but their particular circumstances could not have been more different. Adams, born in 1744 southeast of Boston, was the daughter of a minister and wife of a lawyer. She enjoyed social prominence and relative prosperity. Wheatley was chattel property, captured on the coast of West Africa (most likely in the area between present-day Gambia and Ghana), brought to Boston on a slave ship in 1761, and purchased by pious Congregationalist merchant John Wheatley to work as a house slave for his wife, Susanna. As a Wheatley relative later recalled, the girl cost only a "trifle" because she was sick and very young—she had just lost her front baby teeth. The Wheatleys named her Phillis, after the slave ship on which she arrived, and put her to work.[14]

What Adams and Wheatley shared were intellectual ambition and the talent to become, in very different ways, among the most accomplished women in the colonies. Neither received a formal education. Abigail was typical of middle-class girls in eighteenth-century America and Britain who lacked opportunities for schooling but gained unprecedented access to books. Because Protestant families put a particular value on female literacy for purposes of reading the Bible, even poor families often owned a copy of the scriptures. In addition, with the rise of commercial publishing, more families were able to purchase substantial libraries, and increasing numbers of parents came to see their daughters' literacy as a mark of respectability. Like most American girls, Abigail read British authors: among her favorites were Shakespeare, Milton, Pope, and Richardson. In her teens, she learned French. When she married John in 1764, she gained both an admiring husband and a large library stocked with Scottish moral philosophy, English social critics, and Whig political theory. Corresponding regularly with some of the most educated men in the colonies—her cousin Isaac Smith as he prepared for Harvard, the autodidact Richard Cranch, who courted her sister Mary, and, of course, her suitor and then husband John—Abigail aspired to both learn from and teach men.[15]

Few slaves gained access to the books that were so readily available to Abigail. Phillis had the luck, if one can call it that, of being purchased by devout Congregationalists who supported evangelical efforts to spread the Gospel among Indians and Africans. When they noticed that Phillis was rapidly deciphering the family Bible, they made the unusual decision of allowing their teenage daughter Mary to tutor her. In a letter printed as an introduction to the first edition of Wheatley's collected poems, her master, John Wheatley, emphasized Phillis's precocity: "Phillis was brought from *Africa* to *America*, in the Year 1761, between Seven and Eight Years of age. Without any Assistance from School Education, and by only what she was taught in the Family, she, in sixteen Months Time . . . [could read] the most difficult Parts of the Sacred Writings, to the great Astonishment of all who heard her. . . . WRITING . . . she learnt in so short a Time . . . and has made some Progress in [Latin]."[16] Wheatley thus pioneered what would remain the most likely—if extremely narrow—path to slave literacy: using evidence of remarkable talent to win the sympathy of pious whites.[17]

Wheatley became one of the few American slaves to read the same books as Adams. Though Adams likely read more political tracts and Wheatley more evangelical publications, they shared a British literary culture that emphasized intellectual refinement, particularly the cultivation of sensibility, which both women understood as the obligation to refine reason and affection as a means of better apprehending virtue.[18] The two women also shared a deep interest in revolutionary politics and a location at the center of early conflicts between American patriots and British officials. The Boston Massacre of 1770 occurred down the street from Wheatley's front door (she wrote a poem about it), and Adams's husband defended the British soldiers to prove they could receive a fair trail. Both attended the religious revivals led by the British evangelist George Whitefield in the fall of 1770, though Adams remained moderate in her Congregationalist faith while Wheatley was more ardently evangelical. Further, as these religious and political developments unfolded, quite literally on their doorsteps, both women aimed to shape the course of events through their writing.[19]

In her correspondence with her husband and other leading patriots, Adams raised the issue of whether American independence would offer wives greater freedom within marriage. In the spring of 1776 John was serving as a delegate from Massachusetts to the Continental Congress meeting in Philadelphia and Abigail was managing the family farm in Braintree, southeast of Boston. On 31 March she wrote to her husband in a flush of optimism that the British had finally evacuated and left local residents free to "sit under our own vine and eat the good of the land." Her mind, it seems, then wandered to the laws of marriage that ensured "our own vine" would belong to her husband, despite the investment of her labor in maintaining it. She wrote: "By the way, in the new Code of Laws which I suppose it will be necessary for you to make, I desire you would Remember the Ladies, and be more generous and favorable to them than your ancestors. Do not put such unlimited power into the hands of the Husbands."[20] Appropriating a phrase that John himself had used to begin an unpublished essay on the colonies' struggle, she wrote: "Remember all Men would be tyrants if they could." And finally, tongue in cheek, she threatened that "the Ladies . . . are determined to foment a Rebellion, and will not hold ourselves bound by any Laws in which we have no voice, or Representation."[21] Adams thus subtly, humorously, demanded that adult white women from propertied families—"Ladies"—be able to enjoy the same liberty that men like her husband were demanding for themselves: the right to the fruits of their own labor, the right to consent to the laws that governed them, and the right to resist tyrannical power.[22]

John's response was to compare women—and indeed the majority of adults in the colonial population—to children: "As to your extraordinary Code of Laws, I cannot but laugh. We have been told that our Struggle has loosened the bands of Government everywhere. That Children and Apprentices were disobedient—that schools and Colledges were grown turbulent—that Indians slighted their Guardians and Negroes grew insolent to their Masters. But your Letter was the first Intimation that another Tribe more numerous and powerful than all the rest had grown discontented."[23] Adams thus began a catalog of what constituted disorder rather than liberty with the example of "disobedient" children. His concern was not just with laws but with the expected patterns of deference that he believed should bind families, educational institutions, and workplaces together under the authority of adult white men.[24]

There was another layer to Adams's response that suggests how men could bolster their own sense of mature independence by infantilizing their wives. After comparing Abigail to a "disobedient" child, John went on to explain that men would not give up their "Masculine systems" for fear of being subject to "the Despotism of the Peticoat."[25] This power of the "Peticoat" can be read as women's sexual allure but also, and perhaps more significantly, as the power of a mother over her son. It is the diminutive child, after all, that lives amid a swirl of petticoats. Adams's insistence that a husband must remain "master" of his wife, even if only in "name," thus evokes an underlying need to defend against a return to childish dependence on adult women for nurture. In the spring of 1776, as John struggled to manage an uncertain revolution, he relied on Abigail to manage his farm, raise his children, and console his heart. By comparing his highly competent wife to a child, he reassured himself that he could both depend upon her and remain an adult fully at liberty to govern himself and be "master" of all his dependents.[26]

By retaining common-law precedents, revolutionary leaders went a long way toward ensuring that servants, employees, wives, and children would remain legally dependent on male heads of household.[27] John Adams aimed at more than bolstering domestic hierarchies, however. He was also intent on proving that in affairs of state, all poor men (whether employed or not), all women (whether married or not), and all minors under twenty-one (even those fighting in the militias or army) would be denied political rights.[28] He accomplished this by emphasizing that these three classes of citizens lacked the experiences necessary to cultivate independence and thus resembled young children more than mature men.

Adams's logic can be seen clearly in his response to Judge James Sullivan, who proposed that Massachusetts's new constitution enfranchise every man "out of wardship."[29] In response, Adams compared poor men and all women to children. He divided "the people" into three hierarchical relationships—"old and young, male and female, as well as rich and poor"—in which superiors rightly governed inferiors without their consent because the latter could not be expected to have developed good "judgment" or "independent minds."[30] Adams thus evoked William Blackstone's analogy between the legal dependence of servants, wives, and children in domestic law but went much further in arguing that all poor men and all women shared with children not a similar legal status but a fundamental lack of mature capacity.

Adams argued that Sullivan must recognize "the right of the old to bind the Young," because children "have not Judgment or Will of their own," and "the right of Men to govern Women," because women's "Delicacy renders them unfit for Practice and Experience, in the great Business of Life." Adams then went on to claim that poor men were, like children, "too dependent upon other Men to have a Will of their own" and, like women, "too little acquainted with public affairs." Adams thus classed the majority of the population with children.[31]

At the same time, however, he drew a fundamental distinction between male dependence, which could always be outgrown with time and the acquisition of property, and female dependence, which was perpetual. According to Adams, "Nature" determined that women could never develop the same capacities as men. This natural limit on women's ability to mature explained why they should never be granted political rights even if they were unmarried, of full age, and wealthy.

The age and property qualifications that divided males from each other were of a different order, however, for they were not determined by nature but by human law. "What Reason Should there be, for excluding a Man of Twenty years, Eleven Months and twenty-seven days old, from a Vote when you admit one, who is twenty one?" Adams rhetorically asked. "The Reason is, you must fix upon Some Period in Life, when the Understanding and will of Men in general is fit to be trusted by the Public." The same reason applied, Adams contended, for "fixing some certain Quantity of Property." In other words, age and property qualifications were arbitrary but nonetheless necessary. A few days or a few shillings did not suddenly make a boy a man or a beggar rich, but some limits were required if infants and paupers were to be kept from the polls. Given this, Adams concluded that delegates in Massachusetts would be wise not to modify any of the existing qualifications of voters. If they did, he warned, "there will be no End of it. New Claims will arise. Women will demand a Vote. Lads from 12 to 21 will think their Rights not enough attended to, and every Man, who has not a Farthing, will demand an equal Voice with any other in all Acts of State."[32]

Revolutionary leaders who agreed with Adams had to accomplish two things: first, they needed to define exactly when and on what terms young men and poor men could become the equals of adult male property owners, and second, they needed to clarify that all females—whatever their age, wealth, or marital status—could never grow up to become full citizens. Minimum age qualifications proved useful for both purposes. In retaining some colonial-era age qualifications and modifying others, revolutionary leaders worked on many fronts to map out a series of age-based transitions between boyhood and manhood while also emphasizing the perpetual dependence of all females, whatever their age. The result was that for many purposes, women in the new nation, even if they were single, wealthy adults, found themselves classed with young children. In some states, but not in others, revolutionary leaders also used age qualifications to distinguish white men from black.[33]

When John Adams wrote James Sullivan that women were "unfit for Practice and Experience, in . . . the hardy Enterprizes of War, as well as the arduous Cares of State," he could draw on a set of shared assumptions derived from Enlightenment political theory and common law, but, perhaps more important, he could also rely upon the concrete legal requirement in Massachusetts that at age sixteen all able-bodied white males, and at times black males as well, were required to register for a poll tax and militia duty, age-based obligations that did not fall upon their female peers.[34] By requiring tax payment and military service from boys who were still legal minors, colonial governments benefited from the productive and military capacity of teenage boys while also emphasizing their legal dependence on older and wealthier heads of household. In 1646 Massachusetts set a pattern followed by other New England colonies when the General Court levied a poll tax on every male inhabitant, "servant or othr, of ye age of 16 yeares and upward," with exemptions only for those "uncapable of such rates" because of "sickness, lamenes, or other infirmity." The court also specified that for servants and children "that take no wages, their mastrs or parents shall pay" the tax for them.[35] Militia service functioned in much the same way. All able-boded males from sixteen to fifty years old, with some exceptions, were required to serve in local training bands, but whereas adult propertied men had to provide their own equipment, the law specified that "parents, masters, and guardians shall furnish and equip those of the militia which are under their care and command."[36] By filtering these age-based obligations through male heads of household, Massachusetts legislators created an intermediary stage of citizenship in which young men were classed neither with young children nor with propertied men. The same young men who relied on fathers or masters to pay their poll taxes and equip them for militia duty also relied on heads of household to represent them in town government. Selectmen in Massachusetts were notorious for allowing all householders a vote in local elections, even if they did not meet the state-mandated property requirements, but these same selectmen almost always barred minors under twenty-one and adult sons living with fathers.[37] The result was that most young men continued to obey and be represented by fathers or masters until well into their midtwenties or even later, when they were finally able to set up households of their own.[38]

The age-based obligation to pay a tax and muster for militia duty accorded well with broader cultural expectations that young men in their late teens and early twenties would begin to perform adult tasks while still obeying fathers or masters. The difference was that whereas cultural practices were not sharply defined by age or sexual difference—boys left home at widely varying ages; many girls left home as well—the obligation to pay a tax and muster for militia duty at age sixteen defined a precise moment when boys owed new obligations to the state not expected of their sisters.[39] Massachusetts patriots like John Adams thus grew up with a system of age-based obligations that ensured boys would gain "Practice and Experience" as taxpayers and citizen-soldiers from which their sisters were barred not just by cultural expectations but by law.

In the South, the age-based qualifications for poll taxes and militia duty functioned quite differently but nonetheless revealed a clear belief that free white women, whatever their age, should be classed with young children. In colonial Virginia, for example, where the poll tax functioned as a tax on human property, the House of Burgesses levied a tax on all men but also on all women of color and, at times, female indentured servants who worked in the fields. Burgesses adjusted the age requirement frequently, from a low of twelve to a high of sixteen. In no case, however, did they levy a tax on very young children or on free white women.[40] In setting requirements for militia duty, meanwhile, the House of Burgesses first limited the obligation to white male property owners with no minimum age, then adjusted the age up and down from a low of sixteen to a high of twenty-one.[41] In short, Virginia legislators were quite inconsistent in applying age distinctions but nonetheless ensured that age did not change the obligations of free white females, since they were expected to remain dependent throughout their lives.

Leaders in the new nation retained existing age-based qualifications for poll taxes and militia duty. What changed was their significance. Because Americans redefined themselves as citizens consenting to government rather than as subjects born dependent on the king, the difference between childhood subjection and manhood freedom took on new weight as a matter of practical importance.[42] Militia duty in particular began to function as a path toward full citizenship from which young women were barred.

Revolutionary leaders faced scattered proposals to extend political rights to minors who served in state militias or the Continental Army. Yet Pennsylvania was the only state to grant teenage soldiers the right to vote in general elections, and that only briefly in the spring of 1776 before reverting back to a minimum age of twenty-one in the state constitution drafted later that year. In Pennsylvania, as throughout the nation, constitutional delegates argued that young men made good soldiers but bad voters, precisely because they were accustomed to following orders rather than thinking for themselves.[43] That colonial governments had always required military service of minors helped justify the belief that fighting for American liberty did not qualify an individual to govern himself.

Throughout the nation, delegates to state constitutional conventions required voters to be over twenty-one and to meet either a property or taxpaying requirement. In most states, property requirements were high enough that the majority of young men had to wait until their midtwenties or even later before casting their first ballot. John Adams had a chance to put his theories about the development of "independent minds" into practice when he ensured that the Massachusetts constitution of 1780 limited the right to vote in state elections to "every male inhabitant of twenty-one years of age and upwards, having a freehold estate within the Commonwealth, of the annual income of three pounds, or any estate of the value of sixty pounds."[44] This property requirement was actually higher than had been applied before the Revolution, a reform that delegates to the constitutional convention justified by urging young men of twenty-one to concede that it was "safer for them to have their right of Voting for Representatives suspended for [a] small space of time" than to allow poor men "with less regard to the Rights of Property" to gain political power over their future estates and businesses.[45] Adams thus helped structure political rights to conform to his vision of a private world in which adult men ruled over children, women, servants, and slaves. With age and the acquisition of property, boys, but never girls, could grow up to govern themselves.

Massachusetts and many other states enabled free black men to vote on the same terms as white men, but Virginia, Georgia, and South Carolina required all voters to be white.[46] Vermont was the only state to drop all economic measures of independence, thereby enfranchising virtually every male at age twenty-one.[47]

One state—New Jersey—experimented with woman suffrage. Taking quite seriously the argument that there should be no taxation without representation, revolutionary leaders in New Jersey allowed unmarried women to vote if they met the other qualifications, including being "of full age" and "worth fifty pounds proclamation money."[48] Very few women— mostly wealthy white widows—passed these tests, but their presence at the polls sparked widespread debate. Some, including Abigail Adams, praised the experiment. All other states, however, barred women from voting, either through constitutional provisions requiring voters to be male or through local custom enforced at the polls.[49] Most patriots shared John Adams's view that women, even if they paid taxes, could not develop the capacity to participate in government affairs.

Amid the patchwork of voting requirements that emerged after the Revolution, poor men, black men, and even women could vote in specific localities, but minors could vote nowhere. The age qualification of twenty-one stood out as a clear boundary to full citizenship throughout the nation. Even radical patriots pushing for the enfranchisement of men on the basis of poll taxes or military service excluded minors. For example, the citizens of Northampton, Massachusetts, pushed to enfranchise "every rateable poll being twenty one years of age," thus rewarding those who "have always paid their poll tax, ever since they were sixteen years old." As to why "infants . . . under the age of twenty one years" should not vote, the citizens of Lenox continued, "we ask leave to refer to what Mr. Locke has most judiciously said, on that head, in the sixth chapter of the second book of his treatise of Government, intitled paternal power."[50] Thus did Enlightenment theory intertwine with age-based obligations of citizenship to create a worldview in which young men earned the right to vote by paying taxes and serving in the militia—but not until they reached age twenty-one. In contrast, "women, of whatever age or condition they may be," had no claim to political rights—a situation the male citizens of Lenox found both sensible and just.[51]

In addition to barring minors from the polls, legislators ensured that youth would not govern their elders. Delegates to state and federal constitutional conventions set higher age qualifications for political office, arguing that years of experience were necessary to gain the knowledge and self-control necessary for wielding political power over other men. The federal Constitution specified twenty-five as the minimum age for serving in the House of Representatives, thirty for the Senate, and thirty-five for the presidency. Many state constitutions followed suit.[52]

Taken together, the various age and property qualifications for political rights in the early Republic ensured that dependent boys would not become self-governing men overnight but that they would transition through a series of increasing obligations and rights as they grew older and acquired property. Free black men could make these transitions in some states but not in others, and women only if they lived in New Jersey and were not married. With regard to political obligations, the vast majority of women remained essentially ageless, classed with children throughout their lives.

There is perhaps no better indication that legislators north and south shared an assumption that age mattered primarily for white male citizens than the information gathered in the first census. The census of 1790 divided the population into five broad categories: free white males under sixteen, free white males over sixteen, free white females, free blacks, and slaves. What counted as vital information thus conformed exactly to the general idea that white boys should grow up to become men, while all black people and all women remained dependent throughout their lives.[53] Less clear is the significance of age sixteen to congressmen who two years later set eighteen as a national minimum age for military service while also specifying that militiamen had to be white. This required states like Massachusetts to raise their age from sixteen to eighteen and to exclude blacks, reforms that some military commanders, including George Washington, had been promoting for some time.[54] Evidently, congressmen did not always agree as to when boys should be obligated to serve—whether sixteen or eighteen—but they did agree on the more fundamental point that age qualifications should define what white boys, but not black boys or any girls, owed their government.

Patriot leaders' reliance on age to define the rights and obligations of citizenship is particularly striking given that the revolutionary crisis raised pressing questions about how any individual's age could be known. With regard to militia service in particular, wartime commanders requested that soldiers be over sixteen, which was also the age used by most states for their draft. Continental army recruiters and militia captains, however, often enlisted younger boys if they appeared strong and capable. Masters and fathers complained that servants and sons ran away by pretending to be older than they were. The presence of younger boys in the armed forces required leaders in the new nation to clarify how exactly a person's age could be proved.[55] Massachusetts's militia law of 1792 quite explicitly stated: "In all cases of doubt respecting the age of any person enrolled, or intended to be enrolled, the party questioned shall prove his age to the satisfaction of the Commanding Officer of the company within whose bounds he may reside."[56] With no specific form of proof defined in law, a young man's age was, for the purpose of military service, whatever his commanding officer said it was.

Local officials were quite accustomed to determining people's ages, just as they determined the value of material property. The Massachusetts poll tax law specified that an assessor elected by the freemen of each town was responsible, along with the town selectmen, for counting "the just numbr of their males" liable for the poll tax.[57] In small towns where residents knew each other from birth, assessors and militia captains could rely on personal knowledge to balance the testimony of young men and their fathers or masters. This system for assessing age was imprecise and open to fraud, but no more so than the very similar system for assessing the monetary value of taxable estates. Indeed, Massachusetts assessors must have considered themselves quite adept at estimating ages not only of human beings but also of livestock, for the court set the tax on cows, horses, sheep, pigs, and asses based on age. Even material objects, such as tools, were assessed on the basis of age and wear. That people often lacked official written proof of their age may have struck town leaders as no more problematic than that their cows or saws lacked such proof as well.[58]

Nonetheless, colonial officials in Massachusetts led the way in trying to provide for a system by which citizens could document how old they were. In 1639 the General Court required that towns keep records of births, deaths, and marriages as an aid to adjudicating probate. Individuals could then pay a fee to receive a certificate of their birth. Recognizing that this system was woefully inadequate—more than half of all births went unreported—leaders of the newly formed state tried to increase registration after the Revolution.[59] Massachusetts would continue to serve as a laboratory for the recording of vital statistics, providing models for other states and eventually for the federal government, but in the early national period the majority of citizens lacked any government record of their ages.

More widespread than official registration was the practice of recording births and deaths in a family Bible. Illiterate parents often asked others to write such records for them. In legal cases where age was in dispute, these family Bibles were the most common form of documentary evidence presented in courts of law throughout the nineteenth century. While legislators in Massachusetts would have liked the registration of births to become universal, they were quite comfortable leaving the matter in the hands of local officials. So long as voting, jury service, and office holding, not to speak of estate taxes, remained linked to property, estimating the value of things had higher stakes than judging the age of people. That a few stout boys of fourteen might assume obligations too young, or a few slender youths avoid them too long, did not particularly trouble the revolutionary generation as long as age qualifications functioned overall to separate boys from men and both from women.

Though females in the new nation did not gain the same rights or obligations as their brothers, they did achieve increased access to education. With the expansion of both public schooling and private female academies, young girls developed the training and self-confidence to assert their influence in civil society. They claimed new respect as republican wives and mothers.[60] Abigail Adams, however, remained unsatisfied. She realized that women could never claim the respect they deserved in either public or private life if men continued to treat them as overgrown children. She did not challenge the particular age qualifications that her husband was so busy establishing in law but rather cut to the core of the fundamental assumption behind such laws, which was that women resembled children more than propertied adult men. Adams, who usually wrote only private letters, ventured into commercial publishing in order to voice her conviction that women should not be treated like children. In January 1781 she wrote an anonymous introduction to her friend Mercy Otis Warren's response to Lord Chesterfield's *Letters* (1774), which had become popular for their elegant, if rakish, prose. Adams was incensed by Chesterfield's assertion that women "are only children of a larger growth; they have an entertaining tattle, and sometimes wit; but for solid, reasoning good sense, I never in my life knew one that had it, or who reasoned or acted consequentially for four-and-twenty hours together."[61] Determined to respond to such insult, Adams vented to Warren: "I could prove to this Lordship that there was one woman in the world who could act consequentially more than 24 hours."[62] While Adams never demanded that women serve in the military at eighteen or vote at twenty-one or run for office in their thirties, she was determined that American "ladies" be recognized as adult patriots contributing along with their male peers to the future of the nation.

She did not push as hard for black women and men to gain equal citizenship. Though opposed to slavery as an institution, she benefited personally from a system of racial segregation that enabled her to hire black workers more cheaply than white. Adams managed to weather the economic disruptions of war and its aftermath in part by hiring a black man to work her farm for less money than she would have had to pay a white one, relying on the labor of her father's former slave Phoebe, and indenturing a "very clever black Boy of 15" as a servant.[63] While Adams benefited from the racial hierarchies within her own household and within the nation as a whole, Phillis Wheatley struggled to give voice to the principle that black Americans were as capable as their white peers of developing mature capacities over the course of life and should thus be free to claim liberty and equality as they aged.

PHILLIS WHEATLEY AND THE MATURITY OF AFRICAN AMERICANS

Through her precocious poetic talent, Wheatley established an unprecedented international influence for a person of African descent in the English-speaking world. Yet, in order to publish, she found that she would have to prove her capacity—as a young black woman—to write poetry at all.[64] Her publisher required an "Attestation," which he printed at the front of her book, from the "most respectable Characters in Boston." As the undersigned men—including the royal governor, the lieutenant governor, and the city's leading ministers and merchants, many of them graduates of Harvard—reported, they had examined "a young Negro Girl, who was but a few Years since, brought an uncultivated Barbarian from *Africa*" on the enclosed poems and found that she was "thought qualified to write them."[65] There is no record of this meeting between Wheatley, a slender nineteen-year-old, and the most educated men in the colony, but the central issue was clear: could a young enslaved female claim recognition from these "most respectable" of men?[66]

In her poems, Wheatley subtly but powerfully addressed the assumption that an African, much less a young, female, and enslaved one, should not aspire to the same education as privileged American males. For example, the poem "To the University of CAMBRIDGE, in NEW-ENGLAND" was one in which Wheatley contrasted her own childhood ("'Twas not long since I left my native shore / The land of errors, and *Egyptian* gloom") to the intellectual opportunities offered young men at Harvard ("Students, to you 'tis giv'n to scan the heights / . . . sons of science").[67] These lines drew on European understandings of Africa as a backward and pagan land, but by italicizing the word "Egyptian," which evoked not only the past but also the biblical enslavement of the Israelites, Wheatley identified Africa's problem as slavery. Wheatley thus suggested that Europeans professing to be Christians had become like the Egyptians of old, in that both exploited slaves, and Africans had become like the ancient Israelites, in that both awaited God's deliverance.[68] Wheatley thus set up a complex distinction between the progress of science, which was the birthright of young men at Harvard, and religion, which was the shared heritage of all believers. The force of the poem, however, came from her own identity as a prodigy—which had already been announced in the preface and to which she alluded to in the phrase "not long since." As her readers would have been well aware, male prodigies born in the colonies often attended Harvard in their early teens. While Wheatley could master their curriculum—as displayed in her poems—she remained enslaved. The bold and surprising originality of the poem was that Wheatley claimed her experience growing up in bondage was a source of authority that placed her not only on a par with the young men at Harvard but above them, not only a student of European culture but a teacher.[69]

She had a lesson for these "pupils": "Improve your privileges while they stay." The ultimate test would come, she warned, from a God who offered salvation not to a privileged few but to "the whole human race." She thus claimed both a religious authority and a public voice: "An *Ethiop* tells you [that sin] 'tis your greatest foe."[70]

Wheatley was able to publish her views because a transatlantic network of evangelical women believed her talent provided evidence that missions to convert Africans to Christianity would be effective. The poem that made her famous was an elegy to the Reverend George Whitefield, a British evangelist who died on a tour through North America, soon after both Wheatley and Adams heard him preach in Boston. Whitefield had been the personal chaplain of Selina Hastings, the Countess of Huntingdon, a wealthy British widow and philanthropist.[71]

The countess (though she owned slaves in Georgia) secured the publication of a book by another slave, James Albert Ukawsaw Gronniosaw's *Narrative* (1772). The countess also took an interest in Wheatley and helped arrange to have her collected poems published in London. Wheatley traveled to England in 1773, where she met the Earl of Dartmouth, Benjamin Franklin, and the abolitionist Granville Sharpe—who no doubt mentioned that thanks to the recent *Somerset* decision, she could not be forced back to the colonies as a slave—and would have met King George had her mistress not fallen ill and entreated her to return to Boston. She agreed, apparently in exchange for her freedom. Soon after her book appeared, she became the most famous person of African descent in the Atlantic world—of note to George Washington and Voltaire, among many others.[72]

Like Adams, Wheatley was criticized by a leading American patriot who invoked the political significance of adulthood. The response did not occur in a private letter but in Thomas Jefferson's *Notes on the State of Virginia*, written to answer a set of queries from a French diplomat, the Marquis de Barbé-Marbois, and eventually published in Paris in 1785 (a year after Wheatley's death), in London in 1787, and in America in 1788. Barbé-Marbois asked specifically about Wheatley, whom he regarded as "one of the strangest creatures in the country and perhaps the whole world."[73] Jefferson dismissed her writings as the product of religion without real poetry, "below the dignity of criticism."[74] He went on, following the lead of David Hume, to claim that Africa had never produced a person of genius and speculated that Africans were "inferior in the faculties of reason and imagination," perhaps even "a different species of the same genus."[75]

Jefferson's *Notes*, primarily addressed to a European audience, thus used science to explain how a nation prospering from slave labor could be founded on the self-evident proposition that "all men are created equal." If Africans were not in fact "created equal," then they could not grow up to become full citizens in the new Republic. In his *Notes*, Jefferson reported (erroneously) that Virginia would soon debate legislation providing for slave children to "be brought up, at the public expense, to tillage, arts or sciences according to their geniuses, till the females should be eighteen, and the males twenty-one years of age, when they should be colonized to such a place as circumstances of time should render most proper . . . to declare them a free and independent people."[76] Jefferson thus thought black people could grow up to be independent adults, just not in the same nation as whites.[77]

In 1785, when Jefferson published his *Notes* in Paris, the American states were moving in radically different directions on slavery. Vermont was the only state to prohibit slavery outright in its constitution (1777). In the 1780s, judicial decisions in Massachusetts and New Hampshire, as well as gradual emancipation laws in Pennsylvania (1780), Connecticut (1784), and Rhode Island (1784), slowly undermined the institution. In North Carolina, South Carolina, and Georgia, however, victorious patriots reaffirmed their claims to slave property, and in New York and Virginia, state legislatures refused to act.[78] The federal Constitution, drafted

in 1787, did not mention slavery by name but provided m
ensure the federal government would not meddle with sta
and thus provided protection for southern slave owners that w
until the Civil War.[79]

From these patchwork compromises over slavery, chrono
took on a new significance for both blacks and whites in the No
ual emancipation acts decreed that children of enslaved mothers would be
born "free" but owe service to their mothers' masters until they reached a
particular age. The age differed—from sixteen to twenty-eight—but in all
cases states with gradual emancipation laws did *not* simply declare that the
children of enslaved mothers would be free at the same age as their white
peers. Legislators' primary concern was that masters should gain some
return for their investment in human property, and for this reason gradual
emancipation laws generally specified that children of slaves would owe
service after they reached maturity. Enslaved parents and owners both realized that birthdays had taken on a new significance. Evidence suggests
that black families would sometimes misreport a child's age to strengthen
claims to freedom. While black people did all they could to hurry emancipation, the statutes governing freedom in the North were clear indications
that legislators would not recognize black people's equal claims to adulthood. At a time when most state constitutions did not distinguish between
white and black citizens, gradual emancipation laws created a system in
which white people could control the labor of "free" black children. The
concrete workings of this system may have strengthened the tendency of
whites to regard black people as childlike and dependent, even when they
were nominally free.[80]

States also drew sharp distinctions between the ages at which white
men and white women should be freed from service and able to consent
to marriage. From the colonial period through the mid-1800s, pauper ap-
prenticeships for poor children ended at age twenty-one for boys and sixteen or eighteen for girls.[81] In some states that established gradual emancipation laws, legislators maintained a similar difference, though at much
higher ages, for the female and male children of slaves. For example, New
York's 1799 law required that female children of enslaved mothers serve
until twenty-five, males to twenty-eight.[82] The younger ages for white females were rooted in colonial-era laws that aimed at freeing servant girls to
marry as a means of discouraging illegitimate births. The younger ages for
female slaves reflected a different logic, which was that female slaves cost
less to purchase and maintain and thus represented a lower capital investment for their masters.[83] In the context of the new Republic, twenty-one

as the age for a significant transition for white males but not for young women or children born to enslaved mothers.

Indeed, leaders of the Revolution aimed to simplify the vast array of age qualifications inherited from colonial law by standardizing twenty-one as the age of consent for white males in both civil law and politics. For example, when John Adams drafted the Massachusetts state constitution of 1780, he stripped teenage militiamen of their traditional right to vote for their own officers, limiting participation in these most local of elections to men "of twenty-one years of age and upwards."[84] A 1784 law for the first time required all Massachusetts jurors to be over twenty-one.[85] Legislators in Massachusetts did not display an equivalent concern for setting age twenty-one as a standard for female consent, however. With regard to guardianship, fathers could place both sons and daughters under guardianship until age twenty-one, but with regard to both labor and marriage, revolutionary leaders tolerated an earlier end to paternal control for girls than for boys.[86] For example, a Massachusetts law passed in 1784 provided that minors could not sign labor contracts without the consent of a responsible adult and that those contracts could bind "females to the age of eighteen years, or to the time of their marriage within that age, and males to the age of twenty one years."[87] Two years later, Massachusetts legislators required the consent of a parent or guardian for the marriage of "a male, under the age of twenty one years, or a female, under the age of eighteen years."[88] In Massachusetts, where a 1783 court decision declared slavery unconstitutional, these laws did not distinguish between black and white youth. But they did establish a clear difference between boys and girls. As age twenty-one became more important, it also became more gender specific, marking out a universal transition to personal and political liberty for boys but having little relevance for girls, who were not expected to govern themselves, whatever their age.[89] In states with gradual emancipation laws, age twenty-one became a racially specific boundary as well, marking a transition not to adulthood in general but to white manhood in particular.

In states with gradual emancipation laws, black children entered adulthood with less education and fewer skills than white pauper apprentices. Throughout the North, town officials and overseers of the poor forced white children without other means of support into indentured servitude. Though imposed upon children and poor families, these indentures were a contractual relationship that required masters to provide education and material support in return for the child's labor. There was a presumption that such children would make a transition to full citizenship when their minority ended. In contrast, gradual emancipation laws encumbered masters with no obligation to prepare the children of enslaved mothers for the rights and obligations of independent citizenship. Northerners thus refused to grapple with Phillis Wheatley's assertion that black slaves were capable of developing both reason and moral judgment and therefore needed to be accorded not only freedom but influence, a voice in the public affairs of the new nation.[90]

Denied opportunities by whites, free black people asserted their own claims to full citizenship, building schools, churches, and employment networks that would help their children achieve literacy, moral judgment, and economic competence. In 1794, Absalom Jones and Richard Allen, two formerly enslaved Philadelphians who would go on to found America's first independent black church, published a pamphlet in which they proposed that whites try a very different educational plan from the one recommended by Jefferson: "We believe if you would try the experiment of taking a few black children, and cultivate them with the same care . . . as you would wish for your own children, you would find . . . they were not inferior in mental endowments."[91] As if to prove their point, five years later both Jones and Allen subscribed to a new edition of Wheatley's poems.[92]

Meanwhile, across the Atlantic in Britain, with her attention focused on the revolution in France, Mary Wollstonecraft proposed a similar experiment to the one suggested by Jones and Allen—but the children she wished to "cultivate" were white, European, and female. Their similar strategies resulted not from direct influence but from a shared reaction to the political significance of maturity in the age of revolution.

MARY WOLLSTONECRAFT AND
MEN'S CONTEMPT FOR OLDER WOMEN

In 1785 the Adamses moved to London so John could serve as the first ambassador to the Court of St. James. They chose as their pastor the Rational Dissenter Richard Price, who was also a close friend and mentor of Mary Wollstonecraft. There is no evidence that the Adamses met Wollstonecraft, an obscure educator at the time, but they were soon to hear of her. In 1792 she published *A Vindication of the Rights of Woman*, and two years later John referred to his wife as Wollstonecraft's "Disciple." "Pupil," Abigail corrected him, stressing education over faith.[93] We can only wonder if she thought back to John's letter comparing wives to "disobedient" children, for this tendency of liberal men to infantilize their wives was precisely what Wollstonecraft saw as the greatest barrier to progress.[94]

Wollstonecraft was born in London in 1759 to a family of comfortable means, but her father's drinking, abuse, and failed business schemes soon rendered the family emotionally and financially insecure. As the second child and eldest daughter of seven siblings, Wollstonecraft learned early to care for young children. At nineteen she began to support herself, sampling each of the meager employments open to respectable young women: lady's companion, governess, seamstress, and teacher. In 1784 she founded a girls' school in Newington Green, North London.[95]

It was in Newington Green that Wollstonecraft met Price. His Rational Dissent, later called Unitarianism, provided Wollstonecraft with an understanding of God as a Platonic ideal of reason, justice, and benevolence toward which all human beings could strive. Though she never declared formal membership in a Dissenting church, she abandoned her Anglican belief in original sin for Price's optimistic faith in human perfectibility. This new theology, in turn, focused her attention on encouraging her young female students to develop their full capacities.[96]

Though her school soon failed, she parlayed her expertise as an older sister, governess, and teacher into a career as a writer. Her first book, *Thoughts on the Education of Daughters: With Reflections on Female Conduct, in the More Important Duties of Life*, was released in 1787 by Joseph Johnson, the London publisher favored by Rational Dissenters and radical reformers. Providing a feminine riposte to John Locke's *Some Thoughts Concerning Education* (1693), Wollstonecraft began from the Lockean premise that education formed moral character. While her proposals for female education were not particularly original—she was influenced by Sarah Trimmer, Anna Barbauld, and others—she provided a particularly lucid analysis of how fashionably educated women grew old without ever attaining moral maturity.[97] The "childish" behavior of such women rendered them "insignificant" both to their families and to broader society, she argued.[98]

With Johnson's support, Wollstonecraft soon moved to London to become a full-time writer, reviewer, and translator. She befriended the visionary poet William Blake, debated politics with Thomas Paine, talked with antislavery activists, visited the painter and sexual experimenter Henry Fuseli (for whom she nurtured an unrequited passion), and made the acquaintance of William Godwin, the utilitarian anarchist who would, many years later, become her husband. She also continued to think about pedagogy as Johnson urged his stable of authors to produce for the growing market in children's literature. Wollstonecraft thus found herself in an environment ripe with new ideas about God, liberty, science, and—not insignificantly—childhood.[99]

Her focus shifted to politics with the hopes unleashed by the French Revolution. In August 1789 deputies to the French National Assembly drafted a "Declaration of the Rights of Man and Citizen," which defined the protection of "natural, inalienable, and sacred rights" as the only basis of legitimate government.[100]

All talk in Johnson's bookshop shifted to news from France: the storming of the Bastille, the protests of Parisian market women. In November, Richard Price optimistically sermonized: "Behold the light . . . after setting America free, reflected to France and there kindled to a blaze that lays despotism to ashes."[101] The statesman Edmund Burke, his heart less warmed by revolutionary fire, condemned Price in his *Reflections on the Revolution in France* (1790), thus setting off an acrimonious debate that came to be known as the "revolution controversy" and inspiring Wollstonecraft to author the first published response to Burke, *A Vindication of the Rights of Men* (1790).[102]

In the fall of 1791 Wollstonecraft became concerned that the progress of freedom had stalled. The French Constituent Assembly debated a proposal by Charles de Talleyrand-Périgord for a system of publicly funded schools that would deny education to girls beyond age eight while enabling boys to continue according to their talents. The constitution adopted in September 1791, meanwhile, classified all women—and men without property— as passive citizens, entitled to the protection of the laws but barred from direct participation in government.[103] That month Wollstonecraft began work on a second vindication—this time focused on the rights of women— which she dedicated to Talleyrand.

Though Wollstonecraft's title popularized the concept of woman's rights, her *Vindication of the Rights of Woman* deferred discussion of "the laws relative to women, and the consideration of their peculiar duties," to a proposed second volume (which never appeared).[104] Instead, Wollstonecraft focused on a "few simple principles," the first of which was that women are "human creatures, who, in common with men, are placed on this earth to unfold their faculties."[105]

She argued that otherwise liberal men denied women equal citizenship, not because they thought women lacked reason but because they found girlish beauty sexually attractive and female maturity repellent. Women, for their part, consented to their own subjection because they did not discover "when 'in the noon of beauty's power,' that they are treated like queens only to be deluded by hollow respect."[106]

Wollstonecraft recommended age-graded schooling and cited a "lively writer" who asked "what business women turned of forty have to do in the world."[107] But, in general, she was not concerned with chronological age as a means of defining life stage. Rather, she attacked the attitudinal bedrock that enabled men to treat women like overgrown children. Her goal was not to prove that women were fully mature by age sixteen, twenty-one, or forty but rather to prove the more fundamental point that women and men were both capable of growth throughout their lives.

Wollstonecraft challenged artificial barriers to female maturity in numerous spheres simultaneously: in families, where the laws of marriage required wives to obey husbands; in education, where girls received inferior training to boys; in religious institutions, where male clerics demanded female obedience; in market relations, where employers paid women too little to support themselves; in the state, where men denied women independent political standing; and in civil society, where men discounted women's opinions.[108]

The central problem for Wollstonecraft was not that women were confined to private households. She believed that female duties should center on their families, but she maintained that women could not fulfill these duties if they failed to grow up. Immature women, according to Wollstonecraft, "act as such children may be expected to act:—they dress; they paint, and nickname God's creatures.—Surely these weak beings are only fit for a seraglio!" Though pleasing to men, they could not be "expected to govern a family with judgment, or take care of the poor babes whom they bring into the world."[109] Because men treated women like dependent children rather than rational adults, females were "made ridiculous and useless when the short-lived bloom of beauty is over."[110] Young women, meanwhile, actively participated in cultivating their own childishness because "the adoration comes first, and the scorn is not anticipated."[111] The result was a failure to perform duties as wives, mothers, or useful citizens.

Wollstonecraft illustrated her argument with a lesson drawn from botany, comparing female education to cultivation: "Like the flowers which are planted in too rich a soil, strength and usefulness are sacrificed to beauty; and the flaunting leaves, after having pleased a fastidious eye, fade, disregarded on the stalk, long before the season when they ought to have arrived at maturity."[112] Wollstonecraft did not intend this analogy as a literary metaphor but as a scientific description of the process by which corrupt social relations stunted and blocked female potential. As anyone familiar with botany would have known, luxuriant flowers were short-lived, prone to disease, and sterile but prized for their beauty. Rousseau warned female botanists not to study these flowers because they were "mutilated. . . . Nature will no longer be found among them."[113] Wollstonecraft appropriated his language to argue that women themselves had become like hothouse flowers. In case readers missed the point, she helpfully translated the principles established by botanists into the language of political science: in human terms, the cultivation of beauty resulted in the loss of "abilities and virtues."[114]

Botany was an effective language for Wollstonecraft because the analogy between cultivation and education was well established in pedagogical writings and the philosophical history of the Scottish Enlightenment. More specifically, botany provided an acceptable language for analyzing sex. In the 1730s Carl Linnaeus first detailed the sexual reproduction of plants. What had long been a metaphoric association between flowers and human sexual organs became literal and scientific. Erasmus Darwin's *Loves of the Plants* (1789) scandalously celebrated the wide variety of sexual arrangements illuminated by botanical science and included a frontispiece designed by Wollstonecraft's friend Fuseli.[115]

Wollstonecraft employed the language of botany to expose what she saw as a powerful sexual fantasy shared by many men. Rousseau provided the most vivid example. In describing young girls as coquettes, Wollstonecraft charged, Rousseau "did not go back to nature, or his ruling appetite disturbed the operations of reason."[116] Though he practiced self-denial, he "debauched his imagination."[117] He became, she suggested, sexually aroused by prepubescent girls.

The sexualization of young girls was not a problem limited to ancien régime France, however. "Rousseau," Wollstonecraft pointedly wrote, "is not the only man who has indirectly said that the person of a *young* woman, without any mind . . . is very pleasing."[118] There was also the Scots Presbyterian minister James Fordyce, whose sermons and conduct books praised women but implied "that they are only like angels when they are young and beautiful."[119] Then there were the leaders of the Scottish Enlightenment—John Millar, Adam Smith, and David Hume—whose praise for morally virtuous but dependent women Wollstonecraft compared to the "lullaby strains of condescending endearment."[120]

This ideal of girlish beauty, however, only gained force in practice, for example, when mothers decided not to breastfeed their children in an effort to preserve a youthful shape to their breasts.[121] Wollstonecraft followed Rousseau in advocating breastfeeding as a means of ensuring infants' proper growth, but her explanation for the use of wet nurses stressed women's desire to artificially "preserve their beauty," even if this meant not performing their maternal duties.[122] Where Rousseau saw coquetry as the highest expression of female nature, Wollstonecraft redefined the desire to please men as a source of unnatural corruption.

Ever critical of Edmund Burke, she was quite likely aware of his leering panegyric to "that part of a beautiful woman where she is perhaps the most beautiful, about the neck and breasts; the smoothness; the softness; the easy and insensible swell . . . the deceitful maze, through which the unsteady eye slides giddily."[123] Wollstonecraft argued that given such homage, women understandably tried "to preserve" their "virgin charms" by refusing to nurse their children, an effort that she pointed out was doomed to failure as their breasts inevitably sagged and wrinkled with time.[124] When "superannuated coquettes . . . [can] no longer inspire love, they pay for the vigour and vivacity of their youth," she pessimistically concluded.[125]

Much better, she insisted, to cultivate virtues in youth that would last into old age. By defining individual development as the "grand end" of human life for both sexes, Wollstonecraft took virtues traditionally seen as masculine and repositioned them as aspects of maturity available to both sexes. Whereas the traditional Christian view of maturity distinguished between the ages of the soul and the ages of the body, Wollstonecraft believed that God's providential plan was for body and soul to mature together. Like many Rational Dissenters, she regarded earthly life as a probationary period during which individuals used their reason to gain knowledge of God's eternal goodness and thus prepare for a life of immortality, which she characterized as the highest stage of mature development to which a soul could aspire. According to this revised view of Christian maturity, the human soul was sexless precisely because it was *not* ageless.[126]

Rather than classifying human faculties as masculine or feminine, Wollstonecraft used the language of growth to measure development from weak to strong, narrow to large, immature to mature. According to this logic, "manly virtues" were more "properly" defined as a "scale" for all "mankind."[127] Wollstonecraft thus used maturity to resolve the paradox of sexual sameness and difference that has been fundamental to feminism.[128]

She agreed with Locke that children's lack of reason necessitated a natural stage of subjection, but she emphasized, as Locke did not, that God commanded all of his children—male and female—to develop their own abilities. Let men and women, she wrote, "as children of the same parent . . . reason together, and learn to submit to the authority of reason."[129] Wollstonecraft thus positioned God as a perfected Lockean parent who treated all his children equally, even when earthly parents did not.[130]

Later women's rights activists would argue that women deserved political rights because they were morally superior to men. This was not Wollstonecraft's strategy. Rather, she believed that women needed rights—particularly the right to rely on their own reason—in order to develop their capacities as mature human beings.[131] For Wollstonecraft, a woman who behaved well because she obeyed a husband, a minister, or public opinion was not truly virtuous because she did not rely on her own reason but merely followed the command of another. Whereas Rousseau and the Scottish moralists argued that female dependence conferred moral influence, Wollstonecraft insisted that women could not develop moral sense if they clung to men like overgrown children.[132]

Wollstonecraft argued that women should be free to vote for and to serve as "representatives," to earn their own money, and to remain legally independent within marriage—what we have come to think of as women's rights.[133] She also contemplated how romantic love could become more democratic and sexual desire more meritocratic. For women to develop moral and civic virtue, they would have to be respected for it, and this would in turn require a new valuation of female beauty that placed the mature display of character above the freshness of youth. Physiognomy, the theory that human character could be read in the features of the face, enabled Wollstonecraft to argue that people should look for "the traces of passion" that marked the face as a more elevated form of beauty than the smoothness of youth.[134] Beauty, like other forms of achievement, would then be the reward of individual virtue rather than an arbitrary accident of birth.

It was largely to teach young people to admire character over coquetry that Wollstonecraft made her famous proposal that "day schools, for particular ages, should be established by government, in which boys and girls might be educated together." Students had to be organized by age, for age would create a basis of equality in a school "where boys and girls, the rich and poor, should meet together." From "five to nine years of age," they "should be dressed alike," "submit to the same discipline," get plenty of exercise, and learn basic subjects through active investigation and "conversations, in the Socratic form."[135]

Wollstonecraft's program for national education would turn early childhood into a distinct stage of life free from gender or class distinctions. Adulthood, however, demanded duties appropriate to one's station in life. "After the age of nine," she wrote, "girls and boys, intended for domestic employments, or mechanical trades, ought to be removed to other schools, and receive instruction, in some measure appropriate to the destination of each individual."[136] Wollstonecraft did not seek to overturn all social distinctions.

Her central goal was to reform romantic love among the educated class. Once schools of higher education taught young people to base love on mutual esteem rather than on men's attraction to childish women, "what advances might not the human mind make?"[137] This wish of establishing love between equals was the central reform that previous arguments for liberty and equality had overlooked. It was the heart of Wollstonecraft's "Utopian dreams."[138]

From its first appearance, *A Vindication of the Rights of Woman* sparked debate over Wollstonecraft's sexual prescriptions. Early critics condemned her as immoral, while twentieth-century critics described her as an advocate of bourgeois sexual repression. In fact, she did not seek to repress sexual desire, and certainly not to advance any bourgeois standard of sexual propriety, but she did seek to contain overwhelming sexual passion within a particular stage of life and to direct it toward a particular end. "Youth is the season for love in both sexes; but in those days of thoughtless enjoyment provision should be made for the more important years of life when reflection takes the place of sensation," Wollstonecraft wrote.[139]

Though Wollstonecraft vowed not to marry herself, she argued for the reform of marriage so as to permit the equal independence of husband and wife. Her definition of independence was rooted in her understanding of mature duty and did not necessarily require that the wife pursue paid work. She pictured a rural household where the wife nursed her children and managed domestic affairs while the husband worked outside the home for pay. Wollstonecraft thought "a couple of this description, equally necessary and independent of each other, because each fulfilled the respective duties of their station."[140] Though the wife's work was in the home and unpaid, she exercised her own reason to determine her duties rather than simply obeying her husband as though she were a child. While this image seems to echo conventional praise of domesticity, Wollstonecraft's meaning was more radical.[141] For her, a wife's civil existence could not be incorporated into that of her husband, for how can a being "be virtuous, who is not free?"[142]

The repetitive nature of domestic work, however, was difficult to construe as a form of self-improvement over time. Wollstonecraft resolved this problem by displacing household work onto servants. She pictured a middle-class matron "discharging the duties of her station with, perhaps, merely a servant-maid to take off her hands the servile part of the household business."[143] The displacement of "servile" work onto the "servant" enabled the matron to gain respect as she aged.

Wollstonecraft's relentless focus on self-improvement led her to divide women by social class, both in her educational plan and in her model of household labor. Equally significant, her focus on maturity emphasized generational differences.[144] Even while counseling respect for elders, she hinted that generational conflict might be an inevitable part of social reform, and of female liberation in particular. Writing of parents who lacked virtue, Wollstonecraft wondered: "How indeed can an instructor remedy this evil? For to teach [children] virtue on any solid principle is to teach them to despise their parents." In other words, many women could not become free until they learned to hate their mothers, yet they could only become free by learning to mix love with esteem in the "first affection."[145] This was a paradox that Wollstonecraft did not—perhaps could not—resolve. Where Locke, Blackstone, and Rousseau argued that sons distanced themselves from mothers to become the equals of their fathers, it was much harder to imagine how daughters could do this while also learning to respect female maturity.

In both Britain and America, the initial responses to Wollstonecraft's book were largely positive. Those who chose to criticize her, however, found the equal rights of women as unnatural as those of children. For example, in *Strictures on the Modern System of Female Education* (1799), Hannah More, an evangelical author and reformer, observed, "The rights of man have been discussed. . . . To these have been opposed, as the next stage in the process of illumination, the *rights of women*. It follows, according to the natural progression of human things, that the next influx of that irradiation which our enlighteners are pouring in upon us, will illuminate the world with grave descants on the *rights of youth*, the *rights of children*, and the *rights of babies*."[146] For many readers in the 1790s, Wollstonecraft and More came to symbolize two different approaches to the problem of adult women's citizenship: women as independent beings created equal and endowed with rights versus women as moral exemplars whose virtue resulted precisely from their refusal to compete equally with men in politics and commercial relations. It was still an open question as to which understanding of female citizenship would prevail.[147]

LEGACIES

Adams, Wheatley, and Wollstonecraft shared a common frustration with those who compared the rights of women to the "rights of babies" or argued that women could not make a transition to adulthood on the same terms as men. Each struggled, in her own way, to establish herself as an independent adult in the context of laws that classified all women with children and to win recognition of women's maturity, particularly their intellectual maturity. The varying success with which these three women were able to achieve their goals underlines both the shared concerns that united them and the rigid confines of race, economic status, and class-bound morality that divided them. Further, their later lives reveal that very personal battles were part and parcel of claiming a public influence within international debates. If we privilege their public influence over their private strivings, we lose sight of the very reason they found the issue of adulthood so compelling in the first place: asserting women's maturity required claiming political, economic, familial, and sexual independence all at the same time.

Phillis Wheatley won her freedom in 1773, just as the escalating conflict between Massachusetts patriots and British officials divided her transatlantic network of supporters. Many black people determined that their best chance for liberty lay with the British, but Wheatley chose to stay in Boston and write poems that deftly honored revolutionary leaders and promoted the cause of black freedom. Wheatley corresponded with George Washington, who signed himself her "obedient humble servant," which, though formulaic, was quite a remarkable way for a slave owner to address a young woman recently freed.[148] Despite her international stature, however, freedom for Wheatley, as for all free blacks in the North, meant struggling for subsistence in a context of racial discrimination. In 1778 she married a free black grocer and lawyer named John Peters. Despite their ambitions and some initial success, John fell into debt, and Phillis was unable to secure enough subscribers to print a second volume of poems. Little is known of her life thereafter except that two children died young and, in 1784, her third child was buried along with her in an unmarked grave. She was thirty years old.[149]

Though she had been unable to raise much interest among Bostonians preoccupied with war, her words and achievements continued to influence antislavery activists. One of the first published defenses of her poetic talent against Jefferson's critique was penned by an American land speculator, Gilbert Imlay. His ardent defense of black potential was one of many qualities that convinced Mary Wollstonecraft of his worthiness. The two met in Paris in 1793 as the Terror unfolded and war between Britain and France made all British citizens suspect. Having fallen in love, they convinced the American ambassador in Paris to register Mary as Mrs. Gilbert Imlay, thus making her the citizen of a neutral nation—though, in fact, they never married. This novel arrangement enabled Wollstonecraft to stay in Paris with Imlay, become a mother, and continue to publish under her own name.[150]

In *An Historical and Moral View of the French Revolution* (1794), Wollstonecraft blamed revolutionary violence on the persistence of feudal hierarchies that prevented the French from achieving "maturity of judgment." In 1796, as John Adams prepared to assume the presidency of the United States, amid fears that Jacobin violence could spread to American shores, he first read this book and, over the years, made more marginal notes in it than in any other book in his library: "this weak woman"; "this foolish woman"; "a Savage Theory. A barbarous Theory. Indians Negroes Tartars Hottentots would have refined more."[151] Abigail, if anything, was more anti-Jacobin than her husband, but she read all she could by proponents of female education and circulated these books among family and friends. In 1793 her sister wrote, "I wish you would be so kind as to lend me the Rights of Women."[152]

Abigail was able to give her sister not only "the Rights of Women" but also money—something that under the laws of coverture she should not have been able to do. The Adamses, like all American families during the Revolution, faced shortages and inflation but were in the position of creditors rather than debtors. While John was preoccupied with government service, Abigail was savvy enough to realize that the most promising investment during the war was not land or gold but government securities. These investments paid off handsomely, because the politicians who wielded state and federal power after the war—many of whom were her friends—ensured that the government would fulfill its obligations to creditors, even if this meant demanding high taxes from hard-pressed farmers, organizing mass foreclosures, and, eventually, employing military force to put down the threat of further rebellions.[153] Adams thus established a measure of personal independence within her marriage and public influence in American politics that was contingent on her class position.[154]

Wollstonecraft never had Adams's money, and by refusing to marry, she forswore her claim to bourgeois respectability. In 1795 she returned to London and, as the relationship with Imlay fizzled, supported herself and her daughter through writing. In 1796, with William Godwin, she finally found the blend of romantic love and mutual esteem—the "friendship" between equals—that she had long desired. With Godwin's guarantee of her ongoing independence, she agreed to marry. But their happiness was not to last long. In September 1797, at thirty-eight years old, she died of puerperal fever after delivering her second child (the future Mary Shelley, author of *Frankenstein*). Heartbroken, Godwin published his *Memoirs*

(1798) to honor all Wollstonecraft had achieved, not only in public but in private. His book revealed details—the out-of-wedlock pregnancies!—that had not been widely known. Many were shocked. Others continued, like Abigail, to pass her books from hand to hand.[155]

This was how women's rights worked among educated men and women in the late eighteenth century, through lent books, borrowed ideas, and conversations that never coalesced into a movement but nonetheless sustained new ways of thinking and acting. There were, of course, other modes of making women's rights claims—for example, through working-class protest and slave resistance—but for women like Adams, Wheatley, and Wollstonecraft, a shared print culture was essential.[156]

By 1800 Wollstonecraft and Wheatley were dead. Neither lived long enough to find out "what business women turned of forty have to do in the world."[157] The Federalist Party, through which Adams had exercised her influence, was in defeat and disarray.[158] Thomas Jefferson won the presidency by championing democracy, but his Republicanism did not bode well for the understandings of women's mature citizenship championed by Adams, Wheatley, and Wollstonecraft. At the state level, Republicans began organizing constitutional conventions that replaced property qualifications for the suffrage with age qualifications—but only for white men.[159]

From their very different social contexts, Adams, Wheatley, and Wollstonecraft raised issues that deeply influenced the transatlantic development of women's rights ideas and activism. Each argued that white male citizens claimed revolutionary rights for themselves on the basis of their maturity while classifying other adults as overgrown children. Adams argued that women needed to cast off their childishness to gain respect as patriotic citizens. Wheatley fought to gain respect for African Americans' mature capacity for reason and moral leadership. Wollstonecraft focused squarely on how age structured sexual desire, arguing that women could never become equal citizens as long as men found young girls more attractive than grown women. Later generations of women's rights activists continued to wrestle with these ideas, but the political significance of maturity changed in the United States. As state governments dropped property requirements for suffrage and enfranchised virtually all white men at age twenty-one, full citizenship became a stage of life for white males, and the exclusion of other adults came to seem even more unjust to a growing number of intellectuals and activists.

CHAPTER TWO

DEMOCRATIC CITIZENSHIP
AS A STAGE OF LIFE

In Jacksonian America, no specific birthday was associated with leaving home, completing school, starting work, or getting married. Young people made these transitions at widely varying ages.[1] Yet, delegates to state constitutional conventions replaced property requirements for suffrage with age requirements. Whereas the nation's founders believed that autonomy rested on the material base of property, Jacksonians located a wellspring of independence within men themselves, in "the structure of the mind and in the qualities of the heart."[2] To measure the "mind" and the "heart," politicians turned to chronological age, claiming that white men normally developed the capacity to govern themselves by age twenty-one.[3]

Politicians, especially members of the Democratic Party, turned to age as a measure of civic capacity because it so perfectly suited the Jacksonian-era impetus to cut through class bias and enfranchise the "common man." Laborers, clerks, recent immigrants—that is, the potential voters whose support politicians desired—all could be of the requisite age even if they possessed little else. Counting birthdays was a truly democratic form of accumulation. The result was that by the 1840s, voting had become both a political right and a rite of passage defined by chronological age—but only for white men.[4]

The same politicians who argued that white men normally developed the capacity for self-government by age twenty-one insisted that black men and all women did not. These exclusions were integral, not incidental, to redefining political independence as a normative stage of life. Delegates to state constitutional conventions cited the right of contract as proof that free men over age twenty-one controlled their destiny, in contrast to enslaved men, who supposedly bowed to their masters' will throughout their lives. By alleging that black men tolerated perpetual servitude while white men would not, delegates identified a particular spirit of liberty within white men that did not depend on property.[5] Second, delegates argued that working men used their wages to support dependent women and children. This dedication to protecting dependents, delegates claimed, proved that adult male laborers could be trusted to legislate for the common good even if they had not established independent households but remained tenants and wage earners.[6] Many slaves resisted their masters, and many women earned wages—but positing their perpetual dependence nonetheless proved an effective justification for extending political rights to adult white men while denying them to black men and all women.

For slaves in Jacksonian America, reaching adulthood did not bring a transition to independence but rather an increased valuation in a master's account book. By opening the West to settlement while ending the international slave trade in 1808, politicians increased the importance of interstate slave sales as a source of profit, wreaking havoc on black families and increasing the significance of chronological age and life stage as measures of investment in human property. Between the ratification of the Constitution and the Civil War, approximately two-thirds of a million people were sold from states in the upper South to areas in the lower South and Southwest. Slave owners calculated the price of enslaved people based on many variables—temperament, skills, health, and appearance, indeed all the traits that make an individual. But the shorthand notation of slave sales often listed only name, age, and dollars—the estimate of an enslaved person's age functioning as a rough gauge of size and capacity, which in turn largely determined price. "A boy large enough to plow . . . a Girl large Enough to nurse," as one trader described the logic of treasuring physical growth in men and reproductive capacity in women.[7]

To understand the political significance of chronological age in Jacksonian America, therefore, it is necessary to look at the two arenas in which age figured most prominently: white manhood suffrage and the domestic slave trade. The significance of chronological age was increasing in other arenas as well—educational reformers were pushing for the age grading of common schools, doctors were using age to determine normative patterns of growth, employers were paying more attention to age in structuring wage labor, and middle-class families were beginning to celebrate birthdays. Yet, these economic and cultural developments were still in-choate and unclear.[8] The relevance of chronological age stood out most sharply in the celebration of age twenty-one as a transition to full citizen-ship for white men and as a measure of the value of slave property.

In the face of these developments, disenfranchised intellectuals con-fronted their exclusion from full citizenship in different ways but found common cause in arguing that if democratic equality was a stage of life defined by age, then limiting rights to white men was unjust. Some of these protests, most notably that of Frederick Douglass, argued quite spe-cifically that age twenty-one should become a transition to freedom for all Americans, not just white men. Others, such as David Walker and Marga-ret Fuller, did not mention age twenty-one in particular but rather argued in more general terms that black men or women should be recognized as fully realized adults rather than be categorized with minors. What all these arguments had in common was a critique of the way in which white men claimed rights and opportunities in both public and private based on their status as full-grown men while denying the same to other Ameri-cans, whatever their age or individual capacities.

CHRONOLOGICAL AGE AND WHITE MANHOOD SUFFRAGE

As Democratic-Republicans and Federalists competed for popular sup-port in the early 1800s, politicians (especially Republicans) pushed for state constitutional conventions to expand suffrage to propertyless white men. When these reform-minded delegates turned to age twenty-one as a measure of individual capacity, they did so in response to political im-peratives: the intense partisan conflicts that led to the ascendancy of the Democratic Party in the 1820s, the election of Andrew Jackson in 1828, and the development of the second party system in the 1830s. They were also responding to broad economic and cultural changes that undermined the relevance of landed property to economic well-being. Growth of the market economy, the transition from apprenticeship to wage labor, and migration to cities created a large population of white men who lived off wages and rented homes. By enfranchising these men, competing political factions hoped to gain electoral advantage.[9]

To expand the pool of voters, delegates to state constitutional conven-tions redefined independent citizenship as a stage of life for white men, a process particularly evident in Massachusetts and New York, two states in which the women's rights movement would later flourish. In 1820, when delegates in Massachusetts elected John Adams president of their convention, all rose to remove their hats as he entered the hall and then sat down to dismantle the property qualifications for suffrage that the elder statesman continued to defend. The convention was controlled by conservatives who agreed to extend suffrage to poor men only if property assessments rather than population continued to determine the apportionment of seats in the state senate. With this compromise, advocates for eliminating property qualifications for suffrage carried the convention.[10]

These reformers successfully argued that free men developed the capacity for full citizenship by age twenty-one, in contrast to enslaved men and all women, who did not. Edmund Foster, a Congregational minister and Revolutionary War veteran from Littleton, argued that "men in this commonwealth become freemen when they arrive at twenty-one years of age; and why oblige them to buy their freedom? . . . Men who have no property are put in the situation of the slaves of Virginia; they ought to be saved the degrading feelings."[11] Foster implied that, unlike slaves, free white men over twenty-one were striving to amass property, even if they had not done so yet, and could thus be trusted with ballots. James Austin, a delegate from Boston, agreed, adding that laboring men "support their families reputably with their daily earnings."[12] Delegates thus argued that white men were independent at twenty-one because they were *not* slaves or dependent family members.

No one proposed to enfranchise men under twenty-one. Indeed, in debating whether or not minors in the militia should be allowed to vote for their own officers, delegates took especial pains to clarify that military service should not under any circumstances qualify men between eighteen and twenty-one to vote in general elections. The 1780 constitution, written under the leadership of John Adams, limited participation in militia elections to those twenty-one years and older. Militia commanders at the 1820 convention pointed out that this provision was never enforced until Adams's old colleague James Sullivan held the governorship from 1807 to 1808. Joseph Valentine, lieutenant colonel from Hopkinton, claimed that Sullivan's "prohibition had created great uneasiness and confusion in the militia, and had greatly diminished its spirit." The chair of the committee on the militia, U.S. senator Joseph Varnum, defended the revolutionary-era view that allowing minors to vote in any election was a "violation of general principles" and that twenty-one should be a universal standard for electors. The majority of delegates, however, agreed with Valentine that allowing militiamen to vote for their own officers would boost morale. They revised the constitution so as to allow militia captains to be elected "by the members of their respective companies, without regard to age."

But delegates emphasized that the militia was "a case by itself" and that they had not "opened the door" for minors to vote in other elections. As Samuel Fay of Cambridge argued, "Minors serving in the militia may be perfectly competent to judge of the qualifications for subaltern officers and not competent to judge in other matters."[13] Delegates wanted to encourage teenage boys to perform their military obligation but held fast to the long-established principle that minors lacked the judgment necessary to represent themselves in general government.

Massachusetts was unusual in allowing black men to vote on the same terms as white, a result of the influence of Federalists, who enjoyed large support among black voters. In states like New York where Federalists had less influence, Republicans successfully mobilized arguments for why black men did not develop political capacity with age. The New York state constitutional convention of 1821 was dominated by Bucktails, a reform faction of the Republican Party whose name derived from the fashion of wearing deer-tail hats and whose policies appealed to white working men.[14] As in Massachusetts, those in favor of expanding the suffrage argued that independence resulted from manly character, not property. Daniel Tompkins, vice president of the United States and president of the convention, set the tone when he asserted, "Independence consists more in the structure of the mind and in the qualities of the heart" than in the ownership of property.[15] Reaching age twenty-one necessitated an independent "structure of mind" because men over that age had to become the "framers of their own fortunes."[16] In other words, the capacity for independence was a prerequisite for the contractual relations that enabled a man to amass property, not the result of owning property. Conservative delegates in New York warned that abolishing the property requirement would extend the vote to young single men with no families or permanent residences. Defenders of working men turned this very rootlessness into a virtue, arguing that an unmarried laboring man without property, even if he supported no one but himself, had to be particularly "honest" and "industrious" in order to earn a living.[17]

Massachusetts and New York diverged on the issue of race as a qualification for voting. The strength of Federalists in Massachusetts ensured that the state remained one of the few to allow black men to vote on the same terms as white. New York's Bucktail reformers, however, argued that black men (despite a few respectable exceptions) did not mature in the same way as white.[18] For example, John Ross, chair of the committee on suffrage, argued that black men were "incapable . . . of exercising that privilege with any sort of discretion, prudence, or independence."[19]

After much debate, the New York convention decided to permit black men to vote only if they had amassed a freehold worth $250.[20] Delegates justified the property requirement as an inducement "to make [African American men] industrious and frugal."[21] White men needed no such inducement, however, since these were traits already associated with their stage of life.

In New York, as in Massachusetts, delegates stressed that serving in the militia or army did not qualify minors to vote. General Erastus Root showed a scrupulous concern for "young men coming of age after the [tax] assessment came out, and before October," who, if paying a tax were the only qualification, might not be able to vote "until they were more than twenty-two years of age." So that these men could vote as soon as they reached full age, he proposed adding service in the militia as a qualification but emphasized that this would apply only to those twenty-one and over.[22] Delegates agreed they should enfranchise those who had provided "military service from the age of eighteen to twenty-one," "young men whose patriotic bosoms burn with a love of country," but only when they reached full age.[23]

To prove that voting was a privilege, not a natural right, Federalists pointed out that military service alone had never qualified minors to vote. For example, Elisha Williams from Columbia County asked jokingly if the champions of propertyless soldiers also proposed to enfranchise those only "twenty years of age" and thus make "brave infants voters."[24] Chief Justice Ambrose Spencer went so far as to claim that no one in New York had ever "doubted" the constitutional principle that "no man under twenty-one years shall exercise the right of suffrage"—this despite the fact that "many arrive at maturity of understanding, and are ornaments of society, before they reach that age." The age qualification excluded these worthy voters, Spencer conceded, but was still just, because "it is necessary in establishing laws, to have general rules."[25] In the end, agreeing that age twenty-one was an arbitrary but necessary qualification for electors, delegates abolished property requirements but clung to the rule that voters be legal adults.

As delegates intended, the new requirements for suffrage enfranchised virtually every adult white male. There were a few exceptions. Paupers, "lunatics," and criminals were all understood to lack the control over their own destiny normally expected of adult men. The exclusion of white men from voting was never permanent, however. There was always hope they might reform and assume their status as full citizens. Free black men could vote in some states, especially in New England. Only women were everywhere and always prevented from making a transition to independent citizenship.[26]

In New Jersey, the experiment of propertied women's suffrage came to an end in 1807. Rivalry between liberal and moderate Republicans led to a compromise law limiting the vote to white male taxpaying citizens. Republicans gave up the votes of non-taxpayers and resident aliens, while Federalists sacrificed the votes of free blacks and women. This backroom dealing inspired little protest from women, who had not built the political coalitions that would have been necessary to fight their disenfranchisement. The problem was not only that few women met the property requirement to vote but also that those who did usually enjoyed the privilege for only a brief stage of their lives—either before marriage or after a husband's death. Black women were likely more alarmed by challenges to New Jersey's gradual emancipation law that sought to reestablish slavery in the state.[27]

The phrase "women and children first" would not enter the popular lexicon until the 1850s, when it became part of an unwritten maritime code for rescuing people at sea.[28] Yet the phrase "women and children" recurred frequently in antebellum debates over suffrage because these were the two groups that all delegates agreed could never, under any circumstances, be trusted with the vote. Black men, paupers, lunatics, and criminals might all be capable of becoming independent men. Only women were perpetually classed with minors, whatever their race, wealth, education, or civic responsibilities. What is striking about antebellum state governments' establishment of age twenty-one as a requirement for voting, therefore, is not that it universally enfranchised *all* men but rather that this seemingly neutral measure of human development so thoroughly excluded *all* women.[29]

Young men throughout the North began to celebrate their "virgin vote" as a significant rite of passage.[30] Election officials, meanwhile, faced new pressures to determine whether or not a young man really was twenty-one years old, since age, rather than property, had become the major qualification. Since most municipalities kept no official birth records, election judges determined the age of a potential voter by evaluating his physical appearance (particularly his capacity to grow a beard), relying on personal knowledge of the youth and his family, and asking the young man to take an oath on the Bible swearing he was of full age. In rural communities where men knew each other well, they could generally determine a young man's age through shared recollections. In urban areas with large immigrant populations, where the most heated debates focused on who was or was not a citizen, election judges generally took a young man's word as to his age. Some voters, whether born in the United States or abroad, did not know how old they were. In such cases, election judges had to trust their instinct as to whether the voter appeared to be of full age or not. Because election judges represented competing parties and volunteer challengers from each party stood outside the polling place, partisans kept an eye on each other and generally ensured that local standards, whether strict or lax, fell uniformly across party lines.[31] That age was not established by official documents but by community judgment as to who was a man made casting the first vote all the more precious to young men struggling to make their way in the world—and exclusion from polling places all the more galling for women and black men who found themselves classed with children, whatever their age or community standing.[32]

Even as delegates to state constitutional conventions relied on chronological age, they freely admitted that age twenty-one was an arbitrary boundary in the lives of white males, with many developing competence and patriotism before that age. As politicians were well aware, youth in this period were increasingly mobile, with minors of both sexes leaving home to negotiate their own labor contracts in cities, in factory towns, or on the frontier. Judges accommodated their right to do so through the principle of "implied emancipation," which held that minors independently seeking work had their father's or guardian's implicit consent to do so. Turning twenty-one made little difference in the daily lives of these young workers.[33] Personal writings reveal that young men in antebellum America generally did not consider themselves fully mature until they married and had children of their own, a transition that generally happened somewhere in their midtwenties or even later.[34] Nonetheless, Jacksonian-era political leaders concluded that limiting the vote to white males age twenty-one or older provided an effective means for separating white working men from boys, black men, and all women. By insisting that nearly all white men developed the capacity for full citizenship by age twenty-one while most black men and all women did not, Jacksonians enfranchised the common man while simultaneously adding new fuel to the argument that most adults resembled children throughout their lives. In response, free black men, free black women, and white women intensified their efforts to prove that they were not children. These activists and intellectuals did not dispute the particular age boundaries used to confer obligations and rights on white men—whether eighteen for militia duty or twenty-one for the vote—but rather focused on the more fundamental matter of proving that black men and all women were not overgrown children but fully realized adults.

DAVID WALKER, WOMEN, AND CHILDREN

White men expressed their enthusiasm for "universal" suffrage through rising voter participation, which reached unprecedented levels in the 1820s only to peak even higher during the partisan struggles of the 1840s.[35] The full significance of white manhood suffrage, however, can be appreciated only by looking at the response of those Americans who took an equal interest in politics—who attended speeches, signed petitions, cheered at rallies, read papers, and even paid taxes—but were perpetually excluded from casting a ballot.[36] As they came to appreciate the full burden of this exclusion, they realized that the problem was not simply that they lacked political power but, more fundamentally, that they were unable to claim recognition as adult citizens. If equal citizenship was based not on property but on qualities of the "mind" and "heart," what did the denial of rights say about the character of black men and all women? If all men were "created equal," why did only some people make a transition to independent citizenship at age twenty-one? Between the 1820s and the 1840s, advocates of racial and sexual equality worked out divergent answers to these questions in conversation and conflict with each other.

Free black men were better positioned than black or white women to argue for political equality since they had voted under many revolutionary-era state constitutions. Indeed, their tendency to support Federalist candidates was the main reason Democrats pushed to disenfranchise them. As Democrats developed the self-serving argument that black men were members of a "degraded" race, a substantial coalition of former Federalists, abolitionists, and free black people organized throughout the Northeast to demand that state governments continue to recognize black men "as men."[37] The founding of the American Colonization Society in 1816 as an organized effort to finance the return of black people to Africa further galvanized free black people to defend their equal claim to full citizenship.[38]

The most influential defense of black equality in the face of disenfranchisement and colonization came from David Walker, a Boston merchant who in 1829 published his *Appeal to the Colored Citizens of the World*. Walker was born free in 1796 in North Carolina, the child of an enslaved father, who died before his birth, and a free black mother. He grew to adulthood in the South, a witness to the violence of slavery. By 1825 Walker moved to Boston, opened a used clothing store, joined the African Masonic Lodge and the African Methodist Episcopal Church, and entered the public debate over whether or not black men could qualify for equal citizenship. As an agent for *Freedom's Journal*, the first black newspaper in the United States, Walker was familiar with leading arguments for black equality. His brilliance was to join established traditions of black resistance into a coherent argument against southern slavery, northern prejudice, laws denying black people full citizenship, and proposals by the American Colonization Society advocating the removal of free blacks to Africa.[39]

Walker influentially argued that slavery, prejudice, and colonization proposals alike were based on the belief that black people were not "men." Throughout the *Appeal*, Walker wove together two distinct meanings of the assertion that "we are MEN."[40] His first strand of argument emphasized that all African Americans—men, women, and children—were members of the "human family" and as such deserved to be free.[41] According to this logic, freedom was not a particular stage of life but a fundamental aspect of the general human condition. Because white Americans denied the humanity of "a set of men, women and children," all ages and both sexes had to join in the struggle to prove that "we are MEN, and not brutes as we have been represented, and by the millions treated."[42]

Interwoven with this first strand of argument was a second that responded more particularly to the assignment of rights and obligations on the basis of mature manhood. In this formulation, to be a free man was to be something other than a woman, child, or enfeebled elderly person. Though Walker did not discuss the significance of either age eighteen or twenty-one as a moment when white men took on new rights and obligations, he argued in the strongest possible terms that adult black men had a responsibility to represent and defend their dependent wives, children, and elderly parents.[43] He wrote that black men "feel for our fathers, mothers, wives and children, as well as the whites do for theirs."[44]

Most controversially, Walker insisted that black men would, if pressed, take up arms to defend their liberty. Patrick Henry's revolutionary rallying cry—"Give me liberty or give me death!"—had become a touchstone of American national identity by the 1820s.[45] Addressing black men, Walker asked, "Had you not rather be killed than to be a slave to a tyrant, who takes the life of your mother, wife, and dear little children? Look upon your mother, wife and children, and answer God Almighty."[46] In the highest test of patriotic spirit—risking one's life for liberty—women and children were not partners but dependents whose very weakness inspired men to act.

Walker's simultaneous defense of black manhood as, on the one hand, the general humanity of the race and, on the other, the specific character of adult males should not be seen as contradictory. Walker had set himself the task of responding directly to Thomas Jefferson's *Notes on the State of Virginia*, which "declared to the world that we are inferior to the whites, both in the endowments of our bodies and our minds."[47] Walker was a careful enough reader of Jefferson's *Notes* to notice that the Virginian's argument rested on assertions that black men failed to manifest the same tendency to cherish and protect women. Jefferson alleged that black people desired white people just as monkeys lusted for black women, a claim that drove Walker's outraged determination to refute white people who "held us up as descending originally from the tribes of *Monkeys* or *Orang-Outangs*."[48] That Walker sought to prove the unity of the human race by arguing that black men would risk their lives to protect black women is understandable given the logic of Jefferson's original argument, growing suspicion among white people that God might have created Africans as a separate species, and Jacksonian-era celebrations of manhood citizenship.[49]

Once the parameters of the debate over political equality were set in terms of white manhood as a stage of life, black Americans could most effectively prove that they were part of the human family by demonstrating that black men—and only black men—made a transition to adult independence. To promote the equal rights of black women, even to dwell at length on their economic or intellectual achievements, would be to suggest that the development of black people's capacities followed a different normative pattern than white people's maturation, thus giving credence to the idea of natural racial differences. The problem with black people raising women's rights claims, therefore, was not simply that it would burden the already unpopular cause of racial equality with an even more outrageous claim, nor even that it would require black men to give up authority over their wives and daughters, but, more profoundly, that it would give ammunition to the very theorists of racial difference that black people wanted to refute. As Walker realized, freedom in antebellum America rested on assumptions about manhood as a stage of life.

MARIA STEWART, CHRONOLOGICAL AGE, AND PERPETUAL SERVITUDE

Once state governments decided to base democratic rights on a normative model of human development, black people would have to conform to this model or mark themselves as different in character as well as in color. The first black woman to publicly confront this dilemma was Maria Stewart. Born in Hartford, Connecticut, in 1803, orphaned at age five, and bound out for ten years as a domestic servant, Maria moved to Boston in the 1820s. At age twenty-three she married James W. Stewart, a veteran of the War of 1812 who ran a successful business outfitting ships. The Stewarts involved themselves in the churches and benevolent associations of Boston's black community and became ardent supporters of David Walker. In 1829, after only three years of marriage, James died, leaving Stewart a widow with no children.[50]

Following an intense religious conversion, Stewart felt called to take up Walker's appeal to defend her race. The stakes were high, and not only because Stewart would be taking the unusual step of speaking in public. A year before, Walker was found dead on a Boston street. Though he most likely died of natural causes, rumors at the time spread the fear that he had been—as he predicted he would be—murdered for his outspoken advocacy of slave resistance.[51] When Stewart began her first published essay with the declaration, "I would willingly sacrifice my life for the cause of God and my brethren," she was not making an idle boast; the threat was palpable.[52]

Stewart was fully aware that Walker never intended a woman to risk her life for liberty. To justify her boldness, she identified herself as a widow—in other words, a woman without the protection of a husband—and explained that following her religious conversion she came to "possess that spirit of independence."[53] Stewart located the "love of liberty and independence" in people's "souls" rather than in the character of adult men.[54] If equality inhered in the immortal soul, then she—a twenty-eight-year-old woman who could seem "but a child, inexperienced to many of you"—had as much of a right to publish her views as a middle-aged man like Walker.[55] Further, she distanced herself from martial definitions of republican resistance ("Far be it from me to recommend to you either to kill, burn, or destroy") and aligned herself with republican mothers' duty to educate and influence ("I would strongly recommend to you to improve your talents").[56]

In her first public lecture, delivered at Boston's Franklin Hall in September 1832, Stewart presented a detailed analysis of how racial prejudice distorted not only black manhood but also black womanhood. "Let our girls possess whatever amiable qualities of soul they may," Stewart said; most black women nonetheless "dragged out a miserable existence of servitude from the cradle to the grave."[57] Stewart, like Phillis Wheatley before her, wanted to prove that black people should be free to unfold their capacities over the course of life, but Stewart paid more attention to chronological age and life stage, noting in particular how prejudice and discrimination ensured that black males could not develop independence as they grew older: "Look at our young men . . . souls filled with ambitious fire. . . . They can be nothing but the humblest laborers. . . . Look at our middle-aged men[;] . . . every cent they earn goes to buy their wood and pay their rents. . . . Look at our aged sires, whose heads are whitened with the frosts of seventy winters, with their old wood-saws on their backs."[58] Contrary to white politicians who argued that black males lacked the capacity for manly independence, Stewart argued that black men would make a clear transition to adult independence if freed from discrimination: "Give the man of color an equal opportunity with the white from the cradle to manhood, and from manhood to the grave, and you would discover the dignified statesman, the man of science, and the philosopher."[59]

Yet Stewart could not avoid the question of black men's individual character. Delegates to state constitutional conventions, after all, had defined men's hearts and minds rather than their property as the qualification for equal citizenship. To gain their rights, black men would have to prove that they, in Stewart's words, "possess the spirit of men."[60] Demonstrating independent manhood as a stage of life was one thing that Stewart, as a woman, could not do.

Stewart's frustration at this predicament boiled over in February 1833, when she delivered a lecture in Boston's African Masonic Hall. Standing in a veritable temple to black manhood built by veterans of the Revolutionary War who had led the fight against slavery in Massachusetts, she forthrightly acknowledged that her very presence on the lectern revealed black men's failure of character: had young black men with some money to spare "turned their attention as assiduously to mental and moral improvement as they have to gambling and dancing, I might have remained quietly at home and they stood contending in my place."[61] Stewart's audience let her know their response to this exhortation with hoots, jeers, and a hail of rotten vegetables.

Faced with such hostility, Stewart gave up public speaking, moved to New York, and dedicated herself to teaching and literary study. Her speeches were reprinted by William Lloyd Garrison, however, and widely circulated among abolitionists, particularly influencing white and black members of the Philadelphia Female Anti-Slavery Society. Other free black women did not follow Stewart onto the lecture platform in the 1830s, but many were active in antislavery, mutual aid, reform, and literary societies;

they published in the black press and participated in black political conventions. In a few instances they assumed leadership positions alongside men. More typically they stressed the power of female influence without directly confronting the question of whether or not black women should venture into public to defend the claim that black men deserved the same rights as white.[62]

Free black men, meanwhile, continued to use the dependence of black women and children to prove their equal claims to manhood. For example, in 1837, when Pennsylvania's "reform" constitutional convention moved to disenfranchise black voters, black men appealed to white politicians to recognize their shared need to protect dependents: "Imagine your own wives and children to be trembling at the approach of every stranger, lest their husbands and fathers should be dragged" away and sold into slavery.[63] By the mid-1830s the idea that white manhood was the best measure of citizenship had gained ground, and Pennsylvania's black men lost the right to vote when the new constitution was ratified in 1838.[64] With black men's status as men under attack, black women were understandably reluctant to press the issue of women's rights.[65] Further, by the mid-1830s all Americans had to contend with the arguments of evangelicals and reformers who claimed that God destined men and women for "separate spheres."

MARGARET FULLER, WOMEN, AND CHILDREN

During the 1830s evangelical ministers, advice writers, novelists, journalists, and popular artists all celebrated women's power and influence within their particular sphere. This new idea of woman's "sphere" grew out of the late eighteenth-century British and French celebrations of female virtue that so troubled Mary Wollstonecraft, as well as out of the American glorification of republican motherhood, but added a more rigorous definition of spatial boundaries separating the "private" world of home, family, and church from the "public" world of partisan politics and commercial relations.[66] As educator Catharine Beecher influentially explained, woman's sphere was bounded by "the domestic and social circle"; it was a "private" space in which women were "to win everything by peace and love." An adult man, in contrast, "may act on society by the collision of intellect, in public debate . . . and he does not outstep the boundaries of his sphere."[67] Beecher, a leading advocate of female education and charity work, argued that women could fully develop their mature capacities within woman's sphere.[68] She insisted that the work mothers and female teachers did training young children was a "profession" requiring as much training and deserving as much respect as men's work in "law, divinity, and medicine."[69] Indeed, she envisioned women's moral leadership as the force that would bind the American people together as a strong and thriving nation.[70]

Critics of "woman's sphere," however, argued that women could never fully develop as mature beings unless all avenues of endeavor were thrown open to them as freely as to men. The white abolitionists Angelina and Sarah Grimké controversially insisted that women could not perform their moral duty as Christians and remain within a separate sphere. Sarah in particular drew on the writings of Wollstonecraft but paid relatively little attention to chronological age and life stage, grounding her argument for equality in the Quaker belief that all souls were equal before God.[71] The most influential argument that women could not develop as mature beings if constrained to a narrow sphere came not from an abolitionist but from the transcendentalist educator Margaret Fuller.

In her teaching and in her 1845 book *Woman in the Nineteenth Century*, Fuller argued that the greatest problem women faced was immaturity. Everywhere she looked, "there is no woman, only an overgrown child."[72] According to Fuller, even the most wealthy and educated white women, though members of the economic and cultural elite, remained more like children than fully realized adults.

Fuller, born in 1810, carved out a distinct path for herself as a literary critic and public intellectual. A member of Boston's elite reform circle, Fuller was a close friend of many Garrisonian abolitionists but, though ardently antislavery, did not consider their struggles her own. She instead sought a means by which transcendentalists' romantic faith in self-reliance, intellectual freedom, and spiritual discovery could be achieved by women. Like her close friend and collaborator Ralph Waldo Emerson, Fuller believed in the uniqueness and value of the subjective self. She found the abolitionist women's focus on moral duty to others and their reliance on the Bible unnecessarily limiting.[73]

As one of the most erudite women of her time, Fuller drew inspiration from many sources, especially Johann Wolfgang von Goethe, the German romantics, George Sand, and Dante, as well as from English Platonists and Renaissance writers favored by other transcendentalists. For insights about women's problems, however, she turned to Mary Wollstonecraft. Fuller had quite literally been raised on Wollstonecraft. Her father, the Harvard-educated Republican congressman Timothy Fuller, praised the *Vindication* as a "very sensible & just" guide to improving female education, though he largely ignored its more radical arguments for women's rights.[74] Fuller would not condone sexual fulfillment outside of marriage but demanded sympathy for Wollstonecraft, George Sand, and all other women who "find themselves, by birth, in a place so narrow, that, in breaking bonds, they become outlaws."[75]

Harking back to Kant's definition of enlightenment as reaching adulthood by daring to know, Fuller insisted that women could not know themselves as long as they remained in a limited "sphere," perpetually dependent on men. She was not particularly concerned with chronological age per se but rather with men's tendency to relate to women as though they were children. She noted that the laws of marriage treated the wife "as if she were a child, or ward only, not an equal partner."[76] The problem was not only law but men's attitudes, their "tone of feeling . . . expressed in the common phrase, 'Tell that to women and children.'"[77] Men, Fuller charged, were not "representing women fairly at present" when even the most cultivated men let fall "the contemptuous phrase 'women and children.'"[78]

Women would also need to overcome their own internal limitations. According to Fuller, females remained trapped in a liminal state resembling adolescence: "The present tendency to a crisis in the life of Woman . . . resembles the change from girlhood, with its beautiful instincts, but unharmonized thoughts, its blind pupilage and restless seeking, to self-possessed, wise and graceful womanhood."[79]

To explain women's immaturity, Fuller provided a universal history of mankind. "Man, in the order of time, was developed first. . . . Woman was therefore under his care as an elder. He might have been her guardian and teacher" had he not "abused his advantages" and turned her into a "servant."[80] Fuller found hope for the future in the possibility that every man carried within him the memory of his own mother bent "over him in infancy with an expression he can never quite forget." Gleams of this expression revisited man when he fell in love, married, or saw the mother of his own children. But this thought was "soon obscured by the mists of sensuality, the dust of routine."[81] To respect women's maturity, each man would have to retain rather than repress his childish acceptance of his own dependence on a mother. Fuller's goal was not to reverse the balance of maturation by infantilizing adult men but to achieve the equal status of peers. The time had finally come, Fuller claimed, "when Man and Woman may regard one another as brother and sister." Man had only to "remove arbitrary barriers" so that woman could discover her own possibilities for growth as man's peer.[82]

Fuller saw "symptoms" of the coming womanhood in the separate reforms proposed by Emanuel Swedenborg, a Swiss theologian who recognized women's spiritual capacities; Charles Fourier, a utopian socialist who recognized their capacity for work; and Goethe, a German romantic whose emphasis on self-culture "takes as good care of women as of men."[83] To grow up, however, women needed to cast off the fear of becoming "old maids." For Fuller, the derogatory epithet "old maid" was the flip side of the "contemptuous phrase 'women and children.'"[84] By either infantilizing women as immature beings or denigrating them as already past their prime, men refused to recognize women's capacity as equal adults. Fuller, herself thirty-four years old and unmarried, found hope in the fact that the class of people "contemptuously designated as 'old maids'" and "old bachelors" was growing as society became "so complex, that it could now scarcely be carried on without the presence of these despised auxiliaries."[85] For women in particular, the possibility of dedicating oneself to a great cause rather than to marriage offered a new path into middle and old age. Yet, like Wollstonecraft before her, Fuller believed women should ultimately be able to claim love as well as respect as they grew old.

Fuller painted a highly unflattering portrait of the typical middle-aged matron, "'fat, fair, and forty,' showily dressed, and with manners as broad and full as her frill or satin cloak." Such a woman was unfit to inspire either poetry or art, praised merely for being well preserved, which amounted to being "thought of upholstery wise."[86] A woman with a "care-worn face" might be a better subject for the artists, Fuller speculated. "Yet surely she, no more than the other, looks as a human being should at the end of forty years. Forty years! have they bound those brows with no garland?"[87] Fuller looked to both ancient heroines such as Iphigenia and contemporary notables such as Harriet Martineau as models for women who "at forty . . . would not misbecome the marble."[88]

Even as she emphasized maturity in women, Fuller also invoked the Christian tradition of the soul as childlike, an idea that took on new significance in romantic celebrations of childhood innocence.[89] There was, Fuller argued, one sense in which "the phrase, 'women and children,' may, perhaps, be interpreted aright, [which is] that only little children shall enter the kingdom of heaven."[90] The key to retaining this laudable childishness of the soul was to recognize dependence on God rather than on men.[91] Perhaps influenced by Swedenborg's mystical claim that angels in heaven grow younger with each passing year, Fuller invoked this idea of an inner core free from worldly corruption when she wrote, "The soul is ever young, ever virgin."[92] Fuller could not have been more clear, however, that this childlike spirit had nothing to do with men or courts treating women like overgrown children.

Fuller's most widely quoted proposal was that women should be free to fill any office: "I do not care what case you put; let them be sea-captains if you will."[93] In choosing this example, Fuller not only identified one of the most masculine of all professions but also evoked the popular metaphor of life as an individual voyage that each must chart alone. By claiming that women had the talent to work as sea captains, she also implied that they had the ability to metaphorically steer their own course through life.[94] Indeed, Fuller followed her case for female sea captains with the example of "an old woman" whom a group of travelers found living in "a lonely hut on a mountain." When asked why, she responded that she "'did not know; *it was the man's notion.*'" Fuller commented: "During forty years, she had been content to act, without knowing why, upon 'the man's notion.' I would not have it so."[95] In other words, what was at stake for Fuller was not so much where women could go—this elderly woman, after all, had journeyed to a lofty mountain worthy of any romantic reverie without ever leaving her proper "sphere" of dependence. What mattered was whether a woman could knowingly determine her own path or had to always rely, like a child, upon the guidance of a man.

What American feminists gained from Fuller's *Woman in the Nineteenth Century* was the insight that female maturation required both self-discovery and social reform. This was not just a critique of the idea of separate spheres but more crucially a recognition that democratic politics, law, and market relations penetrated to the core of the self, shaping individuals' spirits, intellects, and desires. This insight largely defined the goals for which white, educated, and economically privileged feminists would struggle.[96] Elizabeth Cady Stanton, Julia Ward (later Howe), Lydia Maria Child, and Caroline Healey Dall all attended Fuller's Boston conversations and then went on, throughout their long careers, to articulate arguments for female development.[97] Indeed, nearly fifty years later, when Stanton gave her widely admired speech "The Solitude of Self," she was still exploring the problem posed by Fuller: how could women be taught, in Stanton's words, that "they must make the voyage of life alone"?[98] Other female activists, including Paulina Wright Davis, Mary Livermore, Sara Underwood, Elizabeth Oakes Smith, and Frances Willard, all identified *Woman in the Nineteenth Century* as the most able exposition of the woman question.[99] Late in the century Charlotte Perkins Gilman adopted Fuller's account of human history to the theory of social evolution, and into the twentieth century feminists would still turn to her as a guide to developing a more authentic self.[100]

Tragically, Fuller died before she could show the world what a more highly developed middle-aged woman could become. In an uncanny reprise of Wollstonecraft's dramatic path, Fuller went to the Continent to support a revolution (in this case Italian revolutionaries' effort to establish a Roman republic in 1849), fell in love, bore a child out of wedlock, and then died at the age of forty. Fuller's untimely death came from, of all things, a shipwreck. The hope that she would show women how to become captains of their own lives sunk off the shores of Long Island in 1850. The two most articulate advocates for women's right to mature—Wollstonecraft and Fuller—both died in the prime of life, leaving others to determine the best course into late middle and old age. Many of Fuller's admirers determined that the path to respect in later life went through politics.

Before they could organize a political movement, however, champions of female development would have to agree that engagement with formal politics was both desirable and necessary. A deeper engagement with the political aspects of individual development came out of abolitionism, particularly Frederick Douglass's effort to build a hybrid strategy of political engagement and moral suasion. Douglass engaged the transcendentalists' romantic idea of maturation as self-culture and self-discovery but from the perspective of a self once held as property.

FREDERICK DOUGLASS, CHRONOLOGICAL AGE, AND THE MARKET VALUE OF SLAVES

Douglass escaped slavery in Maryland to become the most prominent black abolitionist in the country. When he published his *Narrative of the Life of Frederick Douglass, an American Slave* in 1845, Margaret Fuller, then working as a literary critic for the *New York Tribune*, lauded Douglass's "manly heart" and recommended that every American read his book "to see what a mind might have been stifled in bondage."[101] Fuller was not alone in treating Douglass as living proof that an enslaved black man was capable of developing a "manly heart" and great "mind." Indeed, the white abolitionists who promoted Douglass's reputation as an antislavery orator repeatedly staged the drama of his presence in precisely these terms. William Lloyd Garrison, for example, told an audience that they were about to witness not just a speech but the "miracle" by which a "chattel becomes a man."[102]

Douglass willingly took up the challenge of becoming the representative black man, but he wanted to do so on his own terms. In his *Narrative*, Douglass provided a detailed critique of a political and legal system that defined independence as a stage of life for white men while enforcing laws that kept black men in perpetual bondage. He pointed out that age had a different meaning for slaves because owners used chronological age to calibrate slaves' market value as chattel property.[103]

Douglass had been born on Maryland's Eastern Shore in 1818 and raised by his maternal grandmother before moving to the home of his master, Aaron Anthony, who was an overseer for Edward Lloyd, a former governor, a U.S. senator, a Democratic champion of "universal suffrage," and the largest slaveholder in the region. When Douglass was eight years old, he was sent to Baltimore to live with relatives of Anthony's son-in-law Thomas Auld, who in 1827 inherited Douglass from Anthony's estate. Douglass spent the rest of his boyhood in Baltimore, teaching himself to read and making friends with white and free black peers. In 1833, when he was fifteen years old, the Aulds sent Douglass back to the Eastern Shore, probably because they feared his independence. After one failed escape, he succeeded in making his way to freedom with the help of Anna Murray, the free black woman who would later become his wife. He arrived in New Bedford in 1838.[104] When he delivered a speech recounting his experience to an antislavery convention on Nantucket, which Garrison attended, the Massachusetts Anti-Slavery Society hired him as a paid agent. His eloquence was so widely remarked upon that critics began to question his claim to have once been enslaved. To dispel these doubts, Douglass began in 1844 to write his *Narrative*, which he published in May 1845.[105]

The conventions of nineteenth-century autobiography provided Douglass with an opportunity to discuss the way in which chronological age functioned differently for free men and slaves. Whereas eighteenth-century autobiographies usually started with a genealogical review of the author's ancestors, nineteenth-century memoirists increasingly began with their own date of birth.[106] Douglass could not do this. He began his autobiography by stating that he, like most slaves, did not know his true age. "I do not remember to have ever met a slave who could tell his birthday. . . . They seldom come any nearer to it than planting-time, harvest-time, cherry-time, spring-time, or fall-time." Douglass explained that this lack of chronological precision was not the simple result of a premodern, agricultural mindset. Rather, it was "the wish of most masters within my knowledge to keep their slaves thus ignorant." Masters desired that slaves should "know as little of their ages as horses know of theirs."[107]

The masters themselves kept careful records of slave births, but to show slaves such a document would be to inspire them with a sense of their own personhood, to provide a measure for individual development—a state of mind incompatible with the slaves' status as chattel. As Douglass recalled of his own situation, "I was not allowed to make any inquiries of my master concerning [my birthday]. He deemed all such inquiries on the part of a slave improper and impertinent, and evidence of a restless spirit." Douglass recalled that this "want of information concerning my own [date of birth] was a source of unhappiness to me even during childhood. The white children could tell their ages. I could not tell why I ought to be deprived of the same privilege."[108] By the time he wrote his autobiography, Douglass had decided why: his master did not want to treat him like a boy who would grow into a man.[109]

Douglass gave credence to the notion that all white boys looked forward to age twenty-one as an important transition to manhood freedom. He recalled how he befriended poor white boys on the streets of Baltimore and would compare his prospects to theirs: "I would sometimes say to them, I wished I could be free as they would be when they got to be men. 'You will be free as soon as you are twenty-one, *but I am a slave for life*! Have not I as good a right to be free as you have?' These words used to trouble them; they would express for me the liveliest sympathy, and console me with the hope that something would occur by which I might be free."[110]

Douglass not only explored racial inequalities in the use of chronological age as a precise measure of development but also critiqued the racial meaning embedded in popular metaphors of the life course as a voyage. Contemporary white critics regarded Douglass's "apostrophe to freedom" on the shores of Chesapeake Bay as one of the most affecting passages of the book.[111] Douglass constructed this passage around an implicit contrast with the numerous poems, speeches, and sermons depicting manhood as a voyage.[112] He wrote: "Those beautiful vessels, robed in purest white, so delightful to the eye of the freemen, were to me so many shrouded ghosts, to terrify and torment me with thoughts of my wretched condition. . . . You [ships] are loosed from your moorings, and are free; I am fast in my chains, and am a slave! . . . O, why was I born a man, of whom to make a brute!"[113] Douglass thus contrasted the joy felt by white men who saw ships as a metaphor for their own freedom with the sorrow felt by enslaved people who saw only a tragic contrast to their own bondage. Douglass went on to assert that a young bondsman who could not compare himself to a ship setting out of port was not a man at all but a brute.[114]

Douglass's narrative provided a window on what it felt like to have aspirations for liberty and self-improvement but to look forward to a life of perpetual bondage—to know that the passage of years brought a return on investment to a master but no age-based transition to manhood freedom. What this felt like, Douglass explained, was not to be treated like a child by a benevolent patriarch but to be denied humanity, to become a chattel, a "brute."

Like David Walker before him, Douglass found in violence an alternative path to manhood liberty. When Douglass was around sixteen years old, his master sent him to work in the fields. This was typical of slave owners throughout the country, who generally expected adult fieldwork of enslaved people around age sixteen.[115] Concerned that Douglass had become too independent, his master rented him out to Edward Covey, a "farm-renter" with a "very high reputation for breaking young slaves."[116] But Douglass fought back, proving that he could assert his own transition to manhood "in fact" if not "in form." For Douglass, violent resistance became the path through which "a slave was made a man."[117] Douglass thus pointed out the weak point in slave owners' efforts to turn men into property: the same manly strength that increased profits also enabled young men to defend their liberty. Americans, after all, celebrated teenage boys as the backbone of the militias. Black boys too, Douglass warned, could fight to defend liberty, a point that proved prophetic and helps explain why Douglass so eagerly campaigned to enlist black soldiers in Union troops during the Civil War.[118]

Douglass's account of his battle with Covey also invoked and reconfigured the rhetoric of generational relations that underlay accounts of white sons outgrowing their mothers to become the equals of their fathers. In Douglass's account, slavery perverted each of these relations. His father, who never acknowledged paternity, was most likely his master, Aaron Anthony. His mother, forced to work on another plantation, was absent. His aunt Esther became a maternal substitute, but he witnessed her brutal punishment, an event that he later described in language hinting that the violation was a rape and that he too felt the threat of rape. With the sodomitic rape of slave boys by masters and overseers a recognized possibility of plantation life, the young Douglass realized that identifying with his race meant becoming a feminized victim rather than a man. By violently subordinating Covey to his strength, in effect turning a white male into a feminized victim, Douglass put himself in the position of a fully grown man on his own terms and in his own time.[119] He became an independent adult in spirit if not in law.[120]

He remained, however, focused on age twenty-one as the moment when he should gain his emancipation on the same schedule as his white peers. When Douglass approached what he estimated as his twenty-first birthday, he began to feel intense pressure to make a transition to legal freedom before that age: "I was fast approaching manhood, and year after year had passed, and I was still a slave."[121] By chance, his master returned him to Baltimore, where he finally managed to board a vessel and embark on his own voyage of life as a free man. He calculated his age as around twenty, which enabled him later to claim that he spent twenty-one years in slavery, or in other words that he "grew up to manhood" as a slave.[122] Though his owners tried to deny him the transition to manhood at age twenty-one, he had succeeded in becoming a free man by stealing himself.

After publishing his autobiography, Douglass followed the path marked out by Phillis Wheatley, traveling to Britain to gather support and publicize his writings. Douglass secured his freedom when British supporters paid his former master. During his lectures in Great Britain, Douglass spoke to audiences unfamiliar with the workings of the slave trade. He emphasized how slave owners used age and life stage not to facilitate individual development but to value human property. For example, when he arrived in Ireland in 1845, a local reporter described him as a "fine young Negro." Douglass took great offense and explained to his Irish audience, "That is the mode of advertising in our country a slave for sale."[123] The term "prime," which white people often used to define the stage of their greatest achievement, was particularly tainted for Douglass. He quoted from one typical advertisement that listed property to be sold: "*Twenty-seven Negroes in prime condition*; one horse and old wagon."[124] In this advertisement, the description "prime" was applied to the slaves, just as the word "old" was applied to the wagon: an assessment of wear and tear on property.

Douglass dismissed the argument that the relationship between masters and slaves was similar to that between parents and children, rejecting the "honeyed words" that referred to slavery as a "patriarchal" institution.[125] Douglass insisted that even when enslaved people were the biological offspring of their masters, they were not protected like children.[126] The master was not a paternal guide leading the childish slave through life but a shrewd investor concerned with the value of his property.[127]

When traveling through Ireland in 1845, Douglas frequently met the objection that the Irish themselves were "white slaves" and should focus on gaining their own independence from England before working to free the bondsmen.[128] Slavery "is not to have one peculiar right struck down," Douglass clarified; "if it is, all women, all minors, are slaves."[129] To compare slaves and minors would be to fundamentally misunderstand the nature of slavery. Proclaiming himself "an ungrateful fugitive from the 'patriarchal institutions' of the Slave States," Douglass did not want to further any comparison among slaves, women, and children.[130]

Douglass, however, believed that men and women should be free to develop their full potential over the course of life. Around 1841 he met

Elizabeth Cady Stanton and later attributed to her influence his support for women's rights. When Douglass returned from Great Britain in 1847 he moved to Rochester, New York, and began publishing a newspaper, the *North Star*. The masthead included the claim that "Right is of no Sex—Truth is of no Color."[131] For her part, Stanton may have learned from Douglass to pay greater attention to chronological age. Douglass's nuanced analysis of how age functioned to define citizenship for white men but not for black people echoed throughout Stanton's arguments for women's mature capacity. The white female intellectuals who most influenced Stanton—including Wollstonecraft and Fuller—drew upon generalized notions of maturity defined as the unfolding of human potential over time without reference to sharp transitions defined by chronological age. Douglass focused much more concretely on the political significance of age twenty-one, a strategy that Stanton and other white women's rights activists would adopt during the 1840s and 1850s. The struggle for equal adulthood thus emerged out of interracial debate and cooperation between black and white reformers eager to claim the rights, duties, and privileges conferred on young white men at twenty-one but denied to the majority of adults, whatever their age.

In 1848, when Stanton helped organize a women's rights convention in Seneca Falls, New York, Douglass made the trip from Rochester. The two joined together to support the controversial demand that women be given the right to vote at age twenty-one. The two would help to build a diverse coalition of white and black activists all promoting the idea that if state governments were to use chronological age to determine citizens' rights and duties, then they should apply those age qualifications equally to all adults, regardless of race or sex.

CHAPTER THREE

CHRONOLOGICAL AGE AND EQUAL RIGHTS

Between 1848 and 1861, women's rights activists organized a series of local, state, and national conventions at which they raised a broad range of demands, including women's right to vote and run for office, to pursue equal educational and occupational opportunities, to control their property and persons within marriage, and to live by a single standard of sexual morality applicable to both sexes.[1] Organizers modeled these conventions on the national female antislavery conventions held between 1837 and 1839 and the constitutional and political party conventions ongoing throughout the nation, but whereas the former relied on women's power of moral suasion and the latter enforced men's monopoly on electoral power, women's rights organizers sought a means by which women could intervene directly in political debate.[2] This engagement with formal politics focused women's rights activists' attention on age qualifications in law, especially age twenty-one as a nearly universal transition to political rights and contractual freedom for white males.[3]

For example, at the first national women's rights convention, held in Worcester, Massachusetts, in 1850, convention organizer Abby Price observed that conviction for a crime or chronological age were the "only limits" on white men's right to vote or run for office. "Are women," she asked, "to be regarded as criminals, or are they all minors?"[4] Price demanded that state governments grant suffrage to women as to men at age twenty-one. Speakers at these conventions also noted that white men celebrated their right to sign contracts at twenty-one, while slaves and wives lacked the right to contract at all, and free blacks and women faced discrimination in the labor market that severely constrained their ability to achieve adult independence.[5] Other women's rights activists, meanwhile, focused on the obverse side of twenty-one, urging legislators to better protect young girls from sexual exploitation by older men, and particularly to raise the age of consent for marriage to twenty-one, thus bringing it into line with other forms of contract.[6]

Women's rights activists thus used chronological age to draw a sharp line between dependent girlhood and independent womanhood. This was not their only, or even their most important, demand, but the need to distinguish between girls and women on the basis of chronological age surfaced with surprising frequency. Further, as activists struggled to sum up their various goals—for political participation, higher education, meaningful work, freedom within marriage, and personal fulfillment—they repeatedly fell back upon the general claim that all Americans should be free at age twenty-one to pursue their own ambitions over the course of life.

Speakers at women's rights conventions thus placed themselves at the forefront of age consciousness in American culture. In the 1840s and 1850s, some educational reformers, physicians, and advice writers were also using chronological age to establish age-graded common schools, pediatric medicine, and children's literature.[7] Women's rights activists, however, critiqued many of these other age-based reforms, noting that they tended to cultivate independence in young white males while encouraging perpetual dependence for black males and all females. Women's rights advocates, in contrast, promoted the distinctly egalitarian idea that all human beings matured according to a similar schedule and that state governments should apply age qualifications equally to all. In particular, they insisted that black men and all women should be recognized as adult citizens at age twenty-one, just like their white male peers.[8]

This struggle for equal adulthood appealed to activists from various backgrounds with differing political priorities. Women's rights conventions were organized and controlled by educated white married women between the ages of thirty and sixty. Most were the wives or daughters of prosperous farmers, merchants, or professionals.[9] Almost all were abolitionists, though not all of them believed that black people could or should become the political and social equals of whites.[10] Despite the narrow-mindedness of some privileged white women, women's rights conventions brought together a broad range of radical reformers, male and female, black and white, young and old, in no small part because leaders expressed a deep commitment to freeing all Americans at age twenty-one to develop their full capacities.[11] Since age was something all could attain, the struggle for equal adulthood had broad appeal.

Tensions simmered below the surface, however, as black and white activists, both men and women, disagreed as to which reforms should be given priority. White women sometimes suggested that they had a greater claim to equal adulthood based on their education, class standing, or racial superiority. Abolitionists, black and white, insisted that all adults would never be treated as equals in the United States until the nation ended slavery. Older activists, meanwhile, often presumed to speak for younger. These class, racial, and generational tensions at times divided activists from each other, but during this period when advocates for women's rights were few and far between, activists looked to each other for support. A loose coalition with no permanent organizations, they valued conventions as a time to come together and provide an open platform.[12] Speakers found that they could appeal to many by emphasizing the demand that age qualifications apply equally to all citizens, thus deferring the question of innate capacity and social subordination to an indeterminate future when every individual could claim rights and respect as a fully realized adult on the basis of age.

While ideas about equal adulthood flourished within an interracial coalition of women's rights supporters, the notion of freeing and enfranchising all adults struck most Americans as an irrational disregard for natural differences. Politicians, ministers, and mainstream reformers argued that only white men developed the capacity for independent citizenship, while white women needed protection throughout their lives and African Americans were destined for perpetual servitude.[13] The argument that rights and opportunities should be based on age, without regard to sex or race, gained little traction in state capitols, party platforms, higher education, or workplaces during this period. Nonetheless, black and white women's rights activists continued the struggle to prove that they should be recognized as equal adults rather than as perpetual minors.

CHRONOLOGICAL AGE AND STATE CONSTITUTIONS

Several leaders who organized women's rights conventions—including Elizabeth Cady Stanton, religious freethinker Ernestine Rose, and health reformer Paulina Wright (later Davis)—first focused on age, law, and politics during the campaign to win married women property rights in the state of New York. In 1836 the state legislature formed a select committee to consider the issue, and for the next twelve years legislators debated the measure. As Stanton, Rose, and Wright circulated petitions and spoke to state legislators, they gained a greater appreciation for the ways in which mainstream politicians justified discriminatory laws with the belief that white men normally became independent by age twenty-one while black men and all women remained perpetually dependent.[14] Politicians' arguments for white manhood citizenship as a stage of life reached a new peak during the New York state constitutional convention of 1846, when delegates debated men's political rights and married women's property rights.[15] As women's rights activists eagerly consumed news of the convention, they confronted a widespread consensus that, as one delegate succinctly put it, the state had an obligation to protect "the male from infancy to manhood, and the woman from the cradle to the grave."[16]

The significance of age twenty-one as a transition to white manhood citizenship was apparent in debates over black manhood suffrage. Some delegates, including Ansel Bascom, the representative of Stanton's home town of Seneca Falls, pushed to enfranchise black men on the same terms as white men, but those opposed cited the exclusion of women and children to prove that voting was not a natural right but a privilege appropriately limited "to mature age and the male sex."[17] Proposals to extend the vote "without regard to color" were met with jeering questions as to whether "age or sex" should be added, provoking laughter throughout the hall.[18] That the idea of adult black men or adult women voting was as laughable as extending rights to young children deeply offended black civil rights and women's rights activists who contended that being denied the vote was not only unjust but an affront to their mature dignity.[19]

Delegates to the 1846 New York state constitutional convention also debated age qualifications for elected office, in the process revealing their shared assumption that white men developed political capacity by outgrowing the authority of their mothers. The question at hand was whether or not to retain the requirement that all candidates for governor be at least thirty years old. This age qualification received little attention when it was inserted into the New York constitution in 1821. Only one delegate, after all, was under age thirty; 70 percent were between forty and sixty.[20] By 1846, however, the requirement had become controversial. Many New York politicians believed that voters should be free to choose their own candidates, while others clung to the idea that an age limit was necessary to ensure sound government.[21] All delegates to the state convention—even those who opposed the age limit—agreed that a man under age thirty would rarely qualify for governor. As Essex County representative George

Simmons explained: "Under 30 is the age when men are under petticoat government."[22] Before becoming eligible for high office, a young man had "to struggle along ten, or even fifteen or twenty years" in the all-male arena of electoral politics.[23] Delegates thus constructed political authority as something that men developed by leaving women behind.

In the end, delegates voted to retain the requirement that all candidates for governor be at least thirty years old.[24] They generally agreed that a man's capacity peaked in the "middle period of life." This span of years was quite broad, falling sometime between young manhood (under thirty) and old age (over eighty).[25] Tellingly, delegates did not rely on new medical theories of human physiological development. They fell back on hackneyed stereotypes about the rashness of youth and the prudence of age and, most important, cited legal precedents from the federal and other state constitutions, thus recognizing and affirming that age qualifications were rooted in human rather than natural law.[26]

The convention did not consider setting an upper age limit on who could run for governor.[27] Though many delegates regarded old age as a time of impaired capacities, they believed this decline did not set in until quite late in life. One delegate defined "superannuated old dotards" as men over eighty.[28] Another pointed out that when the 1821 New York convention set mandatory retirement for judges at age sixty, "men thrown out by that rule, had exhibited more vigor of intellect after 60, than for ten years before—and the rule was now almost universally condemned."[29] White men could evidently continue to improve themselves until quite late in life, but only if they freed themselves from "petticoat government."

The debate over married women's property rights revealed how clearly delegates understood that their conception of manhood citizenship as a stage of life required the perpetual dependence of women within the home. Opponents of reform successfully argued that while men should compete with each other for individual advancement, they should never be forced to compete with their female peers and especially not with their wives. This issue, more than any other, captured the attention of women's rights activists who had long been involved in a petition campaign to win married women control of the separate property they brought into marriage. Influenced by these petitions, and by the temperance movement, many delegates wanted to protect wives' property from the debts of drunken or profligate husbands. The majority, however, defeated this proposal. They believed that a married woman's economic and social status should depend not upon her own achievements but upon those of her husband. One of the most outspoken opponents of property rights for married women, New York City Democrat Charles O'Conor (himself a bachelor), believed that under the existing law of marriage, "woman, as wife, or as mother . . . had as yet known no debasing pecuniary interest apart from the prosperity of her husband. His wealth had been her wealth; his prosperity her pride, her only source of power or distinction." To prevent wives from competing with their husbands, it was proper to give "the husband the control and custody of the wife."[30]

That this legal arrangement rendered the wife a perpetual dependent, more like a minor under guardianship than an independent adult, did not trouble the delegates, who refused to grant wives control of separate property in 1846. But it did deeply trouble women like Stanton, Rose, and Wright who fervently believed that women, like men, needed to make a transition to independent citizenship as they matured and would never be able to do so if all wives remained classed with minors in law. Supporters of the married women's property act continued to lobby the state legislature, finally securing passage in April 1848. Flush with this success, and further inspired by the democratic revolutions sweeping Europe, advocates for women's rights, led by Elizabeth Cady Stanton and Lucretia Mott, determined to hold their own conventions at which they would attack the underlying assumption that women should remain dependents from "the cradle to the grave."[31] From their involvement in state politics, Stanton and others had learned that they would need to argue specifically that daughters as well as sons should grow up to become independent citizens at age twenty-one.

CHRONOLOGICAL AGE AND WOMEN'S RIGHTS

In July 1848 Elizabeth Cady Stanton, Lucretia Mott, and several other veteran abolitionists called a convention in Seneca Falls, New York, "to discuss the Social, Civil, and Religious Condition of Woman."[32] The three hundred men and women who crowded into the Wesleyan Chapel in that industrial town on 19 and 20 July 1848 included Garrisonian abolitionists deeply committed to human equality, legal reformers campaigning for married women's property rights, supporters of the Free Soil Party organizing to block the western expansion of slavery, and the merely curious.[33] As the organizers knew it would, a convention run by women to advance women's rights gained immediate attention in the nation's press. Journalists publicized the "Declaration of Sentiments," written mainly by Stanton and signed by a hundred participants. This influential document revised the Declaration of Independence to proclaim that "all men and women are created equal" and enumerated the laws, social customs, religious beliefs, sexual practices, and psychological habits that subordinated women to men.[34]

The "Declaration of Sentiments" did not mention age or life stage explicitly. As with Jefferson's original, the claim to being "created equal" dodged the question of how to draw a line between childhood subjection and adult freedom. Further, by framing the "Declaration of Sentiments" as a list of "injuries and usurpations on the part of man toward woman," the abstraction of the singular "woman" occluded differences among women not only of age but also of race and class.[35]

As women's rights activists organized a series of state and national conventions, however, they focused more specifically on age qualifications in law and particularly the significance of age twenty-one as a transition to full citizenship for white men. This concern was most obvious in their demands for equal political rights. As the novelist and critic John Neal urged, "Give to every female, as to every male, at the age of twenty-one, the sacred right of citizenship."[36] In arguing that age qualifications should apply equally to all Americans regardless of race or sex, women's rights activists responded to a new emphasis on chronological age in medicine, education, and popular culture. In 1848, as women's rights activists organized their initial conventions, educational reformer John D. Philbrick opened in Boston America's first fully age-graded common school, a reform that would become widespread over the next two decades.[37] Health reformers were also paying more attention to age, using chronological markers to delineate specific stages of human maturation.[38] Whereas delegates to the 1846 New York state constitutional convention were skeptical about scientific models of human development, speakers at antebellum women's rights conventions were not because they understood that age-based schedules could be used to challenge laws and social customs that treated black men and all women like perpetual minors.[39]

The most important source of ideas about chronological age, however, was black civil rights activists who had long argued that all males should become free at age twenty-one regardless of race. Frederick Douglass, who most clearly articulated this demand for equal adulthood, was a close friend and collaborator of the white abolitionists who led the first women's rights conventions. At the 1848 Seneca Falls convention, when some participants feared that demanding adult women's right to vote would "make the whole movement ridiculous," Douglass allied with Elizabeth Cady Stanton to ensure passage of the suffrage resolution.[40] In the wake of Seneca Falls, Douglass and Stanton collaborated to spread the argument that all citizens, regardless of race or sex, should gain the right to vote at age twenty-one.

Douglass carried the commitment to equal rights for all adults to conventions dominated by black men. At the September 1848 Colored National Convention in Cleveland, Ohio, Douglass sponsored a proposal to admit female delegates on equal terms, and the male delegates voted in favor "with three cheers for woman's rights."[41] During the 1850s, Douglass split with many of his former allies as he came to view the U.S. Constitution as an antislavery document, became more involved in electoral politics, and charted an independent course for his newspaper. Many former allies concluded that Douglass and his close collaborator, the white Englishwoman Julia Griffiths, were doing more harm than good.[42]

Even as Garrisonian women's rights activists attacked Douglass, however, they continued to explore the political significance of chronological age in ways that resonated strongly with the analysis he had developed in the 1840s. In one striking example, the white abolitionist Abby Kelley Foster echoed Douglass's earlier view of twenty-one as a significant milestone in the lives of white males. She spoke, however, from the perspective of a white daughter longing for the opportunity granted her brothers rather than of an enslaved boy envying his free white peers.

In a major speech to the 1853 women's rights convention in Cleveland, Foster asked, "Is it not a deep and lasting disgrace, for a son, after he comes to the age of twenty one, to hang upon the skirts of the household without any employment by which he can render himself independent[?] . . . Now, we must build up such a public opinion, that young women will not dare to hang upon the household after they are of age."[43] Foster thus repeated Douglass's complaint that age twenty-one had become a significant transition for white males but not for other adults. Foster was not consciously quoting Douglass—by 1853, the two had become deeply estranged and critical of each other. Nonetheless, Foster, who had toured as an antislavery lecturer with Douglass in the 1840s, expressed a perspective on the political significance of chronological age that was entirely congruent with Douglass's earlier view.[44] So, more generally, the issue of equal adulthood joined black and white activists in a shared struggle for equal rights even as they often disagreed on specific strategies and priorities.

Black activists who joined the women's rights movement were always a distinct minority at conventions dominated by white women, but they provided crucial support for an understanding of all adults as equal citizens. Some were highly educated freeborn members of the northern black elite with experience fighting for equal educational opportunities for black children and equal rights for black adults. For example, the Garrisonian abolitionist William C. Nell had led the campaign to desegregate Boston's public schools.[45] Robert Purvis had headed the unsuccessful campaign to prevent Pennsylvania from disenfranchising black voters in 1838. Former slave Sojourner Truth, in contrast, could speak about chronological age from her experience of gradual emancipation in New York State.[46]

As black people and their white allies sought to focus women's rights advocates on the need to end slavery and fight racial discrimination, some white activists drew a sharp line between women's rights and black rights. Jane Swisshelm, the outspoken and controversial editor of the *Pittsburgh Saturday Visiter*, signed the call for the first national women's rights convention in 1850 but was dismayed that the antislavery leader Wendell Phillips introduced "the color question."[47] Though Swisshelm considered herself an abolitionist leader and had fought racial discrimination in the North, she was convinced that reformers should organize targeted campaigns to advance single issues.[48] She acknowledged that "Negroes and Women are placed upon the same level in nearly all our Constitutions . . . [and are] disposed of in the same sentence, 'White male citizens.'" This linking of women to black men was, however, the strategy of "the enemies of both proscribed classes." She contended that the "friends" of equal rights would do best to promote black men's rights and women's rights as separate issues rather than claim equal rights for all adults over twenty-one.[49]

Swisshelm held firmly to class and racial inequalities in projecting how women could become the equals of men: "As for colored women, all the interest they have in this reform is *as women*. All it can do for them is raise them to the level of men of their own class. Then as that class rises, let them rise with it. We only claim for a white wood-sawyer's wife that she is as good as a white wood-sawyer—a blacksmith's mother as good as a blacksmith—a lawyer's sister is as good as a lawyer."[50] Whereas Maria Stewart and Frederick Douglass argued that racial prejudice would have to be overturned in order for all individuals to develop their full potential as they aged, Swisshelm did not believe women's rights activists should challenge the prejudices that ensured that black men would not be lawyers.

Going into the 1850 convention, most women's rights activists had a more expansive vision of equal adulthood, which entailed challenging dependencies rooted in slavery, racial segregation, and economic inequalities as well as the subordination of women to men.[51] Given their limited influence within women's rights conventions, however, black activists committed to equal rights for all adults used other venues, such as the black press, antislavery lectures, and personal narratives, to explore how chronological age could define a transition to equal adulthood for African Americans.

CHRONOLOGICAL AGE AND ANTISLAVERY

Two former slaves, Frederick Douglass and Sojourner Truth, were both present at the 1850 national women's rights convention, and both were determined to link women's rights to racial equality. They used their writings and speeches to warn that state governments would never apply age qualifications equally to all citizens so long as white politicians sustained a market in which human beings were assigned a monetary value based on their age or life stage. Douglass stated this point most forcefully in a series of speeches critiquing Senator Henry Clay's 1849 proposal for gradual emancipation in the state of Kentucky.[52] As both pro- and antislavery forces elected delegates to Kentucky's 1848 constitutional convention, Clay drafted an open letter advocating that all slaves born after a fixed date—for example, the first day of either 1855 or 1860—should be freed at age twenty-five, when they would be hired out under the authority of the state for a period of no more than three years to pay their own passage to Africa.[53] As a founding vice-president of the American Colonization Society, Clay believed that free black and white adults could never coexist peacefully in the United States.[54]

Northern whites praised Clay's plan as benevolent, but Garrisonian abolitionists vehemently opposed all colonization schemes.[55] Douglass singled out Clay's use of chronological age not as a compassionate tool to foster slaves' development but as a means by which slave owners could maximize their return on slave property.[56] Clay, Douglass argued, gave masters "twenty-five years in which to watch the New Orleans and Mobile markets, and if they do not see fit to sell [their slaves] during the course of ten, fifteen, or twenty years, just in the last of the twenty-fifth year, when the slave is about to grasp hold of Freedom, their masters can put them on the block and sell them to the highest bidder."[57] For Douglass, white people's willingness to extend black bondage long past the age of twenty-one, and to do so in the name of charity for a dependent race, was a truly horrific denial of black people's desire and capacity for adult citizenship.

Sojourner Truth, the only formerly enslaved woman to rise to prominence in antebellum women's rights conventions, made a similar point when she published her autobiography in 1850. Though white women's rights activists later construed Truth as a symbol of southern slavery, she grew up speaking Dutch in New York's Hudson Valley. She was born around 1797 (like Douglass she did not know the exact date) and named Isabella by parents who had already faced the sale of at least nine of their children. Isabella herself was sold three times to local families, all of whom abused her.[58] As she grew up, New Yorkers debated various plans for gradual emancipation, eventually legislating that slavery would end on 4 July 1827, with the stipulation that children born to enslaved mothers after 1799 would remain indentured until age twenty-eight if male or twenty-five if female—a provision that applied to all of Isabella's five children.[59] Isabella's owner tried to keep her in slavery until the last legal date, but, insisting that he had promised to manumit her a year early, she left with her infant daughter in clear defiance of the law that bound the child to her master. When Isabella's son Peter became one of the many enslaved children sold in violation of the gradual emancipation law, she successfully sued for his freedom. These experiences left her painfully aware that slave owners would postpone or deny black people's claims to freedom beyond the ages set by gradual emancipation laws.[60]

Isabella took control of her own destiny through a spiritual rebirth. On 1 June 1843 she took the name Sojourner Truth and dedicated herself to preaching a perfectionist Christianity that eventually allied her with both abolitionists and women's rights activists. Though unable to read or write, she was inspired by the success of her friend Frederick Douglass's *Narrative* to dictate the story of her life to Olive Gilbert, a sympathetic white reformer. The resulting *Narrative of Sojourner Truth* appeared in 1850. Attending women's rights conventions throughout the 1850s, she both spoke and sold her book at these events.[61]

In her recounting of northern slavery, Truth dwelled at length on masters' reluctance to give up control of slaves who remained profitable. She used the fate of her parents to illustrate how masters freed slaves not on the brink of adulthood, when they were most capable of productive and reproductive work, but in old age, when they could no longer adequately provide for themselves or their families. The result was a travesty of freedom that unfolded not as independent citizenship but as neglect and abuse of the elderly.[62] Truth recalled how her father became prematurely "weak and infirm; his limbs were painfully rheumatic and distorted—more from exposure and hardship than old age." His owners then decided it was "most expedient" to free him and Truth's mother. Her parents thus became secure in their family bonds only "in the decline of life, after the last child had been torn from them."[63] Enslaved throughout the years of his vigorous manhood, freed only when his capacities declined, Truth's father could never provide for himself or his family.[64]

In September 1850, the same year Truth published her *Narrative* and women's rights activists held their first national convention, Congress passed the Fugitive Slave Act, which empowered federal agents to seize alleged runaways in the North and send them into slavery without a jury trail and with no right to testify on their own behalf. Fugitive slave Harriet Jacobs later described the law as the "beginning of a reign of terror to the colored population" of the North.[65]

With the passage of the Fugitive Slave Act of 1850, some black leaders began to argue that championing women's rights was a distraction from the fight against slavery.[66] With regard to chronological age, even those committed to securing equal adulthood, such as Frederick Douglass, resolved that ending slavery for every man, woman, and child was a necessary prerequisite to winning equal political and legal rights for all adults. He made this point most eloquently in his provocative, controversial, and widely quoted Fourth of July oration, delivered in Rochester in 1852.[67]

Nearly five hundred people gathered in Rochester's Corinthian Hall at the invitation of the Ladies' Anti-Slavery Society to hear Douglass speak on the topic "What to the Slave is the Fourth of July?" His bold answer: "a day that reveals to him, more than all other days in the year, the gross injustice and cruelty to which he is the constant victim."[68] Douglass spoke of his frustration at still having to prove that the slave was a "man," but what he meant was not manhood as a particular stage of life but the more general humanity of the race.[69] Slave traders dealt in all ages and sexes: "men, women, and children . . . the old man, with locks thinned and gray . . . the young mother . . . the babe in her arms . . . that girl of thirteen."[70] Worse, by the Fugitive Slave Act "slavery has been nationalized in its most horrible and revolting form . . . and the power to hold, hunt, and sell men, women, and children as slaves remains no longer a state institution, but is now an institution of the whole United States . . . co-extensive with the star spangled banner and American Christianity."[71] The fundamental problem facing the nation, therefore, was the need to recognize that slaves were human beings.

Douglass thus resisted a narrow focus on the rights of adult men in order to paint a more inclusive vision of the freedom owed all Americans. Rather than forgoing the discussion of life stages entirely, he displaced the discussion of chronological age from individual lives onto nations. Addressing his audience on "the birthday of your National Independence, and of your political freedom," Douglass noted that the American Republic was "now 76 years old . . . a good old age for a man . . . but nations number their years by thousands." As a national collective, Americans were "still lingering in the period of childhood." Douglass found "hope in the thought . . . that America is young, and that she is still in the impressible stage of her existence." It was still possible that "high lessons of wisdom, of justice, and of truth, will yet give direction to her destiny."[72] Describing the history of nations in terms of individual life stages was a common literary trope, but when Douglass and other abolitionists did this they argued that the nation as a whole could not mature without acknowledging the equal human potential of all its citizens.[73] For white people as much as for the enslaved, bondage "fetters your progress; it is the enemy of improvement."[74]

Because Douglass believed that freedom had to be won for enslaved men, women, and children before the rights of adults could be settled, he criticized those who focused on women's rights without addressing slavery.[75] He never abandoned, however, his conviction that all human beings, regardless of race or sex, should be free at age twenty-one to claim political rights and personal freedom. This was a basic principle upon which all speakers at women's rights conventions agreed. Even as some white and black activists disagreed about political priorities, debating whether to focus narrowly on women's rights (meaning white women's rights) or commit to a broader struggle for freedom (meaning racial as well as sexual equality), all agreed that white men should not continue to claim rights and opportunities on the basis of age while denying the same to black men and all women.

CHRONOLOGICAL AGE AND
THE PROTECTION OF WHITE GIRLS

While women's rights activists fought to free all Americans to pursue their own destiny at age twenty-one, some also focused on the need to define girlhood as a distinct stage of life requiring special protections until that age. Like Mary Wollstonecraft and Margaret Fuller before them, these activists emphasized that white men infantilized women in part by sexualizing young girls. What these activists added was a specific argument that the age of consent for marriage should be raised to twenty-one for both sexes from the common-law standard of twelve for girls and fourteen for boys.[76] Though few Americans actually married in their early teens, the legal possibility offended women's rights activists who believed that young girls needed to be sheltered from sexual exploitation by adult men. As an alternative to early marriage, activists praised age-graded, coeducational common schools and pushed to reorganize higher education and professional training so that teenage girls could continue to develop along with their male peers.[77]

Elizabeth Oakes Smith was among those who argued most vehemently for the need to raise the age of consent to marriage. In 1850 and 1851 she published a series of essays in the *New York Tribune* that called for giving girls a "fair chance of development," protested the marriage of "baby wives" to older men, and lamented that middle-aged women were often seen as "past all joy, and beauty" at a period of life "when the other sex are in the perfection of their powers." In particular, Smith protested that state governments retained the common-law tradition that girls could consent to marriage at twelve and boys at fourteen. "The very idea of contract presupposes equality," Smith asserted. Yet a teenage bride, "an infant in law, whose pen to a commercial contract would be worthless . . . is party to a contract involving the well-being of her whole future life." Smith, as an older woman writing about how deeply she regretted her own marriage at sixteen to a man twice her age, wanted to create "equality" in marriage by ensuring that the "parties should be of age."[78]

Elizabeth Cady Stanton also argued that the age qualifications for marriage should be brought in line with other types of contract, a point she made in a speech on women's legal status in the state of New York, delivered in February 1854 to the women's rights convention in Albany and then distributed to every member of the state legislature. Noting that under New York law "no man can make a contract for a horse or piece of land until he is twenty-one years of age," Stanton asked, "Upon what principle of civil jurisprudence do you permit the boy of fourteen and the girl of twelve, in violation of every natural law, to make a contract more momentous in importance than any other, and then hold them to it, come what may, the whole of their natural lives, in spite of disappointment, deception and misery?"[79] Some male politicians were also troubled by such a low age of marriage. During the antebellum period, most states either raised the age at which children could marry or instituted an age below which they needed parental consent.[80] Judges, however, generally refused to enforce these restrictions, favoring the common-law tradition over statutory reform and largely upholding individual freedom above regulatory innovation.[81]

Writing from a medical point of view, Dr. Elizabeth Blackwell argued that regardless of state laws regulating the age of consent, "Nature's law" required individuals to postpone marriage until their midtwenties.[82] The first American woman to receive a medical degree, Blackwell attributed the mental and physical diseases of modern women to "imperfect and pre-mature development."[83] In a series of lectures published in 1852 as *The Laws of Life, with Special Reference to the Physical Education of Girls*, Blackwell argued that "the fundamental law of harmonic growth" was "Order in Exercise," by which she meant the sequence through which each faculty should be developed.[84] American girls violated the proper "order" of development because social custom encouraged them to marry before their bodies and minds had been given time to mature. "In America," she wrote, "the large majority of marriages are made too early. A young lady is thought to be getting rather old at 20, but at 25 she is already an old maid; and yet, as a general rule, before the age of 25, she is not prepared to enter on the marriage relation; it is only from 20 to 25 that the body attains its full vigor."[85] The result was that these "early marriages exhaust the vital energy of the mother" and undermined the health of her children. Motherhood and household management, Blackwell argued, "can only be supported by the vigor of a mature woman."[86] If between the ages of six-teen and twenty, girls stayed in school and had some "work to do in the world," then "years of noble usefulness would thus be opened to the young lady on her entrance into adult life . . . which would enable her to enter the married state wisely, and with the full preparation of a mature nature."[87]

At a time when colleges were closed to women (with the exception of Oberlin in Ohio), women's rights activists generally agreed with Blackwell that girls could not mature unless they remained in school longer, prefer-ably as long as their brothers. Convention organizer Paulina Wright Davis lamented the comparatively inferior "training of the girl—we say girl, for before the maturity of womanhood arrives, she is taken home to domestic duties."[88] Similarly, in an 1853 lecture, "Our Young Girls," Elizabeth Cady Stanton argued that "girls are dwarfed in mind and body by a false system of education."[89] To become the equals of their male peers, girls would have to attend not just grammar schools but colleges and professional schools with young men their age.[90] In short, women's rights activists argued that the age-graded, coeducational structure of common schools should be ex-tended to institutions of higher learning as well.

Convinced that all adults should be free after age twenty-one, wom-en's rights activists did not pause to consider whether developing young girls' capacity for independence might lead them to reject the authority of older women. Though activists identified clear differences among chil-dren, adolescents, adults, and the elderly, they saw all ages as allied in a common struggle for the rights of "woman." For example, Elizabeth Cady Stanton, a matron of thirty-seven, addressed "girls" by saying, "In the struggles of our day, you, dear young friends, stand in a most important position. . . . We, who are already in the meridian of life . . . can but warn and advise; to you it remains to usher in the new and happier day for woman." Even as she identified sharp generational differences, Stanton presented girls and middle-aged women as allies in a united struggle.[91] For their part, younger women did not challenge the pretensions of older women who offered themselves as guides and teachers for their "daughters" or younger "sisters who are just entering upon life."[92] At the 1848 Rochester convention, Quaker Rebecca M. Sanford noted that she was a "young bride" and then lauded her audience as "true women of this day and generation."[93] Though she saw herself as young, she did not identify a separate generational identity.[94]

Birth cohort mattered, to be sure. Speakers lauded senior activists, especially Lucretia Mott, as inspiring figures.[95] By the 1850s, they increasingly noted that younger women enjoyed educational and occupational opportunities that had been unavailable to their elders—in no small part because of the success of the women's rights movement itself.[96] Instead of identifying distinct generational goals, however, participants in antebellum women's rights conventions all shared the view that individuals should be free at age twenty-one to develop their full potential. They believed that the prime of life should come in late middle age for women as well as for men, and they looked forward to this time before they reached it. When Stanton was in her early forties, she expressed confidence that she would soon "bring nursing and housekeeping chores to a close."[97] Stanton wrote her unmarried friend Susan B. Anthony, "You and I have a prospect of a good long life. We shall not be in our prime before fifty & after that we shall be good for twenty years at least."[98] The shared commitment to equal rights for all adults and to individual development over the course of life thus prevented generational conflict within the antebellum women's rights movement. Older women fought for the freedom of young adults, and all ages sought the chance to develop their capacities as they grew older. Racial differences, however, were harder to transcend as white women's rights activists, even those committed to equal rights for all adults, often overlooked the struggles particular to enslaved girls and women.

HARRIET JACOBS, CHRONOLOGICAL AGE, AND THE PROTECTION OF ENSLAVED GIRLS

In 1861 the former slave Harriet Jacobs provided a nuanced analysis of the significance of chronological age for female slaves. She published her narrative, *Incidents in the Life of a Slave Girl*, in 1861, on the eve of the Civil War. She was not an outspoken advocate for women's rights, focusing instead on the protections granted white girls and women but denied to slaves. Her effort to express the particular experience of enslaved girls, however, highlighted the ways in which chronological age counted differently for free white and enslaved black girls. Where Frederick Douglass's *Narrative* provided a groundbreaking analysis of chronological age from the perspective of a boy coming of age in slavery, Jacobs specified how things looked different to a "slave girl." Jacobs shifted attention from males and rights to females and protections, arguing that law and custom shielded the sexual purity of white girls and enabled a choice of marriage partner for white women while denying both to slaves. Jacobs invoked chronological age, not because white women underwent a clear transition to adult independence based on age but because describing the extreme youth of enslaved girls subject to sexual abuse was a means of arousing the sympathy of northern readers accustomed to viewing girlhood as a stage of life characterized by sexual purity.[99]

Jacobs aimed to voice the sexual exploitation suffered by enslaved females without adding fuel to racist arguments that they were naturally degraded.[100] Chronological age provided a useful means for invoking what white readers had come to regard as the natural innocence of girlhood, an innocence that Jacobs claimed could not be preserved under laws that made young girls the property of older men.[101] When Jacobs wrote, "I now entered on my fifteenth year—a sad epoch in the life of a slave girl," middle-class readers would have understood her as referring to the typical age of menarche, an age those readers generally believed should be marked not just by a developing body but also ideally, at least for white girls, by a pure mind.[102] When the slave girl is "fourteen or fifteen," Jacobs explained, "her owner, or his sons, or the overseer, or perhaps all of them, begin to bribe her with presents. If these fail to accomplish their purpose, she is whipped or starved into submission to their will. . . . Resistance is hopeless."[103] As Jacobs repeatedly asserted, an enslaved girl could not resist because "there is no shadow of law to protect her from insult, from violence, or even from death."[104]

Enslaved girls became promiscuous, Jacobs argued, not because Africans lacked sexual restraint but because neither fathers and mothers nor husbands could protect them from sexual abuse by white men.[105] Girlhood for slaves was not a protected stage sheltered from sexual activity. "Even the little child . . . before she is twelve years old," Jacobs wrote, "will become prematurely knowing in evil things. . . . She will be compelled to realize that she is no longer a child."[106] Forced to have sex while still in her early teens, the maturing enslaved woman was then denied the right to marry or protect her own children once she became a mother. For daughters of the planter class, motherhood marked the final end of a long process of coming-of-age as adult women—a transition that enslaved women, denied the legal right to marry and vulnerable to separation from their children, could never fully reach.[107]

Jacobs poignantly described how her relatives tried to give her a sheltered childhood but could not do so under slave law. Jacobs's repeated use of chronological age, however, may have had more to do with the concerns of her target audience in the North than with her age-consciousness as a child in the South. Lydia Maria Child, who edited and promoted Jacobs's book, was not only a leading abolitionist but also one of the most influential contributors to the developing field of juvenile literature. Child and her readers were extremely age-conscious, believing as they did in the need for age-graded literature, and particularly focused on the need for mothers to guard the sexual purity of their teenage daughters.[108] Jacobs used chronological age to convince this audience that abused slaves were not promiscuous women, as apologists for slavery would argue, but innocent and vulnerable young girls.

Though Jacobs did not participate in antebellum women's rights conventions, she joined women's rights activists and abolitionists in thinking through the reforms that would be necessary to apply age qualifications equally to all American citizens. Like other antislavery activists, she concentrated on ending the market in human property that rendered any age-based definition of life stages an impossibility for enslaved people whose owners refused protection in childhood and independence in adulthood, insisting instead on maximizing their investment in slave labor. White women's rights activists, even those committed to abolition, often overlooked the significance of chronological age to the market in enslaved people, focusing instead on how state governments, educational institutions, and employers used chronological age to define a clear transition to manhood independence at age twenty-one while classifying free women as perpetual minors. Despite their different priorities, however, black and white activists were engaged in a common debate about the political significance of chronological age. They shared a deep outrage at the ways in which state governments used chronological age to define rights and opportunities for white males while denying equal adulthood to others. Though their priorities and strategies differed, black and white women's rights activists both argued that state governments should apply age qualifications equally to all Americans.

They thus drew a sharp line between dependent children and independent adults. At the same time, however, they also explored the political implications of life course ideals that focused not on age-based transitions between stages but on the need to develop individual potential over the course of life. Women's rights activists, black and white, emphasized that every individual should be free to navigate the journey of life without being confined to any predetermined sphere of activity based on race or sex.

CHAPTER FOUR

THE VOYAGE OF LIFE AND
EQUAL OPPORTUNITY

Antebellum Americans, as they migrated farther west or moved to cities in search of new opportunities, consumed a vast array of advice on how to navigate the voyage of life. Much of this literature was directed at men making their way in an expanding labor market, but some of it was written by and for women. Lydia Sigourney, a popular writer known as the "sweet singer of Hartford," rose to prominence with *Letters to Young Ladies* (1833), then later in life turned to writing for the elderly. Her 1854 collection of poems and essays, *Past Meridian*, which went through multiple printings, suggested that the key to a healthy and productive old age was to remain industrious and to deepen religious faith. For women, she advised cultivating intellectual faculties and recognizing the "beauty of age." Yet she did not ally herself with the women's rights movement, for she, like most Americans, believed that women could develop their capacities without demanding the same opportunities as their white male peers.[1]

Speakers at women's rights conventions could not have disagreed with her more. They contended that women, black or white, could develop their full potential over the course of life only if they broke through the boundaries of woman's prescribed "sphere" and the barriers imposed by racial prejudice to demand an equal opportunity to pursue their own ambitions. In speech after speech, they challenged the spatial metaphors of separate spheres for the sexes and segregation for the races with a temporal idea of maturation.[2] This insistence that a woman's growth necessitated going beyond any fixed "sphere" was what, more than anything, marked women's rights activists as radical. On most other issues they agreed with more moderate reformers who also wanted to expand women's opportunities for intellectual development and moral leadership. Critics often seized on the demands for woman suffrage and black suffrage as the most outrageous proposals, but these goals were but one aspect of women's rights activists' broader demand that every individual be freed from perpetual dependence in order to chart his or her own course through life from young adulthood to old age.[3]

Speakers at women's rights conventions linked their demand for individual development over the course of life to their more specific proposal that age twenty-one become a transition to full citizenship for all Americans. The first strategy emphasized chronological age. The second focused on maturation within adulthood, which activists understood as the longest stage of human life, beginning at age twenty-one and then spanning through midlife into old age.[4] Like other Americans during this period, women's rights activists viewed the stages of later life as depending more on functional capacity than on chronological age. Once a person passed twenty-one, aging became a gradual process with recognizable stages but no agreed-upon chronological transitions.[5]

What galvanized women's rights activists was not the use of chronological age to define the rights and duties of older Americans but the way that law and public opinion shaped the course of life differently for men and women, black and white. In particular, they argued that young white men generally expected that hard work and moderate habits would lead to a peak of achievement in middle age and comfort in old age. Individuals might fail, to be sure, but the cultural ideal was progress and individual development.[6] For those who were not white or male, these activists argued, the prospect was quite different. Activists insisted that free women, black or white, could secure neither economic security nor spiritual satisfaction in later life so long as young girls were told that youthful beauty and the choice of a marriage partner were the keys to their future happiness. Free black men and women, meanwhile, could not pursue their own ambitions because of racial discrimination, while the enslaved could neither improve their lives nor choose their own marriage partners.

Black and white women's rights activists developed their understanding of life's voyage through debate and mutual influence. They strongly agreed that all human beings should be given an equal opportunity to chart their own course. What they did not agree on, however, was how to best achieve this goal. Some believed that the priority of the women's rights movement should be to enable educated women to compete equally with their male peers. Antislavery activists emphatically disagreed, arguing that ending chattel slavery was a far more urgent priority. Still others focused on the needs of wage-earning women trying to navigate a labor market that offered few options for self-support. Despite these different priorities, however, activists could all rally around the general principle that every individual should have the opportunity to determine his or her own path through life free from artificial restraints based on race or sex.

IMAGINING THE STAGES OF A WOMAN'S LIFE

In antebellum America, white manhood citizenship was a stage of life with a clear beginning at age twenty-one but no fixed end. Legislators and jurists, though convinced of the need to set minimum ages for taking up rights and duties, were much more reluctant to set maximum ages. With regard to suffrage, delegates to state constitutional conventions recognized that some elderly men lost the mental capacity for informed consent, but they left this determination in the hands of judges and election officials.[7] The federal government did not recruit men over forty-five for military service, but the prevalence of middle-aged commissioned officers demonstrated that white males could continue to serve their country beyond any fixed age.[8] A few states experimented with setting a mandatory retirement age for judges, but these limits remained controversial as people protested the removal of qualified individuals.[9]

This reluctance to use chronological age to define a transition out of productive adulthood and into dependent old age mirrored a general cultural understanding that human beings could remain active and engaged until quite late in life. While some Americans denigrated the elderly and promoted a cult of youth, most believed that those who worked hard when young could look forward to the reward of material success and health in later life. Advanced old age might bring physical and mental decline, but even then, many hoped to find comfort and spiritual solace. Even those who emphasized the negative sides of aging tended to fix the period of decline after age seventy.[10]

The cultural assumption that individuals should reach a peak of achievement in middle age and then continue to find comfort and spiritual fulfillment in old age can be found in visual representations of the steps and stages of life, which were popular in antebellum America. These pictorial representations followed two conventions. The first divided the stages of life into separate frames, while the second pictured life as a rising and falling staircase. This imagery had ancient roots but in nineteenth-century America often took the form of glorifying the material success and cultural influence of an expanding middle class.[11]

For example, *The Four Seasons of Life*, a set of 1868 prints by Currier and Ives, pictured the ideal also found in antebellum advice books that men and women should move through life's stages in tandem, their fates linked through romantic love and companionate marriage (see figures 1–4). Boys and girls frolic together in *Childhood, "The Season of Joy,"* then settle down to the serious commitment of courtship and marriage in *Youth, "The Season of Love."* In *Middle Age, "The Season of Strength,"* a powerful man and his boisterous son stride into a well-appointed home where the man's wife, two daughters, and infant child eagerly greet his return. In *Old Age, "The Season of Rest,"* a dignified elderly couple bask in the warmth of a fashionable parlor, imparting wisdom to their granddaughter.[12] Though joining husband and wife in every season, the sequence marks out clear differences in how men and women moved through stages after childhood—the young woman leans on her companion; the middle-aged woman stays at home; the old woman knits while her husband reads a newspaper. These differences express the idea that women depended upon men throughout adulthood and that their relation to the market and politics was mediated through the ambition of their husbands.

The other popular convention for representing the life course was as a rising and falling staircase with steps arrayed at regular intervals, often ten years apart. These images of the steps of life, which originated in sixteenth-century Europe and were ubiquitous in America by the 1830s, represented the physical changes and social attributes associated with aging while communicating a clear expectation that a virtuous life would lead to a peak of success in the middle years. Some of these images pictured men and women moving through life together, while others divided them into separate frames.[13] In either case, the attributes associated with males displayed military, political, and commercial achievement, while those associated with females drew attention to marriage, motherhood, and household work. For example, in *The Life and Age of Man*, printed by James Baillie in 1848, the same year as the Seneca Falls convention, a young white man energetically mounts the steps of life as he seeks military glory and then commercial success (see figure 5). The peak of his life comes at age fifty, when strength begins to fade but wit confers new powers. The apex of the image, however, is not the man himself but the American flag held aloft at age forty and proudly associating his individual journey of life with the fate of the nation.

Figure 1. Currier and Ives, *The Four Seasons of Life: Childhood, "The Season of Joy"*
(c. 1868), courtesy of the Library of Congress, Washington, D.C.

Figure 2. Currier and Ives, *The Four Seasons of Life: Youth, "The Season of Love"*
(c. 1868), courtesy of the Library of Congress, Washington, D.C.

Figure 3. Currier and Ives, *The Four Seasons of Life: Middle Age, "The Season of Strength"* (c. 1868), courtesy of the Library of Congress, Washington, D.C.

Figure 4. Currier and Ives, *The Four Seasons of Life: Old Age, "The Season of Rest"* (c. 1868), courtesy of the Library of Congress, Washington, D.C.

The companion print of the *Life and Age of Woman* depicts a much more demure and restrained young lady, a wedding gown and child marking her ascent to a matronly peak at fifty years (see figure 6).[14] The engraver etched sharper wrinkles on her face than that of her companion, consciously or not emphasizing the loss of girlish beauty. The poems accompanying the two images emphasize the male's individual growth and decline ("At forty nought his courage quails / But lion-like by force prevails") and the female's relationship to other people ("[at forty] bearing fruit, she rears her boys / And tastes a mother's pains and joys"). Tellingly, a woman makes a brief appearance in the life of man, supporting him in infancy. The artist thus evokes the principle that men grew up by leaving their mothers behind. The female infant is not pictured in her mother's arms but alone in a cradle. Rather than leave her mother, she becomes a mother herself a few steps further along. For both the man and woman, the very last steps of life are full of suffering, but these begin at age eighty in a life that stretches to one hundred years. Such popular representations of aging thus offered both men and women the hope of success in middle age followed by a slow, if inevitable, decline while at the same time expressing the idea that men should pursue their own destiny while women should marry their future to men's.

So well known were these images by the 1840s that temperance activists parodied them to warn that prodigal habits in youth would result in early decline and premature death. In 1846 Nathaniel Currier popularized this view in his depiction of *The Drunkard's Progress*, where an intemperate man climbs steps of intemperance before a rapid decline that ends with suicide. Beneath the arched stair, a grieving wife and young child are left wandering without support.[15] Temperance activists brought this understanding of women's vulnerability into women's rights conventions, building close alliances between the two movements.

Women's rights activists, however, made the more radical argument that all wives were vulnerable in later life, even those who married successful and hardworking men. They regarded the popular imagery of the life course that linked women to men through marriage as nothing but a sham, concealing the force of laws that stripped wives of their property and stifled their ambitions. Paulina Wright Davis forcefully made this argument at the 1853 national women's rights convention held in Cleveland, Ohio. For her, the central problem with imagining the course of female life was the inability to picture a woman moving through life alone or achieving any individual ambitions after marriage.[16]

Davis was the wealthy childless widow of a successful Utica, New York, merchant and the wife of an antislavery Democratic congressman from

Figure 5. James Baillie, *The Life and Age of Man, Stages of Man's Life from the Cradle to the Grave* (c. 1848), courtesy of the Library of Congress, Washington, D.C.

Figure 6. James Baillie, *The Life and Age of Woman, Stages of Woman's Life from the Cradle to the Grave* (c. 1848), courtesy of the Library of Congress, Washington, D.C.

Rhode Island. During the 1840s she joined the campaign for New York's Married Women's Property Act and toured the state lecturing on female anatomy, and then from 1853 to 1855 she edited the *Una*, one of the first newspapers dedicated to advancing women's rights. Her wealth, social connections, and poise made her an effective organizer and propagandist. While her interest in female anatomy may have helped focus her attention on aging, her main concern was not with the biological process of growing older but with social conventions that defined youthful beauty and girlish dependence as the achievement of true womanhood.[17]

Davis asked her audience to imagine a series of images laid out on canvas to represent the normative stages of a white woman's life. The first canvas pictured the "marriage hour," when the husband, by valuing "girlish beauty" and "entire dependence" as the height of femininity, "invested [his bride] with his ideal of womanhood, while she was yet a child." As a result, this woman gained the most respect when she had not yet matured in "years and development," and later stages of life could bring only decline and disappointment.[18]

Since the bride remained dependent on her husband, time passed without maturation. "In the next scene, the child wife appears withering away from life. . . . The occupation of business, ambition, and the ennobling pursuits of life, are forbidden her by general consent." The woman had only two routes into middle age, neither very appealing. In the third picture, she could either become "the heartless votary of fashion, a flirt, or—that most to be dreaded, most to be despised thing—a married coquette." Or, if she realized that her "beauty of person has faded away, she may be found turning from these lighter styles of toys, to a quiet kind of handmaiden piety and philanthropy." This woman never learned to follow her own conscience and as a result found neither peace nor salvation in old age. In the final canvas, as "the angel of death" approached, one look at the old woman's eyes showed that "there is a falseness and wrong that must be removed." This "falseness" was the ideal of womanhood that overvalued dependence and youth, leaving no room for development as an independent adult.[19]

When Davis imagined four "canvases," she broadly invoked the whole tradition of representing the stages of life but more specifically alluded to one of the most famous series of paintings in antebellum America—Thomas Cole's *The Voyage of Life* (see figures 7–10). In 1848, the same year as the Seneca Falls convention, up to 500,000 people (the equivalent of half the city's population) gathered in New York City to see Cole's four-part allegory. Over the next twenty years, thousands more purchased cheap engravings of the series, which outstripped portraits of George

Figure 7. Thomas Cole, *The Voyage of Life: Childhood* (1842),
courtesy of the National Gallery of Art, Washington, D.C.

Figure 8. Thomas Cole, *The Voyage of Life: Youth* (1842),
courtesy of the National Gallery of Art, Washington, D.C.

Figure 9. Thomas Cole, *The Voyage of Life: Manhood* (1842),
courtesy of the National Gallery of Art, Washington, D.C.

Figure 10. Thomas Cole, *The Voyage of Life: Old Age* (1842),
courtesy of the National Gallery of Art, Washington, D.C.

Washington in popularity. Noting the "magic influence of this series on the public mind," the Presbyterian minister and educator Gorham Abbot described the paintings as "an Epic Poem—the hero, or heroine of which is the beholder."[20] Yet one wonders how white and black women identified with Cole's allegory, since sex and race difference were central to the drama of *The Voyage of Life*.

In the first canvas, titled *Childhood*, viewers beheld an infant setting out on the stream of life. The baby's white skin practically glows against a jet-black background, evoking race as a critical determinant of individual destiny. The sex of the infant is as yet unclear, but the next three canvases present maturation as a process of increasing sex differentiation. The second, titled *Youth*, shows a young man who is still rather effeminate. In the third stage, all sexual ambiguity is gone; the image is not called *Adulthood* or *Middle Age* but more specifically *Manhood*. In a written description accompanying the paintings, Cole explained that the demons in the gathering clouds are "Suicide, Intemperance, and Murder, which are the temptations that beset men in their direst trouble."[21] The last image shows that men who successfully restrained themselves and placed their faith in God would find a safe harbor in old age.

The Voyage of Life was commissioned by Samuel Ward, a prominent temperance reformer and father of Julia Ward Howe (who became a leading women's rights activist after the Civil War).[22] Cole provided a visual representation of the successful life course promulgated by evangelical Protestants and temperance reformers, who stressed the importance of self-control, faith in God, and religious feeling. Cole's image highlights the voyager's emotional response as a force turning the individual toward God.[23] Perhaps because women hearkened to the evangelicals' sentimental appeals in greater numbers than men,[24] the Reverend Gorham Abbot assumed that women found meaning in Cole's allegory. While Cole stressed dependence on God, however, his was a specifically masculine form of dependence. Cole explained that in middle age "the helm of the boat is gone," illustrating the voyager's "dependence on a Superior Power."[25] Cole's voyager was nonetheless captain of his own craft, an individual independent of any earthly authority but his own conscience. He reacted to the stormy vicissitudes of a sex-specific stage of life known as "manhood." In old age, his extravagantly flowing beard linked him to the biblical patriarchs, whose authority was based on age, gender, and (as many interpreted the story of Ham) racial inheritance.[26]

In contrast to the male voyager, the feminine presences in Cole's allegory do not gain wisdom or find salvation with the passage of time. One is an idealized feminine form, a youthful beauty, her face unworn by cares, her body promising fertility, and her upturned gaze betokening devotion to another person: the wooden figurehead of the boat, a representation of the "Hours." Significantly, she does not weather the storms of "manhood" but has broken off and sunk. The other feminine presence is a guardian angel.[27] In *Childhood*, the infant depends on her to steer the boat, her whiteness a shield for his—just as mothers were credited with forming the character of white male citizens.[28] Childhood ends precisely when the voyager takes "the helm himself" to pursue his dreams of "glory and fame." The angel hovers behind "with an air of solicitude" for the individualized male.[29] Cole thus presents a course of life that was specifically male and an ideal of femininity that was not fully human.

Paulina Wright Davis's four canvases clearly evoked and contrasted with Cole's. Davis's woman was trapped in interiors and defined by her relationships to others, while Cole's lone voyager charts his course through the American wilderness. Further, Davis rejected Cole's image of women as angelic comforters of men, arguing that women also needed to face the vicissitudes of life alone: "Give her strength, power and ability to stand alone, ere you demand of her duties from which an angel might shrink."[30]

Women's rights activists repeatedly evoked the competing possibilities of life's voyage as a "ship wreck" or "safe harbour."[31] In an 1861 speech titled "Fashionable Women Shipwreck," Elizabeth Cady Stanton compared a white woman in a divorce case to a voyager blown "by an adverse wind . . . on the shoals of stern hard ruin." Like Cole's youth, this woman pursued "promises of happiness as she stepped on the threshold of womanhood," only to have her "bright dreams of life's future" dashed on the rocks of middle age.[32] This was a sex-specific form of ruin, however, for she placed her faith in marriage and depended upon a husband who later abandoned her to a court system dominated by men. To prevent this "total wreck of helpless woman," Stanton felt a duty to speak "of wrongs which my daughter may tomorrow suffer in your courts where there is no . . . woman's presence to protect" her.[33] Throughout her career, Stanton repeatedly argued that women could not depend upon men to guide and protect them on life's voyage.[34] Here she suggested that older women had a duty to protect their daughters from the dangers of depending on men.

Cole's allegory, like Stanton's, stressed the disillusionment of youthful hopes in middle age—a common theme of romanticism.[35] But many Americans saw only Cole's image of youth, and engravings of this particular panel greatly outstripped reproductions of the entire series in popularity. Many read the image out of context as a representation of hope in an era of Manifest Destiny.[36] Women's rights activists repeatedly evoked Cole's image of youth. Lucy Stone, for example, proclaimed, "Laying her hand upon the helm, let woman steer straight onward to the fulfillment of her own destiny. Let her ever remember that in following out the high behests of her own soul will be found her exceeding great reward."[37] While Cole's entire allegory stressed dependence on God, his image of youth concisely expressed the popular notion, also evoked by delegates to state constitutional conventions, that every man entered a stage of life in which he was expected to chart his own course.[38]

REFORMS NEEDED FOR WOMEN TO DEVELOP THEIR POTENTIAL OVER TIME

Women's rights activists challenged the metaphor of woman's sphere with new metaphors that defined womanhood, like manhood, as a path, pilgrimage, or voyage during which individuals discovered their full potential.[39] Others relied on metaphors of physiological maturation, as when Paulina Wright Davis declared, "I ask only freedom for the natural unfolding of [woman's] powers, the conditions most favorable for her possibilities of growth."[40] In all cases, the metaphors used by these activists redefined womanhood as a process of development unfolding over time.[41] As Abby Price summarized the central demand of the women's rights movement: "In the name of eternity . . . we ask our brothers no longer to proscribe [woman's] sphere" but to allow each woman "to develop all her faculties, as an individual."[42]

Abby Price was thirty-six years old when she began speaking at women's conventions. As a poet and lecturer, she knew personally of women's fight for remunerative and rewarding work. In 1850 she and her family were members of Hopedale, a socialist cooperative community in Milford, Massachusetts, when she delivered a keynote address to the first national women's rights convention in Worcester. In her speech, Price articulated three practical reforms regarded as crucial by all antebellum women's rights activists. First, women of all ages should have access to a greater range of paid employments; second, wives should be independent within marriage; and third, mature women should be able to claim respect for their achievements and join their male peers in positions of political leadership. Without these reforms, women could enjoy no real growth or development.[43]

Price and her allies wanted women to be able to choose their own paths through life, but to do so they would need access to a greater range of paid employment. Women's rights activists protested the practice of "excluding [women] from those [occupations] which are most lucrative; and, even in those to which they are admitted, awarding them a compensation less— generally by one-half to two-thirds—than is paid to men for an equal amount of service rendered."[44] Activists were particularly concerned that paid labor did not enable women to attain financial security in later life. Abby Price, focused as she was on achieving "pecuniary independence" for women, pointed out that "very few . . . who throng the crowded paths frequented by Woman's patient feet, are enabled to save anything for the contingencies of the future."[45] Price argued that female as well as male wage earners should be given the chance "of maintaining an honorable independence."[46]

Women's rights activists recognized the professions as a means of achieving public stature in middle age. "I speak from the experience of many years," said forty-four-year-old Harriet Hunt. "My path has been public, as a physician for my own sex and for children." Twice denied admittance to Harvard Medical School because of her gender, Hunt campaigned to open medical training to women. Unmarried professional women like Hunt recognized themselves as models of a new kind of female maturity, but, significantly, they did not condescend to housewives. Hunt, for example, believed that medical education would be useful in training young women for either paid work or motherhood.[47] Indeed, antebellum women's rights activists expected most women to marry, and many were married and mothers themselves.

Much of their imaginative energy went into reconfiguring marriage as a path of individual development for white wives. "A true marriage," according to women's rights leader Henry Blackwell, "will involve no subjection. It will not limit thoughts, nor fetter activities. It will complete, not destroy, the individuality of women."[48] Blackwell came from an extraordinary family of reformers, all committed to antislavery and women's rights. His two sisters were among the few women to practice medicine in the United States, while his brother married Antoinette Brown, the first American woman to be ordained as a minster. When Henry Blackwell married Lucy Stone in 1855, the two publicized their unusual marriage as a demonstration of women's rights principles. Stone kept her maiden name—indeed, later brides who did so were known as Lucy Stoners—and excised the word "obey" from her marriage vows.[49] Many women's rights advocates shared Blackwell and Stone's concern for finding ways women could both marry and pursue individual ambitions over the course of life.

At women's rights conventions in the 1850s, Ernestine Rose insisted that wives' labor would be devalued, their financial security would be in jeopardy, and their personal dignity would be eroded until married women had equal rights to all marital property. Rose, a Jewish immigrant and leading freethinker, had refused an arranged marriage in Poland, sought an education in Germany and England, and then joined the campaign for New York's Married Women's Property Act.[50] Though some states had granted wives control of the separate property they brought into marriage, husbands continued to own all property gained after marriage. Women's rights activists argued that this was deeply unjust since wives' unpaid labor contributed as much to family fortunes as husband's paid labor.[51] As Rose asserted forcefully, "The mass of people commence life with no other capital than the union of heads, hearts, and hands. To benefit of this best of capital, the wife has no right. If they are unsuccessful in married life, who suffers more the bitter consequences of poverty than the wife? But if successful, she cannot call a dollar her own."[52] Whereas Charles O'Conor had argued at the 1846 New York constitutional convention that the husband's "prosperity" should be the wife's "pride," during the 1850s women's rights advocates asserted the belief that wives should be able to revel in their own achievements and control the fruits of their own labor.[53]

The inequality of inheritance rights was also a major issue in the women's rights movement. Throughout the antebellum period, convention participants pointed out that dower, the portion of marital property legally guaranteed a widow during her life, was an inadequate right—"a pitiful life interest only in one-third of his real estate, provided he leave any"—which did not recognize wives' financial contribution to the marriage and did not provide women with adequate security in later life.[54] Precisely because the timing of death remained capricious, wives faced the possibility of being left "in the middle of their days, without adequate means of support."[55] Wives could not, in effect, plan for the future. Clarina Howard Nichols, who struggled to support herself and her children after a failed first marriage and then joined her second husband in working as a newspaper editor, felt deeply the need for equal inheritance rights.[56] As Nichols complained, "O men! in the enjoyment of well-secured property rights, you beautify your snug homesteads, and say within your hearts, 'Here I may sit under my own vine and fig-tree; here have I made the home of my old age.' And it never occurs to you that no such blissful feeling of security finds rest in the bosom of your wives."[57] This issue of inheritance united both the women like Nichols who earned money from paid labor and the vast majority of white women's rights activists who depended for financial support upon the success of their husbands.[58]

Women's rights activists believed that even in cases where widows were well cared for financially, their years of hard work hardly yielded proper independence and respect. Quaker abolitionist Lucretia Mott told of a man who complained bitterly that he had "to *keep his mother* a good many years, and she lived to be ninety years old!" When asked, the man admitted that his mother had been "a very industrious woman. His father and she commenced life poor, but gathered together this great estate by their united industry." When pointedly asked how he could then claim that he "kept" his mother, he "saw the injustice of his past position, and was disposed to make some redress for the wrong done his own mother in making her, in her old age, dependent upon him." Mott wanted industrious older women to be seen no longer as burdens on male relatives but rather as models of individual achievement.[59]

With a romantic faith in individual genius, women's rights activists often argued that it was up to truly exceptional women to settle the question of woman's proper sphere. They frequently mentioned the names of prominent women in history—writers, scientists, queens (usually, but not always, white)—as evidence of the heights women could scale when they broke free from artificial restrictions.[60]

Their central goal, however, was to make marriage and motherhood paths to public leadership. Abby Price looked forward to a time when "experienced and virtuous matrons, who have passed through years of domestic duties with fidelity and care, shall sit in the Councils of the Nation wisely to control and direct their deliberations."[61] Seeking to redefine marriage and motherhood as a distinct phase of a woman's life rather than her entire destiny, women's rights activists tried to open leadership positions to white middle-aged matrons. Henry Blackwell believed that girls "should be trained for an active, independent life, before and after those years when children are to be reared."[62] Price agreed, noting that "those women who are married, and have the care of families, have duties and responsibilities that rest peculiarly upon themselves," but later in life no one should say to them, "Keep your minds and attention within that narrow circle, though your mature and ripened intellects would fain be interested in whatever concerns the larger family of man."[63] Conceiving of motherhood as a stage of life was, in part, a strategic response to the conservative argument that expanded opportunities would cause white women to neglect their family responsibilities. John Neal met this charge directly, declaring that if white women were allowed to run for office, "the probabilities are, that not a married woman would be thought of under a certain age."[64] The end of child-rearing, recognized as distinct from menopause, would mark a change of life, a time when white women could pursue public careers. Elizabeth Cady Stanton pointed to the life of Lucretia Mott, a mother and reformer in her late fifties: "There is no such thing as a sphere for sex. . . . The same woman may have a different sphere at different times. For example, the highly gifted Quakeress, Lucretia Mott, married early in life and brought up a large family of children. . . . Her children settled in their own homes, Lucretia Mott has now no domestic cares. . . . Who shall tell us that this divinely inspired woman is out of her sphere in her public endeavors[?]"[65] Equality for women did not mean following a male-defined career, but it did mean the equal chance to develop over the course of one's life.

Stanton recognized that gender equality would be achieved only when models of successful aging changed for white men as well as for white women. Experience in the home should be taken as a necessary qualification for political leadership, a view that ran counter to the conception of male political leaders rising to prominence through public competition with other men. "Children need the watchful care and wise teachings of fathers as well as of mothers. . . . Having done their duty at home, let them together sit in our national councils."[66]

Women's rights activists admitted that extreme old age weakened both mind and body.[67] But, as Blackwell noted, contempt was generally much greater for old women than for old men. The "customary epitaph applied to an imbecile, incompetent man, is 'old woman,' or 'granny.'"[68] If a white middle-aged man embodied competence, then an elderly woman personified imbecility.[69] While some elderly men were regarded as dotards, older white men who retained their masculinity and intellectual vigor could still win respect.

These activists believed that patriarchy was a system of both age and gender privilege that valued older men. They eagerly took up the first glimmerings of evidence—just emerging in this period and discredited in later generations—that the most ancient of human societies were matriarchal.[70] Price noted that wives and mothers participated in public and religious functions in the past, and she looked forward to the time when they would do so again.[71] Matriarchal theory retained the age privilege inherent in patriarchy but elevated older women as well as men. As the forty-six-year-old poet and lyceum lecturer Elizabeth Oakes Smith contended, "The maiden may be fair; the mother holy and tender; but the mature woman, grand in her serene wisdom, giving the law, not only to her household, but to the country also, is more than this—she is beautiful, august."[72] Smith promoted a new standard of female beauty—one that would improve, rather than decline, with age—and embraced a new standard of human achievement that valued traditionally feminine experience (raising children, managing a household) as a source of wisdom and power.

RACIAL HIERARCHIES AND THE POTENTIAL FOR GROWTH

Black women's rights activists fervently supported the goal of giving all individuals an equal opportunity to develop their full potential over the course of life. But just as the women's movement gained momentum in the 1850s, black people had to contend with scientific experts offering new evidence that Africans were naturally incapable of developing the same potential as Europeans and would always remain childlike beings, whatever opportunities they might be given. Over the next decade, American scientists and women's rights activists would form two separate camps competing to define individual development, the scientists stressing natural limits and the activists fighting to break what they saw as artificial barriers. The stakes were high, as defenders of slavery and racial segregation seized upon racial science as proof that black people could never reach the same degree of maturity as whites and were therefore better suited to perpetual servitude than to equal citizenship.[73]

Where Thomas Jefferson had speculated in the 1780s that Africans might be a separate species, inferior in body and mind, antebellum American scientists claimed to have found concrete proof that God separately created different races, endowing them with faculties best suited to their particular environments. This theory of separate creations, which came to be known as polygenesis or the American school of ethnology, was never widely accepted. Most Americans, scientists and laypersons alike, clung to the biblical description of all human beings as the descendants of Adam and Eve. They explained racial difference as the product of variable degeneration or the curse of Ham. Many who rejected the theory of separate creations nonetheless accepted new evidence that African Americans could not develop the same potential for full citizenship as people of European descent.[74]

For example, Louis Agassiz—the Swiss-born Harvard zoologist who accepted his professorship at Harvard in 1848, the same year women's rights activists gathered in Seneca Falls, and published his views on race in July 1850, a few months before the first national women's rights convention in October—argued that God endowed all human beings with the same basic faculties but created the races separately, resulting in "different faculties" being developed over the course of life. As a result, "those higher attributes which characterize man in his highest development are exhibited in the several races in very different proportions."[75] Providing Africans with the same opportunities as Europeans would do little to change these fixed patterns of individual development. It was, Agassiz claimed, "mock-philanthropy and mock-philosophy to assume that all races have the same abilities . . . and that in consequence of this equality they are entitled to the same position in human society."[76] That God endowed all human beings with the potential for growth was, of course, precisely what many women's rights activists, black and white, were contending as proof of their claim to equal citizenship.

Agassiz relied upon the research of others, most importantly the Phila-delphia doctor Samuel George Morton. A pioneer of craniometry, the sci-ence of measuring skulls, Morton believed that people with bigger brains were more intelligent and that accurately measuring brain size was the key to understanding racial difference. In the 1830s Morton influentially claimed that, on average, Europeans developed larger brains than Na-tive Americans and Africans. Though both his data and his assumptions were discredited by later scientists, his findings garnered widespread in-terest.[77] The hierarchical metaphors employed by polygenists like Agas-siz and Morton invoked both physical and temporal measures, describing Europeans as having either grown bigger or progressed further than Afri-cans. In either case, those of European heritage appeared as more mature adults, having attained a higher degree of physical, moral, intellectual, and cultural development.[78]

Many who rejected Morton's theory of permanent racial differences were nonetheless impressed by his method for measuring variable intelligence. For example, George Combe, a Scottish phrenologist who influenced Eliza-beth Cady Stanton, Lucretia Mott, and Frederick Douglass, accepted Mor-ton's evidence that Africans' brains were smaller than Europeans' brains but attributed this fact to environment and predicted that with "greater ex-ercise of the mental faculties in freedom," Africans' brains would "increase in size."[79] With even progressive-minded reformers like Combe promoting Morton's findings, advocates for black equality faced increasing pressure to prove Africans could mature in the same way as whites.

Further, by the 1850s many white Americans who defended the biblical account of a unitary creation nonetheless interpreted the new data on brain size as proof that African Americans never fully matured.[80] For example, John Bachman, a South Carolina minister and natural history enthusiast, united scripture and science in his defense of slavery by reasoning that the African was an "inferior variety of our species," just as "our child . . . who looks up to us for protection and support is still of our own blood notwith-standing his weakness and ignorance."[81] The Virginia sociologist George

Fitzhugh, one of the most influential defenders of southern slavery and an early champion of the French sociologist Auguste Comte, understood society as an organic whole in which the most developed individuals should guide those who were less mature. Fitzhugh promoted slavery as a paternalistic relation in which "the master occupies toward [the slave] the place of a parent or guardian." The adult slave, Fitzhugh wrote, was "but a grown-up child, and must be governed as a child."[82]

The most influential promoter of the view of African Americans as a childlike race was not an apologist for slavery but its leading critic: the novelist Harriet Beecher Stowe. Younger sister of educator Catharine Beecher, Stowe supported an end to slavery and the colonization of blacks to Africa. Her antislavery novel *Uncle Tom's Cabin* first appeared serially in the *National Review* in 1851 and then became the best-selling book of the century, second only to the Bible. Throughout her novel, Stowe praised what she called "the childlike simplicity of affection" of the black race.[83] In case readers missed the point, Stowe explained in her *Key to "Uncle Tom's Cabin"* that black people were "confessedly more simple, docile, child-like and affectionate than other races" and were thus more receptive to "the divine graces of love and faith."[84] These childish qualities made Africans devout Christians, since they realized the need for all people to depend on God, but just as surely rendered them incapable of achieving equal citizenship with white Americans. Stowe advised in *Uncle Tom's Cabin*, "Let the church of the north receive these poor sufferers in the spirit of Christ . . . until they have attained somewhat of a moral and intellectual maturity, and then assist them in their passage to [Africa], where they may put into practice the lessons they have learned in America."[85] The most influential antebellum attack on slavery thus promoted the argument that Africans could never mature into independent citizens on equal terms with whites.

By the 1850s, those who would defend the equal capacity of all Americans to mature over the course of life had to counter scientific racists like Agassiz and romantic racists like Stowe, both of whom categorized black Americans as childlike beings incapable of attaining the same degree of development as whites. Black women's rights activists such as Frederick Douglass, Sojourner Truth, and Frances Harper mounted a concerted attack upon the hierarchical measures of individual development that classified some adults as forever stunted in their capacity for growth. They took up Phillis Wheatley's argument that religious faith was the highest goal toward which a human being could strive and used it to attack antebellum theories of racial hierarchy.[86]

Douglass took on American ethnologists on their own terms, directly confronting Agassiz and other scientific racists in a major speech titled "The Claims of the Negro Ethnologically Considered." The first African American invited to speak during commencement at an American university, Douglass used his address at Western Reserve College in July 1854 as a chance to influence scientific understandings of racial difference.[87] Douglass ultimately rested his claims to justice upon the Bible, juxtaposing the infinite love of God for all his children to the racial distinctions drawn by white men.[88] Yet Douglass also employed the tools of ethnology, joining a long line of black intellectuals who had been challenging the findings of American scientists.[89] For Douglass, the political implications of polygenesis were clear: "For, let it once be granted that the human race are of multitudinous origin, naturally different in their moral, physical, and intellectual capacities, and at once you make plausible a demand for classes, grades and conditions, for different methods of culture . . . and a chance is left for slavery, as a necessary institution."[90] The whole question of democratic equality, in other words, hinged on the issue of whether or not all human beings had the same inherent capacities that could be developed over time.

Douglass's main point was that Africans were as capable of reaching great heights as Europeans if given an equal opportunity to do so. In the most general terms, he accepted a ranking of European civilization as superior to African and then argued for Africans' power to develop as civilized beings.[91] In terms of craniometrics, he accepted that prominent intellectuals had larger brains and called for measuring the heads of leading black thinkers such as Martin Delaney and Samuel Ward. Though Douglass mentioned men, his strategy of accepting hierarchies of growth and arguing for black people's ability to attain "the very best type" was the tactic used by educated white women's rights activists who claimed that women were capable of developing the same potential as their male peers.[92]

By the late 1850s, however, Douglass focused on male development in a speech on "self-made men," which he first delivered in 1859 during a tour of Illinois and Wisconsin and then revised and reprised over the next thirty-five years.[93] In the late 1850s Douglass joined the lyceum circuit, traveling the country to give paid lectures to large audiences. In contrast to the earnest activists gathered at reform conventions, lyceum audiences expected to be entertained as well as enlightened, and Douglass obliged by speaking on subjects other than slavery. Most radically, he—a black man and fugitive slave—assumed the privilege of advising whites on "what I think sound and important views of life."[94] Life-course advice was a well-established genre developed by preachers, moralists, and politicians. Within the black community, black lecturers and authors advised members of their own race. But for a black man to offer such advice to whites was an innovation.[95]

In his popular speech on "self-made men," Douglass displayed his familiarity—and discomfort—with popular metaphors for human life. He presented a catalog of such tropes, saying, "To the sailor, life is a ship. . . . To the farmer, life is a fertile field. . . . To the architect, it stands out as a gorgeous palace or temple. . . . To the great dramatic poet, all the world is a stage, and men but players." Rejecting all these, Douglass settled on the metaphor of life as a continuous process of education: "To all mankind, the world is a vast school. From the cradle to the grave, the oldest and the wisest, not less than the youngest and simplest, are but learners; and those who learn most, seem to have most to learn."[96]

He argued that while industry was the key to success, any comparison of the achievements of white and black men would have to take into account the arresting force of slavery and racial prejudice. He also argued that true achievement was measured not by individual success but by dedication to a great cause: "We all need some grand, some soul-enlarging, some soul-sustaining object to draw out the best energies of our natures and to lift us to the plains of true nobleness and manly life."[97] While women too could pursue a grand cause, Douglass did not say so. Nor did he explore the contributions that wives made to "self-made" men. Further, he downplayed the essential support women lent to his own success.[98]

Douglass's support for women's rights did not extend to a reconfiguration of marriage. In 1853 Douglass explicitly opposed a resolution urging state legislatures to make husbands and wives joint owners of marital property: "It seems to me not altogether fair to give the wife an equal right to the disposition of the property. The husband labors hard, perhaps, while the wife lives in luxury."[99] That Douglass accepted this stereotype and focused on married men as "self-made" while giving no credit to their wives showed his unwillingness to question the private forms of power that prevented married women from gaining respect and independence as they aged. A more probing examination of both gender and racial hierarchies within the human family came from black women, most notably Sojourner Truth and Frances Harper.

BLACK WOMEN AND MORAL MATURITY

Like Douglass, Truth ridiculed the pretensions of craniometric scientists, but she did so in terms that emphasized the practical wisdom of women. In 1851, at the Women's Rights Convention in Akron, Ohio, Truth mocked craniometric expertise with measures any domestic servant would use in the kitchen. Truth said: "As for intellect, all I can say is, if a woman have a pint and a man a quart—why can't she have her pint full? You need not be afraid to give us our rights for fear we will take too much,—for we can't take more than our pint'll hold."[100] According to Truth, even uneducated cooks could see that men should grant women rights precisely because women might have smaller brains and thus could not take more than their share.[101] Further, by self-consciously identifying herself as illiterate— "I can't read, but I can hear"—and then displaying her knowledge of the Bible, she asserted that the infinite wisdom of God was a greater source of truth than the experiments of learned scientists. Noting that Jesus "never spurned woman from him," Truth suggested that it was sinful for white men, so much less perfect in their development than their savior, to deny women rights because they might have smaller brains.[102]

Truth told her audience that the greatest problem with measuring intelligence by volume was that it led sons to reject their mothers. Truth reminded people that Jesus came into the world through "God who created him and woman who bore him" and then asked, "Man, where is your part?"[103] In Truth's account, the whole idea of sons becoming full citizens by outgrowing their mothers and joining their fathers was a violation of God's plan, which made Jesus's mother the source of redemption. After having rejected hierarchical measures of intelligence, Truth returned to a metaphor of higher and lower at the end of her speech, asserting that "women are coming up blessed by God and a few of the men are coming up with them."[104] In this redefined hierarchy, men would not reject their mothers to become self-made but would join in partnership with women.

At the 1853 women's rights convention held at the Broadway Tabernacle in New York City, Truth asserted in even stronger terms that sons had a Christian duty to respect their mothers by granting them rights. She warned young roughs in the audience that they were defying the fifth commandment by insulting older women onstage: "Sons hiss their mothers like snakes, because they ask for their rights. . . . 'Honor your father and your mother.' . . . I can see them a-laughin', and pointin' at their mothers up here on the stage. They hiss when an aged woman comes forth."[105] Generational standing was, for Truth, a divinely ordained source of authority, whereas the pretensions of white manhood citizenship violated God's plan by setting sons above their mothers.

Truth's most dramatic evocation of motherhood as a source of political authority came in 1858 when members of the Democratic Party disrupted a series of speeches Truth delivered in Indiana. Calling out from the audience, they asserted that Truth was not really a woman and demanded that she show the women present her breast in order to prove her sex. Truth responded by dramatically infantilizing her attackers, bearing her breast to the entire audience while describing how slavery wore out the bodies of black women in the support of white manhood citizenship. Reportedly, she told the rowdy men "that her breasts had suckled many a white babe . . . grown to man's estate . . . and she quietly asked them, as she disrobed her bosom, if they, too, wished to suck!"[106]

Frances Harper went even further than Sojourner Truth in using the Bible to question hierarchies of individual development. To do so, Harper drew upon an understanding of Christian adulthood in which childlike faith was the greatest source of wisdom—a form of wisdom that, she suggested, black women often developed in middle and old age. By this metric, white Americans and black men who trumpeted their superiority to those with fewer advantages fell far short of the highest stage of human development.

Harper was born in Baltimore on 24 September 1825 to free parents whose names are not known. Orphaned by the age of three, she was raised by her maternal uncle William Watkins, a leading abolitionist, educator, and member of the AME Church.[107] As a student at her uncle's school, the William Watkins Academy for Negro Youth, Harper received one of the most advanced educations of any American woman of her time, but when she completed her studies in 1839, the only job she could find to support herself was working as a domestic servant. Making the best of her limited opportunities, she accepted a job in the home of a Quaker bookseller, who opened his library to her. It was during this period, when still in her early teens, that Harper published her first poems. In 1845, when she was twenty years old, she marked her literary coming-of-age with the publication of her book of poems *Forest Leaves*.[108] Harper then worked as a teacher before moving to Philadelphia and dedicating herself to the antislavery cause and the Underground Railroad.[109]

On her twenty-ninth birthday in 1854, she started work as an abolitionist lecturer for the State Anti-Slavery Society of Maine, making her one of the first black women employed in this capacity. One month after her first antislavery lecture, she released her second book of poetry, *Poems on Miscellaneous Subjects*, which sold 10,000 copies and established her reputation as the leading African American poet of the nineteenth century. Throughout the 1850s she built her reputation as an antislavery orator and poet, often weaving her poems into her lectures. Though she did not speak at women's rights conventions during this period, concentrating her work on the antislavery movement, she met many abolitionists also active in the women's rights movement. In her lectures, poetry, and essays, she developed a complex analysis of race, sexual difference, and individual development over the course of life.[110]

When Harper first began working as an antislavery lecturer in the 1850s, her view of human development was clearly influenced by women's rights activists and abolitionists. Like them, she argued that the natural course of human development was distorted by slavery, which "dwarfs the intellect, stunts its development, debases the spirit, and degrades the soul." Pointing to signs of intellectual improvement among free blacks as "the first step of a mighty advancement," Harper employed a progressive model of development that imagined individuals and races maturing through a series of hierarchical stages.[111]

Yet Harper qualified this hierarchical model of human development in a contemporaneous essay, "Christianity," in which she argued that moral perfection could be found at all stages of development.[112] The power of Christian truth came precisely from the fact that it was "adapted to [man's] mind in its earliest stages of progression, and its highest state of intellectuality." Harper argued that philosophy, science, and literature might "cultivate the intellect" but were only "idle tales compared to the truth of Christianity."[113] She thus severed the link between intellectual refinement and moral discernment, undercutting hierarchical models of human development even as she championed intellectual progress. Harper clung to an older belief that stressed the importance of the immortal soul in an aging body, and she spent much of her essay refuting the notion that individual life stages had any bearing on the great questions of life. Harper believed that Christianity offered "truths that a child may comprehend"; it was "the staff of decrepit age, and the joy of manhood in its strength."[114]

The immortal soul, in Harper's vision, was not ageless but, more specifically, young. According to Harper, the central trait of an idealized childhood—loving dependence on a benevolent parent—was the ideal state in which the soul approached the heavenly father. For example, in her poem "The Dying Christian," Harper likened a dying woman to

> a child oppressed with slumber,
> . . . her trust in her Redeemer,
> And her head upon His breast.[115]

Harper drew upon a particular understanding of Christian maturity, first articulated by Augustine in the fourth century and centered on the idea that perfect adulthood was a transcendent ideal embodied only by

Christ. This understanding of maturity cited New Testament passages suggesting that adults should be like children, since childlike traits such as wonder and trust were also the essential qualities of faith.[116] This was not the only available biblical interpretation of childhood and adulthood. Sojourner Truth, for example, cited biblical passages that draw a sharp distinction between childhood obedience and adult authority, particularly God's command to "honor thy father and thy mother."[117] Harper, however, preferred the confounding of childhood and adulthood in descriptions of Christian faith as childlike. She was not arguing that rights be extended to actual children but rather that adults who were denigrated as childlike in dominant political discourse should instead be recognized as possessing the moral qualities most needed to make America a Christian nation.[118] She used this model of Christian adulthood to remind Americans, black and white, male and female, that childishness was not the particular nature of dutiful black slaves or dependent women but a goal that the Bible and church fathers enjoined on all Christians.

Harper was one of many educated black women who worked as teachers and led Sunday school classes. She was deeply concerned with developing the full potential of actual children through greater educational opportunities.[119] In her poems and speeches, however, this was not her focus. Rather, she used the idea that childlike faith was the highest stage of Christian maturity to challenge the denial of citizenship to adults who resembled children. Because the New Testament definition of faith as childlike long predated evolutionary theory, Christian maturity provided Harper with a model of individual development distinct from the racialized understandings of Africans as a childlike race.

Where Frederick Douglass asserted black men's capacity to become the equals of white men, even as he sought justice for the whole human family, Harper argued that the efforts of black people to gain respect on the same basis as white men would only make them complicit in a system that licensed the oppression of the weak by the strong. In an 1859 essay titled "Our Greatest Want," published in the *Anglo-African* magazine, she criticized black people who worshiped at the "shrine of success." Rather than staking any claims on the advancement of adult men, Harper pointed to the needs of enslaved women and children. "The respect that is only bought by gold is not worth much," she insisted. "It is no honor to shake hands politically with men who whip women and steal babies."[120] Harper implied that to gain citizenship on the basis of manhood was to be complicit in the oppression of those excluded from the category, especially black women and children, who were excluded by their lack of whiteness and lack of manhood.

The only hope for the vast majority of black people was to build a better society dedicated not to self-advancement at the expense of others but to self-sacrifice for the good of others. The only measure of this highest stage of human development would be "to make every gift, whether gold or talent, fortune or genius, subserve the cause of crushed humanity."[121]

Harper's rejection of earthly success was part of a larger Christian tradition. As she explained in an 1859 letter to the abolitionist William Still, "the nearer we ally ourselves to the wants and woes of humanity in the spirit of Christ, the closer we get to the great heart of God."[122] By this understanding of success, the "humblest and feeblest of us can do something."[123] If manhood and womanhood were based on self-sacrifice, then not only the most developed but also the "feeblest" could achieve great things. She constructed an ideal of self-sacrifice that combined the religious imagery of Moses and Christ with the biographies of abolitionists and slaves who risked death to win freedom. This model of success as self-sacrifice was one that both abolitionists and slaves could achieve, whereas material goals such as fame and wealth often were out of reach.[124]

Harper was careful to distinguish between self-sacrifice to the greater cause of humanity and the false teaching that black people were created to serve whites. In the "Bible Defense of Slavery," she lamented that

> A "reverend" man, whose light should be
> The guide of age and youth,
> Brings to the shrine of Slavery,
> The sacrifice of truth!

Rather than Christianizing slaves, masters created "heathens at [their] doors."[125] True Christianity demanded self-sacrifice for, rather than oppression of, the weak.

Harper also rejected the notion that women's nature demanded their self-sacrifice to men. Her short story "The Two Offers," published in the *Anglo-African* magazine in 1859, downplayed race in order to focus specifically on the question of what kind of sacrifice should define a woman's life. The story centered on two cousins whose racial identity is ambiguous but who clearly represented divergent paths through womanhood. Laura Lagrange was a daughter of privilege whose central goal in life was marriage; Janette Alston lost an early hope of marriage but learned to support herself as an author. At the beginning of the story, Laura was considering two marriage proposals. Janette advised her to decline both, since she obviously loved neither suitor. Laura replied, "If I refuse there is the risk of being an old maid, and that is unthinkable."[126]

The rest of the story was an effort to think through the status of the old maid and to redefine single womanhood as more fulfilling—and more womanly—than a self-sacrificing marriage. In the process, Harper demonstrated that she had fully absorbed the women's rights argument that women need to look beyond youthful romance in order to develop their full capacities and reach their peak of achievement in later life. Harper added the caveat that self-development brought fulfillment only insofar as its purpose was to better serve the weak and oppressed.

When Laura said that becoming an "old maid" was unthinkable, Janette forced her to think through the question of whether there was not "more utter loneliness in a loveless home, than in the lot of an old maid who accepts her earthly mission as a gift from God, and strives to walk the path of life with earnest and unfaltering steps."[127] Laura questioned whether Janette was a true woman, reproaching, "I do not think you know anything of . . . the deep necessity of woman's heart for loving." Harper revealed that Janette in fact had greater depths of feeling than Laura.[128] Whereas Laura carefully calculated which marriage offer would entail more material rewards, Janette "had at one period of her life, known the mystic and solemn strength of an all-absorbing love." Estrangement and then "death" had left her alone.[129]

Janette possessed the youth, beauty, and capacity for love of a romantic heroine, but she took a more unusual path: she quite happily became an old maid. She found an outlet for her passionate nature in literature, where "her genius gathered strength from suffering. . . . Men hailed her as one of earth's strangely gifted children."[130] Whereas most romances ended with either marriage or death, Harper picked up her story ten years later to show how the heroines had changed. The dramatic structure—and didactic message—of the story centered on the contrast between the dreams of youth and the experience of later life. After ten years, Janette had not married but had attained a glorious womanhood. "The bloom of her girlhood had given way to a higher type of spiritual beauty. . . . Her inner life had grown beautiful, and it was this that was constantly developing the outer. Never, in the early flush of womanhood, when an absorbing love had lit up her eyes . . . had she appeared so interesting."[131] Harper thus affirmed the argument made by Mary Wollstonecraft and echoed by antebellum women's rights activists that the beauty of older women had greater depth and interest than that of young women. Harper also implied that Janette was an old maid by choice since she was presumably "interesting" to men.

The "once-beautiful and light-hearted Laura," in contrast, lay on her deathbed. She had sacrificed herself for a husband who was "unworthy of the deep and undying devotion of a pure-hearted woman." As a suitor, he had "bowed at her shrine, a willing worshipper," but "he looked upon marriage not as a divine sacrament for the soul's development and human progression, but as the title-deed that gave him possession of the woman he thought he loved." Laura learned "the bitter agony that is compressed in the mournful words, a drunkard's wife."[132]

Harper used the event of Laura's death to editorialize on women's education for dependence, echoing many themes developed by white women's rights activists in the previous decade. "You may paint [woman] in poetry or fiction, as a frail vine, clinging to her brother man for support, and dying when deprived of it; and all this may sound well enough to please the imagination of school-girls, or love-lorn maidens," Harper wrote, implying that such romantic notions were suited only to the immature. She argued that "the true aim of female education should be, not a development of one or two, but all the faculties of the human soul."[133]

Invoking the metaphor of life's voyage, Harper wrote that "to trust the whole wealth of woman's nature on the frail bark of human love, may often be like trusting a cargo of gold . . . to a bark that has never battled with the storm."[134] Harper clarified that women could not depend on men to chart their destiny. Women as well as men must make the voyage of life with Christianity as their guide. In other words, while the soul's childlike dependence on God was desirable, women's dependence on men was not.

Whereas many writers argued that women could find happiness only by sacrificing their individual ambition to the care of a husband and children, Harper used Laura to show what a waste such a life could become. In contrast, Janette sacrificed herself to the greater good of humanity and in the process found self-fulfillment. She did not seek self-aggrandizement. "She had a higher and better object in all her writings than the mere acquisition of gold, or acquirement of fame."[135]

The dramatic force of Harper's story was to prove that the status of "old maid" was not deficient but could become womanhood in its most perfect form: enabling sacrifice for the higher good rather than for just one family. "True, [Janette] was an old maid, no husband brightened her life with his love, or," Harper sardonically added, "saddened it with his neglect." The greater loss was that "no children nestling lovingly in her arms called her mother." Yet she found womanly happiness, "not vainly striving to keep up her appearance of girlishness, when departed was written on her youth. Not vainly pining at her loneliness and isolation: the world was full of warm, loving hearts, and her own beat in unison with them." Happy in middle age, she continued to find satisfaction; "as old age descended peacefully and gently upon her, she had learned one of life's most precious lessons, that true happiness consists not so much in the fruition of our wishes as in the regulation of our desires and the full development and right culture of our whole natures."[136]

For Harper, Janette's self-sacrificing path through adulthood was gender-neutral. Harper likened Janette to a soldier with "a high and holy mission on the battle-field of existence," a metaphor she would repeatedly apply to women after the Civil War as if to underline that both women and men could achieve the status of citizen-soldiers when the battle was over morality.

The Civil War, however, irrevocably altered understandings of adult citizenship by offering the chance for black males to prove that they were, in Frederick Douglass's words, "men among men." Where antebellum women's rights activists crossed racial lines to argue for equal rights for all citizens and to promote the individual development of all, the Civil War and Reconstruction opened a path to citizenship through governmental institutions that used sex and age to define rights and duties. The politics of aging in America would never be the same.

CHAPTER FIVE

COMPETING MEASURES OF
MATURE CITIZENSHIP

During Reconstruction, Radical Republicans forever altered the political significance of age twenty-one by pushing for the enfranchisement of all men without regard to race. The Fourteenth Amendment to the Constitution (passed by Congress in June 1866 and ratified in July 1868) placed the power of the federal government behind the idea that males normally made a transition to full citizenship at age twenty-one, while females did not. The final wording of section 2, which introduced the word "male" and age twenty-one into the Constitution for the first time, reduced congressional representation for any state that denied the right to vote to "the male inhabitants of such State, being twenty-one years of age . . . in the proportion which the number of such male citizens shall bear to the whole number of male citizens twenty-one years of age in such State."[1] The logic of the amendment thus deliberately and decisively rendered adult males the only population that counted for purposes of political representation and rewrote the nation's fundamental law so as to clarify that states had no obligation to extend political rights to women or minors.

Women's rights activists responded in different ways to this change. Most regarded the elimination of racial qualifications for the vote as an essential step toward winning equal rights for all adults, but a vocal minority refused to accept any reform that sustained the classification of women with children.[2] Three of the activists who had most thoroughly explored the significance of adulthood in the antebellum period—Frederick

Douglass, Elizabeth Cady Stanton, and Frances Harper—took the lead in articulating divergent views on the political significance of maturity during Reconstruction. Douglass urged his allies in the women's rights movement to recognize that while winning equal rights for all adults was the ultimate goal, black men urgently needed the vote to prove their equality with other men and to protect their dependent wives and children.[3] Stanton, drawing on a mix of crude racism and cutting-edge sociology, particularly the writings of August Comte, argued that if anyone needed the vote it was the most "intelligent" and "virtuous" women in the nation, and if any adults should be classed with children it was "ignorant" and "degraded" men. Stanton invoked a hierarchical "scale of being" with multiple metrics—educational attainment, moral refinement, social status, the progress of civilization, racial difference, and generational standing.[4] She relied variously on these different measures of "higher" and "lower" orders depending on context but always argued that by any criteria that really mattered, manhood suffrage amounted to "exalting the son above the mother."[5]

Harper, meanwhile, insisted that the life of Christ provided the only true model of individual development.[6] The lesson to be learned from the Bible, she argued, was that the highest stage of human maturity was reached when an individual put aside ambition for wealth or power and instead worked with Christian humility for the good of "all God's children." By this measure, Harper contended, white women's rights activists boasting of their own superior development while trampling on the rights of others were more like children than mature adults. Freedmen came closer to the mark when they offered to protect freedwomen and children, but they too retained an immature tendency to put personal ambition above service to others. Freedwomen in the South, precisely because they could boast of neither manhood nor superior education, came closest to realizing the ideal of Christian maturity, Harper maintained. The federal government, she argued, denied freedwomen a political voice at its own peril, for they were most likely to have developed the type of wisdom necessary to securing the nation's future. Harper insisted that women's rights activists not stand in the way of enfranchising adult black men but work steadily for winning black women rights as well. She found few allies as other reformers continued to debate the relative maturity of black men and privileged white women.[7]

Whereas antebellum women's rights activists could unite around the shared goal of enfranchising all adults at age twenty-one regardless of race or sex, debate over the Reconstruction amendments to the Constitution divided those willing to support the extension of manhood citizenship to African Americans from those who refused to accept the further classification of women with children. Debate turned on a fundamental disagreement as to what should qualify an individual as an adult citizen: manhood as a stage of life, superior education, or a commitment to social justice. In an effort to promote their own maturity, activists intensified their tendency to infantilize others. The seeds of this debate were sown during the first months of the Civil War as black men presented themselves for military duty.

THE RELATIVE MATURITY OF BLACK
SOLDIERS, WHITE MOTHERS, AND FREEDWOMEN

On 12 April 1861 the Confederates fired on Fort Sumter. Within days Douglass called for raising black troops both to end slavery and to prove black men "were not wanting in manly spirit."[8] For the first two years of the war, however, Douglass watched with growing frustration as the Lincoln administration tried to placate border states and northern conservatives by refusing black volunteers.[9] In promoting black enlistment, Douglass abandoned his earlier general references to the "manhood of the race" and instead incarnated black masculinity in the "iron arm of the black man."[10] This phrase evoked neither an old man nor a boy but a man at the height of his physical strength. Douglass further suggested that courage and physical strength were measures of masculinity by which black men, toughened under slavery, surpassed white men. As he warned fellow Unionists, "We are striking the guilty rebels with our soft, white hand, when we should be striking with the iron hand of the black man, which we keep chained behind us."[11]

In this pugilistic construction of national identity, there was little room for women and children. Interestingly, in a historical lecture delivered after the war, Douglass mentioned that women had served as soldiers in the past and that fighting was "among woman's latent powers."[12] Yet during the war he stressed the dependence of women and children, who relied on men for protection.[13] Metaphorically, the nation was a house on fire, and "when helpless women and children are to be rescued from devouring flames a true man can neither have ear nor heart for anything but the thrilling and heart rending cry for help."[14] Like David Walker in his *Appeal*, Douglass urged men to prove their love of liberty by protecting their dependents, the difference being that by 1863, Republicans in power were listening.[15]

In January 1863 Lincoln declared slaves in the rebel territories "forever free," and the Union army began recruiting black men as soldiers. Douglass signed up as a recruiting agent for the Fifty-Fourth Massachusetts Volunteers, the most prominent black regiment. Federal draft legislation called for able-bodied men between the ages of twenty and forty-five, thus including men who had not yet reached the age of contract along with those who were solidly middle-aged.[16] Recruiting agents like Douglass, however, targeted volunteers in their teens and twenties—"young men and strong men," recruits in "the full fresh bloom of youth and manly vigor."[17] Following common usage, Douglass sometimes referred to these volunteers as "boys." Yet he was clear that this diminutive was not meant to invoke childishness or servility; they were, in his words, "full-grown black men."[18]

Rather than offering a transition to equal manhood, however, the Union army enacted policies that ensured that blacks would remain subordinate within a white-dominated hierarchy. Black soldiers received three-fifths the pay of whites, and the highest-ranking blacks received less than the lowest-ranking whites. Further, Secretary of War Edwin Stanton refused to commission blacks as field officers, accepting them only as surgeons and chaplains who would not command whites. Union officials argued that black men lacked the capacity for leadership and that white soldiers opposed placing blacks higher than themselves in the chain of command. Early in 1865 the War Department finally commissioned the first black officers; only a handful served.[19] In August 1863 Douglass resigned his position as a recruiting agent in protest over the army's discriminatory policies.[20] He insisted that the government give black soldiers "a fair chance of winning distinction and glory in common with other soldiers."[21]

Throughout the war Douglass continued to support equal rights for women, but his theoretical commitment to universal rights was increasingly overshadowed as he conflated black manhood, independent citizenship, and increased opportunities into a single goal that could be reached through military service—a path open only to males. Indeed, when Douglass brought up black women's rights during the war, it was in relation to their rights as dependents on the military pensions of their husbands. He protested the fact that states routinely granted pensions to the wives and children of white recruits while refusing support to the families of black soldiers. Douglass sought this same status—what could be called the right to dependency—for black women. "Your mothers, your wives and your sisters ought to be cared for," Douglass told potential black recruits.[22] Douglass's engagement with the institutional structures of the

Union army thus led him to frame his claims for equality in terms of gender and age difference, seeking equal independence for adult black men and equal dependence for black women and children.

As the war drew to a close and politicians turned their attention to freedmen and freedwomen's civil and political rights, Douglass still supported equal citizenship for all adults but argued that the nation's first priority was to extend manhood suffrage to black men. In January 1865 he told the Massachusetts Anti-Slavery Society that "no class of men can, without insulting their own nature, be content with any deprivation of their rights." He supported woman suffrage but claimed "that question rests upon another basis." Since no women voted, they could remain perpetually dependent without insult.[23] For adult males, the vote was required to prove that they were men. Further, hierarchical measures of intellectual and moral development had nothing to do with manhood suffrage. The typical freedman was ignorant, Douglass conceded, but "he knows as much when he is sober as an Irishman knows when drunk."[24] To prove black manhood, Douglass drew upon familiar stereotypes of ignorant and immoral voters—the illiterate, the hooligan "engaged in a street fight," "Pat, fresh from the Emerald Isle"—to insist that white men regularly voted without meeting any test of intellectual or moral capacity and that freedmen could easily meet this standard even if they were illiterate and unaccustomed to freedom.[25] In short, Douglass insisted that it was time for black men to claim the same political rights as white men at twenty-one.

As long as slavery persisted, Stanton agreed with Douglass that the most pressing issue for human rights was "recognition of the manhood of the slave."[26] In 1861 women's rights activists stopped holding conventions. As Stanton explained, it was "impossible . . . to think or speak on anything but the War."[27] Two years later she joined with other women's rights activists to found the Women's Loyal National League, dedicated to supporting the union and petitioning for the abolition of slavery.[28] The league organized a massive petition campaign for a constitutional amendment banning slavery. As Stanton, Susan B. Anthony, and Matilda Joslyn Gage later reported in the *History of Woman Suffrage*, "women of all ages" joined the league "from the matron of threescore years and ten to the fair girl whose interest in the war had brought her premature sadness and high resolve."[29] In gathering petitions, however, the league limited eligible signers to women "above the age of 18 years," corresponding to the age of military service for young men.[30] While Douglass championed the fitness of young black soldiers for full citizenship, Stanton and Anthony created a means by which women too could demonstrate their commitment to the Union.[31] In presenting the first 100,000 signatures to the Senate in February 1864, Charles Sumner described the petitioners as "a mighty army."[32]

Meanwhile, Dorothea Dix, the sixty-year-old reformer who served as superintendent of nursing for the War Department, imposed novel age requirements on her female recruits. In an effort to placate critics who alleged that opening military hospitals to female nurses would lead to sexual improprieties, Dix sought to capitalize on the assumption that young men were not sexually attracted to middle-aged women. In an army circular issued in July 1862, Dix announced that "no candidate for service in the Women's Department for nursing . . . will be received below the age of thirty-five-years, (35) nor above fifty." She further specified that "matronly persons of experience, good conduct, or superior education and serious disposition, will always have preference."[33] Dix, who developed a reputation for playing favorites, bent the rules for women who, though under her age requirements, appeared sufficiently "matronly."[34] For example, Sophronia Bucklin, who later wrote about her "resolve not to be kept from the great work because no wrinkles seamed my face, and no vestige of gray hair nestled among my locks," was able to find a local recruiter who, perhaps impressed with her plain and sober demeanor, did not ask her age. Dix later declared Bucklin "altogether too young" but kept her on nonetheless because she was a serious and efficient worker.[35] As long as a woman appeared sufficiently "matronly," Dix would overlook age, much as army recruiters accepted younger boys who were as tall and strong as older men.

Women rejected by Dix on the basis of their youth found that they could volunteer directly with local regiments. Indeed, as the war progressed, women of all ages filled the dire need for nursing care.[36] Whatever their age, many of the women who worked in army hospitals emphasized the maternal nature of their responsibilities for the "boys" under their care. A matronly air not only defused sexual tensions but also provided nurses with some claim to authority, as mothers if not as equal citizens. Those who employed this strategy included established women's rights activists such as Jane Swisshelm and Mary Livermore. Ultimately, however, service in military hospitals may have done more to reveal the limits of mature women's authority than to expand its bounds, as male doctors and government officials continually reminded older women of their subordination to men.[37] This was certainly the lesson Stanton, Anthony, and Gage took from the war, noting in the *History of Woman Suffrage* that though Dix was "appointed" to her office by the U.S. government, she "found herself as a member of a disenfranchised class, in a position of authority without the power of enforcing obedience."[38]

When abolitionists who favored equal suffrage for all adults began to argue that black men deserved rights as men, Stanton objected. Her alarm turned to outrage in December 1865 as Republicans in Congress began to debate measures that would eventually become the Fourteenth Amendment. Refusing to exert direct federal control over suffrage qualifications, Republicans proposed penalizing with reduced representation in Congress any state that disenfranchised black men. Congressmen considered wording that would encompass all adults but decided not to sanction states that denied votes to adult women. This decision infuriated Stanton and others who felt that women's contribution to the union cause had proven their capacity for full citizenship.[39]

Stanton did all she could to convince Republican leaders that adulthood rather than manhood should determine political rights. To press her argument, she made a fateful choice: she decided to attack the political capacity of adult men by invoking scientific and popular theories of racial difference. In December 1865 Stanton and her close ally Anthony urged readers of the *National Anti-Slavery Standard* to send a petition for woman suffrage to their congressmen that read: "We would call your attention to the fact that we represent . . . intelligent, virtuous, native-born American citizens."[40] Stanton and Anthony thus linked intellectual and moral maturity to the widespread idea that white native-born Americans had developed a greater capacity for self-government than had other types of people. This was a potent claim at a time when many Republicans had nativist tendencies, northern immigrants tended to vote Democratic, ethnological charts ranking human differences circulated widely, and the popular press trafficked in ethnic and racial stereotypes.[41]

The letter she wrote to accompany her petition was a frank announcement that she and her allies would no longer cooperate with abolitionists. "The representative women of the nation have done their uttermost for the last thirty years to secure freedom for the negro," Stanton claimed, "and so long as he was lowest on the scale of being we were willing to press *his* claims." But, she warned, they would not support Republican efforts to elevate "the black man . . . above the educated women of the country." They would not "stand aside and see 'Sambo' walk into the kingdom [of equal rights] first."[42] As to the argument that black men needed the vote to protect their wives and children, Stanton claimed to speak for "two millions of Southern black women" whose emancipation would become "another form of slavery" if their husbands and fathers claimed the "absolute power the statute laws of most of the States give man."[43] Stanton thus countered Douglass's argument that black men required the vote to protect their dependents with the assertion that adult women needed political equality to protect themselves.

Stanton's denigration of black men profoundly altered the racial valence of arguments for female maturity, alienating black people, abolitionists, and Republicans even as she continued to campaign for universal rights. Her central argument, however, was not focused on race per se but rather on maturity. She was arguably more troubled by what she saw as the childish selfishness of leading Republicans than by the "ignorance" of black men. As Stanton wrote her cousin, the abolitionist Gerrit Smith, the nation's founders understood that the word "male" had no place in the Constitution, but "the recreant sons of the Fathers" had decided to "mar that glorious bequest." Before it was too late, Republicans needed to "recant this foul insult to the mothers of the republic."[44]

By early 1866, Stanton had articulated an ideological answer to universal manhood suffrage. If, as Douglass argued, no class of men could remain politically dependent without "insulting" their nature, then, Stanton countered, "educated, virtuous, native-born" women could not submit to the authority of "degraded" men without betraying their racial heritage, and "mothers" could not submit to the authority of wayward "sons." Mature development, not manhood, rendered perpetual dependence an intolerable state.

In May, when women's rights activists gathered for the first national convention since the outbreak of the war, delegates still retained a shared commitment to winning equal rights for all adults, but deep fissures of resentment separated those who supported the Fourteenth Amendment from those opposed to it. Abolitionists and Republicans would not tolerate suggestions that black men lacked the mature capacity required of adult citizens, while those committed to proving women's maturity would not sanction the further classification of women with children. In the midst of this acrimonious debate, Frances Harper addressed the first national women's rights convention held since the Civil War in order to argue that neither manhood nor racialized measures of individual development offered a truly democratic qualification for citizenship. Harper indicted both men and privileged women for pursuing their own self-interest and insisted that the most moral citizens were those whose suffering had attuned them to the needs of the weak. According to Harper, black women, despite their lack of formal education and in the face of racial theories denigrating their moral capacity, had in fact attained the highest stage of maturity in that they recognized the true meaning of social justice and democracy better than their more privileged peers. If anyone was qualified to protect those who could not protect themselves, it was the freedwomen in the South.[45]

The 1866 convention was Harper's first. She explained that she had been drawn to the movement because of her personal struggle to establish adult independence under laws that construed wives as perpetual dependents. Half a year before the war, on 22 November 1860, she married Fenton Harper, a widower with three children. She contributed her earnings from royalties and lecture fees to the purchase of their farm near Columbus, Ohio. Throughout her marriage, she continued to agitate against slavery, cared for her stepchildren and daughter Mary, and earned money by making "butter for the Columbus market." On 5 May 1864 Fenton died suddenly. Her husband's creditors seized all the household possessions including her "means of support . . . the very milk-crocks and wash tubs from my hands." Harper was left to contemplate the inequity that, "had I died instead of my husband, how different would have been the result!"[46]

By focusing on her husband's death, Harper highlighted an iconic moment of divergence in the course of manhood and womanhood. Already a major issue for the antebellum women's rights movement, the inequality of inheritance law became only more significant in the wake of wartime deaths. Harper's personal story demonstrated that black women as well as white suffered from these laws. The central conclusion of her speech was that "we are all bound up together in one great bundle of humanity."[47]

Some women's rights activists, however, were focused on breaking this bundle apart into more and less developed strata. Stanton delivered a keynote speech in which she argued that educated women had a duty to demand the vote so that, as moral leaders, they could advance the progress of civilization and, as mothers, "guard the youth of the nation."[48] In response, Harper poked fun at the notion that white women's moral purity would make politics a force for good: "I do not believe that giving the woman the ballot is immediately going to cure all the ills of life. I do not believe that white women are dewdrops just exhaled from the skies."[49] She boldly told women's rights activists that they could not deny rights to those less strong than themselves and claim to be moral at the same time: "Society cannot trample on the weakest and feeblest of its members without receiving the curse in its own soul."[50]

After directly castigating white women for ignoring the struggles faced by black women, Harper concluded by arguing that white women did not deserve the vote because they were educated and moral but rather needed the vote in order to *become* educated and moral: "Talk of giving women the ballot-box? Go on. It is a normal school, and the white women of this country need it. While there exists this brutal element which tramples down the feeble and treads down the weak, I tell you that if there is any class of people who need to be lifted out of their airy nothingness and selfishness, it is the white women of America."[51] Harper thus suggested that Stanton's favored class of "intelligent, virtuous, native-born" women were actually childlike beings lost in daydreams and following selfish impulses.[52]

Harper grounded her appeal for social justice in her experiences traveling in the South during Reconstruction as a lecturer for the AME Church. She attracted both white and black audiences but focused her efforts on black schools and Sunday schools.[53] She often held meetings exclusively for freedwomen in order to talk "about their daughters, and about things connected with the welfare of the race."[54] By collaborating with white women's rights activists, she sought to include black women squarely within arguments for woman suffrage.

CHRONOLOGICAL AGE AND THE IDEA
OF ARBITRARY BUT NECESSARY QUALIFICATIONS

At the 1866 women's rights convention, Harper supported Anthony's proposal to form a new organization dedicated to winning equal rights for all adults.[55] The American Equal Rights Association (AERA), as Anthony explained, should begin with a campaign in New York to "strike out from our Constitution the two adjectives, *'white male,'* giving to every citizen, over twenty-one, the right to vote."[56]

On the evening of 27 June 1867 a large crowd gathered in the New York state assembly chamber to hear Stanton and Anthony present their case for universal suffrage to members of the New York state constitutional convention.[57] The meeting was presided over by Horace Greeley, editor of the *New York Tribune*, liberal Republican, and chair of the convention's suffrage committee. Many women's rights activists saw Greeley as an ally because his paper was the only mainstream daily that provided them with favorable coverage. That night in Albany, Stanton and Anthony offered several compelling arguments for woman suffrage and black manhood suffrage, most importantly that voting was an "inalienable right." Greeley challenged this natural rights argument by shifting attention from black men and women to the case of minors and immigrants denied the vote for fixed periods of time. "When does this inalienable right commence for young men and foreigners?" Greeley demanded. "Have we the right to say when it commences?" Anthony responded that the state certainly had a right to set age and residency requirements but that those should apply equally to all human beings. "If you have the right to vote at 21 years, then I have," Anthony contended. "All we ask is that you should let down the bars, and let us women and negroes in, and then we will sit down and talk the matter over."[58]

When faced with arguments that voting was a natural right, Greeley brought up the state's right to set age qualifications for suffrage because he knew that he could count on Anthony to concede that even if age twenty-one was an arbitrary distinction between citizens, some age qualification was necessary or else New York state would have to welcome young children at the polls, a contingency that even the most radical champions of "universal" suffrage did not support. Once Anthony allowed that the state had "the right to say" that a young man must be twenty-one or older before he could vote, she had in effect disarmed all of her own arguments for universal suffrage, for she had acknowledged that voting was not a natural right but a privilege that states could regulate at will. Further, she had conceded that paying taxes, serving in the military, and displaying clear political competence did not entitle a citizen to vote, since young men indisputably did all these things before they turned twenty-one. As American politicians had been doing since the Revolution, Greeley invoked age twenty-one as an arbitrary but necessary distinction between boys and men in order to justify the state's right to impose other qualifications on electors, even if these might also be arbitrary.

As had happened before the war, Anthony's proposal that the state should apply age qualifications equally to all citizens fell flat as Greeley successfully used the disenfranchisement of young men to prove that American citizens did not have an inalienable right to vote. Over the next months, much to Greeley's frustration, Democrats beat him at his own game by successfully arguing that if the state could prevent women and minors from voting, then there was no reason to enfranchise adult black men either.[59] The requirement that voters be twenty-one years of age was central to these debates over citizenship, not because politicians or reformers thought that teenagers should vote but precisely because of the widespread agreement that they should not. Given that every state barred soldiers and taxpayers from voting if they were under twenty-one, both Republicans and Democrats could cite the age qualification for suffrage as proof that states had no constitutional or moral obligation to, in Anthony's words, let "women and negroes in."

Whereas delegates to New York's antebellum conventions treated age twenty-one as a universally agreed-upon qualification for electors, two delegates to the 1867 convention proposed enfranchising young men between eighteen and twenty-one.[60] Republican Marcus Bickford, a staunchly pro-Union newspaper editor who raised large numbers of volunteers during the war, argued that soldiers were full-grown men and deserved to be treated as such. Democratic superior court judge Anthony L. Robertson, meanwhile, submitted his resolution as an alternative to black manhood suffrage, contending that "white 'boys' of eighteen" were more competent than black men over twenty-one. No delegate even bothered to argue against these resolutions, which were easily defeated by a margin of three to one.[61] Delegates paid more attention to woman suffrage because Anthony, Stanton, and other members of the AERA had built a powerful lobby, but delegates eventually defeated the woman suffrage resolution by an even larger margin of more than five to one.[62]

The only reform with a solid chance of passing was black manhood suffrage. Republicans controlled the convention and argued that black men deserved the right to vote because of their military service. Democrats, however, successfully countered this argument by pointing out, in the words of Judge Homer Nelson, that on "the rolls of that army which fought so bravely . . . [were] long lines of honorable names of young men between the ages of eighteen and twenty-one" who could not vote.[63] Claiming that "we all know young men between the ages of eighteen and twenty-one, numbers of them, who would cast as intelligent a vote as perhaps any of us could cast, and yet they are excluded," Nelson argued that the age qualification, like the other "various exclusions," was "an arbitrary line," but "it must go somewhere."[64] Even Republicans who supported universal suffrage used the disenfranchisement of minors to prove that voting was not a natural right, as when Stephen Hand thundered: "Who gives you the right to say that the age of twenty-one years is the precise period of a man's life when he shall attain the privilege of the elective franchise? The fact shows that the right belongs to society . . . coming together here in this Constitutional Convention."[65] The convention decided, after months of debate, to do nothing to reform suffrage. The Fifteenth Amendment, ratified in New York in 1869 and passed in 1870, brought interracial democracy to New York state.[66]

Thwarted by Republicans, Stanton and Anthony began an appeal to Democrats. When Greeley's Republican-controlled committee insisted that woman suffrage was too "revolutionary" a proposition, Stanton and Anthony convinced the Democrat George William Curtis to present a petition headed with the signature "Mrs. Horace Greeley."[67] The convention erupted in laughter, the New York papers had a field day, Greeley never forgave Stanton or Anthony, and Republican leaders lined up behind the committee's argument that woman suffrage was too "revolutionary" to consider.[68]

Stanton and Anthony, who would soon start a newspaper called the *Revolution*, went from New York to Kansas, where the state legislature had submitted three referenda to the white male electorate, one to strike the word "white" from suffrage requirements, one to strike the word "male," and one to disenfranchise voters suspected of disloyalty to the Union during the Civil War.[69] Henry Blackwell and Lucy Stone were already in Kansas, campaigning for universal suffrage as representatives of the AERA.[70] Stanton and Anthony arrived in September to find Republicans quoting from Greeley's report, accusing Stone and Blackwell of being free lovers, and asking men if "they wanted every old maid to vote."[71] Either classed with minors or written off as old maids, Stanton and Anthony found little support for the idea that they should claim adult citizenship on the same terms as men.[72]

Taking a step that would have widespread repercussions, Anthony joined forces with presumed Democrat George Francis Train, an eccentric and ambitious man who made a fortune in railroads, gained a political following for being pro-Union but against the Emancipation Proclamation, and cultivated a theatrical image as a public speaker. Train was typical of Democratic leaders, popularly known as Copperheads, who adapted Darwinian theories of evolution to argue that black men were unfit for independent citizenship. Stanton and Anthony saw Train as a source of money and a link to Democratic voters, especially Irish immigrants, but other leaders of the AERA were shocked and outraged by his racism and open attacks on the Republican Party.[73] By welcoming Train's support, Stanton and Anthony made fully clear that they would accept racist measures of black people's potential and support the Democratic Party if doing so would aid the cause of white women's rights.[74]

In November, Kansas voters retained the word "white" in their voting qualifications by a margin of three to one and the word "male" by an even greater margin.[75] Stanton and Anthony arrived back in New York to intense criticism for associating with—in William Lloyd Garrison's words—"that crack-brained harlequin and semi-lunatic, George Francis Train!"[76] The organizational structure of the AERA continued to provide a united front, but key leaders could no longer find common ground. Stone, Blackwell, and Douglass, among others, would not forgive Stanton and

Anthony for allying with Democrats and racists.[77] Stanton and Anthony, meanwhile, cast themselves loose from their Republican and abolitionist allies, using Train's support to launch the *Revolution* and cultivate a base of support among educated middle-class readers.[78]

COMTEAN POSITIVISM, RACISM, AND WOMEN'S RIGHT TO GROW OLD

A banner announcement in the first issue of the *Revolution*, published 8 January 1868, declared that the paper would advocate "Educated Suffrage, Irrespective of Sex or Color . . . Deeper Thought; Broader Ideas; Science not Superstition." Stanton led with an article on the Kansas campaign, blaming abolitionists, black men, and Republicans for the defeat of woman suffrage and thereby placing those groups outside the purview of deep thought and science. In her first editorial she explained that the *Revolution* was "a fitting name for a paper that will advocate so radical a reform as [the enfranchisement of women] involves in our political, religious, and social world." She thus invoked Republicans' opposition to woman suffrage as the very reason people devoted to "new thought" and "progress," all those "who are tired of the old grooves," should support it. "What thinking mind," she wondered, "does not feel that we need something new and revolutionary in every department of life." The nation needed "wise rulers" who might "leave the dead letters of the past and in calm, regular steps of progress secure the health and happiness of the people." A short unsigned item then added the observation that Charles Sumner, leader of the Radical Republicans, seemed "to think that all we need to make us a nation, is a black boy, in the Federal family—forgetting that a mother is of some importance."[79]

The first issue of the *Revolution* set the pattern that would follow: advocacy of educated suffrage, promotion of "science" as the key to progress, biting critiques of Republicans, and virulently racist denigrations of black men all thrown together to prove that suffrage should be based on maturity rather than on manhood. Over the next two years, contributors to the *Revolution* would relentlessly defend white women's superior development and, by trafficking in crude racism, sacrifice the ability to collaborate across the color line in a shared struggle for equal adulthood.

In editing the *Revolution*, Stanton was joined by Parker Pillsbury, former editor of the *National Anti-Slavery Standard*. Anthony was the "Proprietor and Manager." Train provided the initial funds, and the paper dutifully published his arguments for an inflationary currency and Irish freedom.[80]

While former allies attacked Stanton, Anthony, and Pillsbury for allying with Train and opposing Republicans, the editors found support among a circle of New York intellectuals who shared their interest in sociology.[81] Stanton's sociology was typical of many old-stock intellectual elites who used scientific expertise to justify their own continued authority in the face of challenges by popular political parties, labor unions, and new money elites. What Stanton took from social science, however, was more specific. She turned August Comte's law of tripartite development into an argument that leading priests and politicians—"Saxon fathers . . . the best orders of manhood"—were lagging behind in the scale of development because they clung to outmoded ideas about women. In the pages of the *Revolution*, Stanton relegated most white male leaders to the lower orders of manhood, above blacks, Irish, and Chinese to be sure, but not above scientifically minded women like herself.[82]

Early in 1868 Stanton's cousin Gerrit Smith had urged her to read Auguste Comte, the French founder of positivism who coined the word "sociology," and Stanton had enthusiastically responded to Smith's challenge.[83] In April, Stanton and Pillsbury printed new translations of Comte's *Système de politique positive* (1851–54), enabling English-speaking readers to form their own opinion regarding his views on women.[84] Their selections focused on Comte's argument that human morality is divided into three parts, represented by three segments of society: intellect, represented by male philosophers; activity, represented by the male proletariat; and affection, represented by women. Comte argued that woman's unique office is to inspire social unity through affection and love within the family; however, he opposed woman's suffrage and any effort to gain higher pay for women's work.[85]

After printing Comte verbatim, Stanton then offered her readers a detailed model for how to transform positivism into an argument for women's rights. She reported on a visit to Smith's home in Peterboro, New York, where she astounded gathered Comteans with a positivist argument for women's political empowerment. "It was most gratifying to see the despairing looks of Comte's disciples," she wrote, "when . . . after days of communion with the French philosopher, we declared he was on our side of this question." Stanton proved to Smith's friends that "Comte's principles, logically carried out, make woman the governing power in the world."[86]

Stanton borrowed a strategy from Mary Wollstonecraft's critique of Rousseau by arguing that Comte was right in his general understanding of human nature and society but wrong about women. Indeed, immediately following Stanton's report of her debate about Comte, she reprinted

Wollstonecraft's entire critique of Rousseau from *A Vindication of the Rights of Woman*.[87] Stanton thus associated herself with Wollstonecraft's earlier reinterpretation of a leading French philosopher.[88]

While rejecting Comte's views on female dependence, Stanton wholeheartedly embraced his "fundamental law" of tripartite development. In his *Cours de philosophie positive* (1830–42), Comte distinguished three stages through which the human mind passed in both its historical and individual development: the theological, the metaphysical, and the positive.[89] Because Comte positioned ministers and politicians as representing the theological and metaphysical stages, respectively, his developmental hierarchy perfectly suited Stanton's desire "to take this long-debated problem of woman's sphere entirely beyond the control of popes, poets and politicians, of Bibles, belles-lettres and Blackstone, into the realms of pure science." Unlike Comte, who argued that only mature men could become positivists, she looked to women who had "grown too wise" to believe that God or political necessity dictated their subordination.[90]

In essence, Stanton rewrote Comte's stages of social progress to argue that man governed the theological and metaphysical stages when immature passions reigned.[91] Stanton identified immaturity with the "masculine element" and argued that it was time for woman—as the figurative mother of the race—to lovingly but firmly discipline men's childish impulses.[92]

The generational metaphor was no accident, for Stanton's rereading of Comte challenged the idea that men matured by leaving behind their dependence on mothers. Stanton, embracing the idea of inherent differences between the sexes, argued that men's moral development was naturally stunted because men were more individualistic and selfish than women. Men's selfishness, Stanton argued, drove the progress of civilization in more violent times but rendered men incapable of resolving the class and racial tensions that threatened America in the nineteenth century. Social progress required men to acknowledge their dependence upon "the mothers of the race" for moral guidance. Where law and social custom regarded women as perpetual minors, Stanton's rereading of Comte positioned men as perpetual children in need of maternal authority. "We do not blame man for his injustice to woman more than our baby for upsetting the inkstand on a valuable manuscript," Stanton condescended; "they are alike ignorant of what they have done."[93]

Stanton and Pillsbury printed excerpts from other authors who were reading Comte in the same way.[94] They tirelessly promoted *Sexology as the Philosophy of Life*, by Elizabeth Osgood Goodrich Willard, an American writer and contributor to the *Revolution*.[95] Like Comte, Willard argued that sexual difference was a fundamental natural law, the feminine element representing aggregation, and the masculine, segregation. Unlike Comte, Willard concluded that society would be out of balance until the feminine element participated in government.[96] The *Revolution* also printed the historical research of spiritualist Matilda Joslyn Gage, who argued that the development of civilization in past ages was governed by men, ruling through physical force, while future progress would be achieved by women, representing the "moral element" of society.[97]

Throughout the late 1860s Stanton advocated the view that "Comte, the distinguished French writer, in his Positive Philosophy, shows clearly that the first step towards social reorganization involves the education and elevation of woman." She also cited John Stuart Mill, Herbert Spencer, and Jules Favre, among others, as leading thinkers who recognized the importance of women's moral leadership.[98] Stanton particularly saw Mill and his collaborator Harriet Taylor as supporting women's right to develop their full capacities.[99] But her rereading of Comte was the backbone of her argument that women needed the vote more than black men did.

The use of Comte to promote white supremacy was not new. Southern slave owners were the first Americans to enthusiastically embrace Comtean ideas of social order and hierarchy. Emphasizing that black people were naturally suited to dependence and white men to leadership, southern Comteans praised the slave system as a model of social harmony.[100] While Stanton may not have read such arguments directly, she absorbed their import along with the scientific and popular racism that permeated American culture.[101] Stanton certainly used positivism to argue that white women were more qualified for adult citizenship than black men. Her main emphasis, however, was on using Comte to argue that educated women should develop and assert their mature wisdom. As she wrote in a response to David Croly, the editor of the *New York World* and a leading American disciple of Comte, "The present position of woman, as the inferior and dependent of man, is an entire perversion of the natural order. Woman, as the mother of the race, is the rightful governing power."[102]

In an effort to foster female development, Stanton also filled the *Revolution* with her own editorials, articles from regular contributors, and letters from readers that linked proper female aging to the achievement of sexual equality. The editors printed numerous pieces on young girls that analyzed how their development was perverted to suit male desires and recommended healthy diet, exercise, and expanded opportunities as the remedy.[103] Stanton critiqued the early age of marriage and railed against older men who seduced and abandoned girls.[104] Like Mary Wollstonecraft, contributors to the *Revolution* critiqued the way in which male prejudice devalued female aging.[105] They assured their readers that older women would gain more respect as they won greater rights and opportunities. Discussing the dignified appearance of the fifty-two-year-old actress Charlotte Cushman, Stanton noted that "her gray hair was tastefully arranged without dye or head dress." According to Stanton this signified more than personal style: "It is a great step towards freedom when woman has the right to grow old and feels herself no longer bound to seem young when she is not."[106]

The *Revolution* printed several articles on what journalist Sara Willis, known by the pen name Fanny Fern, memorably called "The Modern Old Maid." Willis, who was in her midfifties and had lost her first husband to death and taken the radical step of divorcing her second, argued that as a result of expanding opportunities for women in philanthropy, the arts, and the professions, the contemporary woman "doesn't care whether she is married or not."[107] While Fern celebrated new possibilities for aging spinsters, other contributors argued that public opinion had not changed and continued to regard "old maids" as eccentric and selfish, even though many were involved in philanthropy and politics.[108]

For her part, Stanton argued that middle age was a stage of life when women—married or single—were well fitted to devote themselves to politics. While she had made this argument in the antebellum period, during Reconstruction she placed it in a Comtean frame. Insisting that the "primal truth of sex in mind, now recognized by the leading thinkers on both continents," was an argument for woman's enfranchisement, she pointed out that maternity was no barrier to women's political leadership.[109] Indeed, Stanton predicted that as knowledge of science grew, woman's reproductive cycle would become highly scheduled: "When we apply the same laws of science to the propagation of the human family as to the lower animals, women will not marry before twenty five, nor have children but at intervals of four or five years. As to holding office," Stanton continued, "the public life of most men begins at about forty years of age, after which period most women might be relieved from all domestic cares, as at that time their children are grown up and married, or in school." Science, Stanton predicted, would bring a convergence of life stages for middle-aged male and female political leaders.[110]

Stanton and other contributors to the *Revolution* also searched for models of vibrant, politically involved men and women in their seventies, eighties, and nineties.[111] As she had earlier in her life, Stanton pointed to Lucretia Mott as a paragon of successful aging. At seventy-six, Mott's "voice [was] still stronger and her step lighter than many who [were] juniors by twenty years."[112] Contributor Adele Summers attributed the existence of "flabby old" women to lack of physical and mental exercise and argued that suffrage would keep women interesting and attractive into old age.[113]

While Stanton used the pages of the *Revolution* to encourage what she saw as proper female development, many of her former allies became increasingly critical of the hierarchical measures of maturity celebrated in its pages, particularly Stanton's willingness to denigrate black and immigrant voters. In May 1868 the AERA gathered for its annual meeting, and Frederick Douglass directly confronted the arguments Stanton had been laying out in the first issues of the *Revolution*. He emphasized his own continued support for enfranchising all adults on equal terms but then suggested that women could tolerate, perhaps even benefit from, perpetual dependence while men could not. Eliding black women, he acknowledged that white women found their dependence on male relatives degrading but then emphasized the privileges they received: "The Government of this country loves [white] women. They are the sisters, mothers, wives, and daughters of our rulers; but the negro is loathed," Douglass said.[114] Stanton rejected this view, arguing that "we have tried the government of class and caste and they have uniformly failed." Women could not depend on men to represent them.[115]

Following the AERA meeting, in August 1868 Stanton heard of a case that perfectly illustrated her point. Hester Vaughan was a young emigrant from England, seduced, abandoned, and then found lying next to her dead baby; on scanty evidence a Philadelphia jury sentenced her to death for infanticide. "If that poor child of sorrow is hung," Stanton editorialized in the *Revolution*, "her death will be a far more horrible *infanticide* than was the killing of her child."[116] Far from protecting female dependents, white male power seduced and abandoned young girls, Stanton alleged. Tying her own critique back to Wollstonecraft's earlier analysis, she reprinted on the same day a section from *A Vindication of the Rights of Woman* asserting that the "libertinism of man leads him" to mistake "the little artless tricks of children" for mature womanhood.[117]

In December 1868, when Congress debated a proposed Fifteenth Amendment to the Constitution that would prevent states from denying suffrage on the basis of race but allow sex to remain as a barrier, Stanton became ever more strident in her denigration of male voters.[118] It was hard enough for women to bear the laws of "Saxon fathers," she argued, but the amendment brought in "all the lower orders, natives and foreigners,

Dutch, Irish, Chinese, and African."[119] She derided "Patrick and Sambo and Hans and Young Tung," thus invoking stereotypes of Irish, black, German, and Chinese men familiar from both ethnological illustrations and Thomas Nast's popular caricatures for *Harper's Weekly*.[120]

At the same time, Stanton more fully explored the generational hierarchy between mothers and sons. Her main critique of the Fifteenth Amendment was that it created an "aristocracy" of sex, meaning that it empowered one class based on an arbitrary distinction.[121] Of all possible aristocratic systems, she argued, "that of sex is the most odious and unnatural, invading as it does our homes . . . dividing those whom God has joined together, and exalting the son above the mother that bore him."[122] In other words, the mistake of the Fifteenth Amendment was not just that it enfranchised the lower orders of men but that it failed to recognize wives as the peers of their husbands and mothers as the guardians of their sons. This was a grave error, according to Stanton, because "all the recent revelations of science" showed that "it is only through the infusion of the mother soul into our legislation, that life will be held sacred, capital and labor reconciled, . . . [and] labor [made] profitable and honorable to all."[123]

By 1869 Stanton had managed to construe most men as childlike—because they were either black, immigrants, poor, or Republican. She developed this rhetoric of infantilization even as she continued to insist that all adults should be granted the right to vote at age twenty-one and that all individuals should be encouraged in their free and unfettered development. She insisted that the Declaration of Independence presented the right idea of government, "that all mankind are equal; not equally wise, strong, or good, but that their rights are equally sacred, and that laws should be framed for the highest development of all alike."[124] These ideas certainly had no place in orthodox positivism, which regarded equality and individual freedom as metaphysical illusions that must be transcended.[125] Stanton, however, never fully abandoned democratic rhetoric even while she embraced Comte's elitism. She believed educated, mature leaders should provide the ideas for government, but she always imagined this leadership as benevolently leading toward the higher development of all.[126]

By the May 1869 meeting of the AERA, women's rights activists' shared commitment to enfranchising all adults at age twenty-one could no longer contain the various tensions that divided leaders from each other.[127] The rhetoric of infantilization—Republicans' references to dependent wives and children, Stanton's dismissal of male voters as the "black boy in the Federal family" and of the elevation of "sons" above "mothers"—drove former allies apart even as they all continued to insist that granting universal rights at age twenty-one was the best policy.[128]

At the AERA's May 1869 anniversary meeting, Stephen Foster demanded that Stanton resign, since she had "publicly repudiated the principles of the society" by editing a paper that had "adopted as its motto Educated Suffrage" and by bringing "George Francis Train on this platform with his ridicule of the negro."[129] Though the majority voted for Stanton to remain, Douglass objected to her "employment of certain names such as 'Sambo,' and the gardener, and the bootblack." He then staked out a clear position in support of the Republican Party and the Fifteenth Amendment, claiming that he could "not see how anyone can pretend that there is the same urgency in giving the ballot to woman as to the negro. With us, the matter is a question of life and death." Evoking the brutality of racial violence both north and south, he argued that black men needed the vote because "their children are torn from their arms and their brains dashed out upon the pavement." When a member of the audience called out, "Is that not all true about black women?," Douglass answered, "Yes . . . but not because she is a woman, because she is black."[130] When the question was one of "life and death," Douglass reasoned, men needed the vote to protect their dependents.

Anthony, Stanton, and their allies refused to countenance the notion that women needed to be protected like children. Instead they argued that, in Anthony's words, "if you will not give the whole loaf of justice to the entire people . . . then give it first . . . to the most intelligent and capable portion . . . because in the present state of government it is intelligence, it is morality which is needed." Further, Anthony continued, men could not "understand" women any more than slaveholders understood slaves. Just as slaveholders thought, "'The negro is a poor lovable creature, kind, docile, unable to take care of himself, & dependent on our compassion to keep them' . . . [m]en feel the same today." But women, Anthony insisted, were no more willing to live in a state of perpetual dependence than enslaved people had been. "There is not a woman born," she claimed, "not one who consents to eat the bread earned by other hands, but her whole moral being is in the power of that person."[131] Women, like black men, had a burning need to be recognized as mature beings capable of supporting themselves.

The controversy at hand was whether or not to support the Republican Party and the Fifteenth Amendment, but the deeper issue at stake was who counted as an independent adult and on what basis. Did all men need to be recognized as adult citizens in order to protect their dependent wives and children? Or, did every individual who had developed "intelligence" and "virtue" deserve to be recognized as an adult citizen, regardless of sex?

Lucy Stone tried to find a middle way, fully supporting the Fifteenth Amendment but also noting that "Ku-Kluxes here in the North in the shape of men, take away the children from the mother . . . [and] *any* father . . . whether he be under age or not, may by his last will and testament dispose of the custody of his child." Because manhood suffrage would not protect children and immature men had too much authority, Stone concluded that "the influence of woman will save the country."[132] Stone's compromise of supporting the Fifteenth Amendment while still demanding woman suffrage appealed to the majority of AERA members. The issue, however, would not rest, as Phoebe Couzins, a young white law student from St. Louis, rose to dispute Douglass's evocation of black male protectors with the claim that "the black men as a class . . . have learned the lesson of brute force but too well, and as the marriage law allows the husband entire control over his wife's earnings and her children, she is in worse bondage than before."[133]

Representatives of white wage-earning women recognized that the debate over what qualified an individual for full citizenship was not serving their needs, since they were neither men nor the most highly educated women. They attempted and failed to gain a space for discussing a resolution "looking to the amelioration of the condition of the working woman."[134] Delegates from the Boston and New York Working Women's Associations protested what they saw as an "attempt to exclude the discussion of the relations of capital and labor."[135] Their failure to define the agenda was symptomatic of a larger shift. Even as Anthony focused her comments on economic independence, she and Stanton mobilized a Comtean logic that defined intellectual and moral development, rather than economic independence, as the best measure of maturity. For the next two decades, these leaders would focus narrowly on encouraging educated women to develop their full potential as professional and political leaders, sidelining the concerns of wage-earning women for shorter hours and better pay.[136]

Frances Harper, one of the few black women to attain a leadership position within the AERA, took on the task of explaining why black women supported manhood suffrage even as they saw the need for women to gain the power to protect themselves from ignorant citizens—including white women who were, by her account, neither educated nor virtuous. She reported that in Boston "there were sixty women who left work because one colored woman went to gain a livelihood in their midst." She thus challenged Stanton, Anthony, and Couzins to explain how enfranchising white women would enable all women to achieve independence. She supported Douglass's assertion that gaining federal protection for the rights of black men was more urgent than enfranchising supposedly educated and virtuous white women.[137] "When it was a question of race, she let the lesser question of sex go. . . . She would not have the black women put a single straw in the way, if only the men of the race could obtain what they wanted."[138]

Following this debate, Stanton, Anthony, and Pillsbury left the AERA to found the National Woman Suffrage Association (NWSA), based in New York, the first formal organization dedicated to woman suffrage, while six months later Lucy Stone and Henry Blackwell founded the American Woman Suffrage Association (AWSA), based in Boston and loyal to the Republican Party. Stone and Blackwell raised funds to publish the *Woman's Journal*, which had a larger circulation and lasted much longer than the *Revolution*.[139] Harper and Douglass lent their support to the AWSA. These national organizations would remain divided until 1890, and it would take until 1920 to amend the Constitution so as to provide women a nationally recognized right to vote at age twenty-one.

IRRECONCILABLE MEASURES OF MATURITY AND THE LOSS OF EFFECTIVE COALITIONS

By the time she founded the NWSA, Stanton was thoroughly invested in comparative measures of individual development. Indeed, even when she called for amending the Constitution so as to enfranchise all adults at age twenty-one, she focused on the needs of what she regarded as the best specimens of womanhood. She announced the NWSA's campaign for a Sixteenth Amendment by proposing that a petition for woman's suffrage be carried to the nation's capital "by young girls of twenty-one years of age—one from every State—strong, well-developed, with sensibly large waists," who would put to rest any doubts that women themselves wanted the vote.[140] The needs of Americans who were less "well-developed" had become, in her eyes, less pressing.

Stanton and Anthony remained focused on the *Revolution* until May 1870, when they resigned, exhausted and in debt, ready to devote more time to writing and lecturing. Both noted that it was time for "younger hands" to take over.[141] Yet Stanton editorialized, "Do not think, dear readers, that we propose to die or pass our time in idleness . . . far from it, we shall speak and write in the future as in the past."[142] While Stanton was eager to escape the strain of producing a newspaper on a deadline, she wanted to retain her position as a leading source of suffrage ideas. Indeed, she seemed to envision her future as that of a female version of Comte's positivist philosopher. Fed up with political campaigns and petitions for woman suffrage, Stanton announced that she would no longer listen to the "puerile objections" of male voters.[143] Over the next years, Stanton sharpened her arguments that "the worst indignities against woman" were rooted in the legal principle of women's "perpetual guardianship" and that the time had come for woman to become an equal, adult citizen.[144]

Practically speaking, she and Anthony took to the lyceum lecture circuit, which in the years after the Civil War developed into the most popular entertainment of the day and a new opportunity to make money. Anthony estimated that between 1870 and 1880, she delivered about two hundred paid lectures every year. This work enabled her to clear her $10,000 debt accrued as publisher of the *Revolution*. Stanton joined the lecture circuit in 1869, presenting herself as both leading suffragist and middle-aged matron dispensing advice on "Our Young Girls." In 1870 Anthony turned fifty and Stanton fifty-five. Lecturing opened up a new career to both in middle age, providing them with a platform from which to promote their views on women's mature capacity and, equally important, to join the nation's leading men in a forum where those with education and talent met as relative equals. In 1873 *Harper's* ran a cartoon showing the two women amid the nation's leading personalities. Having lived through years of ridicule in their youth, they became famous in middle age.[145]

Building a reputation as a lyceum lecturer did not, however, leave much time or energy for the unremunerated and often unrewarding work of building organizational alliances. Many of the prominent leaders of the AERA—including Douglass and Harper—traveled the lecture circuit, but they did so alone, not together. The NWSA and the AWSA each organized competing national conventions, but speakers expected to be paid, and organizers began to charge admission fees. Rather than debating each other on an open platform as they had before the war, women's rights activists focused on crafting speeches that would appeal to a large audience.[146]

Stanton's success as a lyceum lecturer gave her little incentive to question her strategy of promoting the mature capacity of the most educated and advantaged white women. The price she paid was to cut herself off from the strategies and political insights of working-class and black Americans, even as she continued to see parallels between their condition and that of white women. For example, in 1873 she claimed that "the white man's 'wards' have all alike, Africans, Indians, women and Labor been crippled by his guardianship and protection." Rather than recognize the ongoing struggles of African Americans for adult citizenship, however, she alleged that their emancipation was complete and suggested the same approach could be applied to other races. She concluded that the more difficult struggle was to prove that women should achieve adult independence: "This is all we ask for woman, the same advantages, opportunities, and code of laws man claims for himself . . . no 'protection.'"[147] Stanton fully believed that this program would benefit all women, but she was no longer listening to those who suggested that racial and economic dependencies were the most pressing issues, or that in the face of deprivation and violence, enhancing men's power could in fact benefit a whole community.[148]

In response to Republican arguments that men would protect women, Stanton adopted a hierarchical language of individual development that not only cut her off from powerful allies but also discounted the wisdom of working-class and black women, leading her to articulate a narrow understanding of what female maturity entailed. Stanton did not see wage-earning women, positioned in her rhetoric as working "girls," as a source of political insight, even as she campaigned on their behalf. In 1868 Stanton and Anthony founded the Working Woman's Association, hoping to secure a new constituency for woman suffrage.[149] At the first meeting Anthony explained that the goal was "the elevation of woman in the sphere of labor."[150] Even as Anthony worked to organize and empower wage-earning women, however, she tended to refer to them as "girls." A reporter from the *New York World* noted that most who attended a Working Woman's Association meeting were between fifteen and twenty-five years of age, but some were middle-aged and older. To refer to them all as "girls" was certainly condescending and may explain, at least in part, why Stanton and Anthony soon focused on the needs of educated, professional, and older self-supporting women rather than on wage-earners' struggles for better pay and working conditions.[151]

Nor did Stanton notice the freedwomen and children in the South, many of whom regarded the vote as a form of communal property, who were rebuilding political institutions along with black men. Though she still paid respect to leading black activists such as Frances Harper and Sojourner Truth, Stanton largely lost sight of the fact that freedmen and freedwomen in the South were exploring many of the same issues she tackled in the *Revolution*.[152]

For example, Stanton's Wollstonecraftian argument that elite men maintained sexual inequality in order to seduce young girls certainly had relevance to the black girls in the South who so often bore the brunt of rape. In opposition to the Fifteenth Amendment, Stanton argued that "Saxon men," who had "held the ballot in this country for a century," had not protected women but sexually exploited them: "Society, as it is organized today under the man power, is one grand rape of womanhood." Stanton's analysis of how a "young girl" could find no protection under man-made laws had much in common with Harriet Jacobs's analysis of enslaved girls' fate under slave law, but with one crucial difference: Stanton imagined rape victims as white and some of their assailants as black. Thus Stanton reprinted in the *Revolution* the story of a white girl "fourteen years of age" and "a negro on the farm [who] effected her ruin." Stanton then asked a loaded question: "With judges and jurors of negroes, remembering the generations of wrong and injustice their daughters have suffered at the white man's hands, how will Saxon girls fare in their courts for crimes like this?"[153] Focused on denigrating black manhood suffrage and championing "the higher classes of womanhood," Stanton failed to notice that precisely because black men had seen their daughters raped by white men, they might be her best allies in challenging the abuses of "Saxon" men. Stanton missed this because her theory of politics envisioned wisdom as flowing only from the top down. "Gerrit Smith and Wendell Phillips teach this lesson" of denigrating womanhood "to the lower orders of men who learn truth and justice from their lips." That those lower orders might be able to teach Saxon rulers about "truth and justice" never occurred to her as she construed them as immature and childlike others in need of maternal guidance.[154]

Harper, in contrast, directly confronted the legacy of white men's rape of black girls, arguing that it was only by acknowledging this history and redeeming the maternal authority of freedwomen that justice would fully triumph. Harper's brilliance was that she engaged all the multiple registers of Stanton's developmental hierarchies and, in each one, positioned freedwomen above white women. For example, Minnie, the mulatto heroine of Harper's serial novel *Minnie's Sacrifice*, which appeared in the *Christian Recorder* in the summer of 1869, gained wisdom by choosing to identify with the race of her enslaved mother rather than of her planter father. "There are lessons of life that we never learn in the bowers of ease. They must be learned in the fire," Minnie reflected. First among these lessons was that "any society, however cultivated, wealthy or refined, would not be a social gain to me, if my color and not my character must prove my passport of admission."[155] Harper thus contended that as long as national citizenship was based on whiteness, it could not also be based on intellect or virtue. Hierarchical measures of education, wealth, and moral development meant nothing, she pointed out, if skin color rather than character was required for admission to the higher orders.

Harper's most probing engagement with Stanton's hierarchies of development, however, concerned whether or not freedwomen deserved the respect Stanton claimed for the "mothers of the race." This was an important question, since under slave law children followed the condition of the mother, and mixed-race southerners most commonly had white fathers and black mothers. The central story of *Minnie's Sacrifice*, and of Harper's more famous 1892 novel *Iola LeRoy*, was that the greatest political capacity resulted from an acknowledgment of enslaved maternal ancestors. For Minnie, this choice meant recognizing her biological mother, identifying as colored, and sacrificing herself to a Christlike death at the hands of white supremacists. Harper also suggested that leading white Americans could, in an ethnological sense, choose to acknowledge that their heritage of liberty passed through a black maternal line. Harper embedded in the novel the story of a young woman descended from Patrick Henry. A commissioner of public schools was delighted to employ the descendant of "one of the first families of Virginia" until her recommender added: "She is colored."[156] This capable woman was refused the job of teaching in the public schools because her connection to American liberty had to be traced through a black mother and was thus, in the eyes of the commissioner, no connection at all.

By publishing in the *Christian Recorder*, the official journal of the AME Church, Harper addressed her story to a black audience, but the theme of her fiction was the same one she had raised at the 1866 national women's rights convention: enslaved people, despite a system that denied them formal education, upward mobility, and the power to follow individual conscience, had through religious faith developed intellectual and moral maturity that surpassed that of more privileged Americans. In *Minnie's Sacrifice*, Louis, who was raised by a white planter only to discover that his mother was black, reflected that the enslaved "as a race had lived in a measure upon an idea; it was the hope of deliverance yet to come. Faith in God had underlain the life of the race." Louis thus claimed religious faith as an intellectual exercise, an "idea." He observed that when "some of our politicians did not or could not read the signs of the times aright these people with deeper intuitions understood the war." What they understood was that it was a war for freedom.[157]

Through the character of Minnie, Harper was able to directly explore how black women would lead "another army" that, even more than Union regiments, would ensure that the South would be "rightly conquered."[158] As the fictional Minnie told her husband Louis, "To-day our government needs woman's conscience as well as man's judgment." This argument, which convinced Louis, echoed Stanton's but with two crucial differences: the first shown by Minnie's conviction that black women, not white, represented the very best of feminine "conscience," and the second demonstrated by Minnie's declaration that she "would not throw a straw in the way of the colored man."[159] ·

By weaving the same phrases through political speeches to predominantly white activists and in fiction written for the black press, Harper sought to build biracial support for the moral leadership of black women as the key to national progress.[160] In the poetry she wrote during Reconstruction, Harper developed a model of leadership that construed the highest stage of individual development as neither manhood nor educational attainment but commitment to serving the needs of the weak. In "Moses: A Story of the Nile," written in the late 1860s, Harper described the Old Testament hero as a great leader precisely because he gave up his wealth and status as heir to the throne of Egypt in order to cast his lot with his enslaved kin. Drawing on traditions within the AME Church and within Unitarianism, a denomination she would formally join in 1870, Harper linked Moses and Jesus as deliverers from slavery and sin.[161]

That Moses died without reaching his goal but secure in the knowledge that others would reach it strengthened Harper's argument that earthly reward was not what defined success: "His life had been a lengthened sacrifice, / A thing of deep devotion to his race." When death approached, Moses "bowed his meekened soul" to God's will.[162] In the striking adjective "meekened," Harper compressed her vision of civic leadership: a true leader was not strengthened by his power but humbled before God.

> Let haughty rulers learn that men
> Of humblest birth and lowliest lot have
> Rights as sacred and divine as theirs.[163]

It was no accident that Harper wrote "Moses" in the late 1860s, just as the AERA was cleft by debates over whether educated women or all men were more deserving of citizenship rights. For Harper, the lesson to be learned from the story of Moses was that

> . . . the strongest hands
> Should help the weak who bend before the blasts

Of life, because if God is only one
Then we are the children of his mighty hand.[164]

In other words, citizens deserved justice not because they were men, or highly developed women, but because all were "children" of God, sharing a common humanity that transcended race but also sharing a profound dependence that put the abuse of earthly power to shame.[165]

In 1872, with the publication of her long narrative poem *Sketches of Southern Life*, Harper provided an answer to why black women, as much as black men, needed political rights and economic independence. The heroine, Aunt Chloe, was an elderly slave woman who lacked education, wealth, and status but nonetheless displayed the ideal type of moral refinement and steadfast dependence on God that Harper prescribed for all. Chloe, wizened by experience but childlike in her simple faith, illustrated why hierarchical models of human development based on manhood, education, wealth, and power often excluded the truly virtuous.[166]

Chloe's story began with the moment that defined the rest of her life:

> I remember, well remember,
> That dark and dreadful day,
> When they whispered to me, "Chloe,
> Your children's sold away!"

Harper used this incident to illustrate how both black and white women lacked control over their own lives. Chloe's master died in debt, and his wife, though benevolent, could not prevent creditors from seizing her slave property.[167] Though both confronted laws that rendered women insecure, the mistress lost her property while Chloe lost her children.

The scene also defined one of Chloe's central character traits: she soldiered through life supported by her faith in Christ. Though she felt "as if a bullet / Had shot me through and through," she did not die of grief. Uncle Jacob told her to depend on Christ: "Just take your burden / To the blessed Master's feet." God would grant "justice in the kingdom" if earthly masters would not.[168] Aunt Chloe and Uncle Jacob were both examples of the wisdom gained by slaves without formal education. While educated whites read newspapers and debated the war, Jacob asked "the Spirit, / If God is good and just," and "something reasoned right inside" that slavery could not last.[169] Jacob would often tell his fellow slaves, "Children don't forget to pray."[170] As God's children, they did not need book-learning to know the truth.

In contrast, Thomas, the son of Chloe's mistress, learned what was right by reading the news. He was "kind at heart" but nonetheless joined the Confederate army and died in battle. Harper presented Thomas as eager to prove his manhood; he told his mother that

> None but cowards . . .
> Would skulk unto the rear,
> When the tyrant's hand is shaking
> All the heart is holding dear.

Thomas, however, mistook the nature of tyranny. As a result, he gained the appearance of manhood without its moral core. "His uniform was real handsome; / He looked brave and strong," Chloe remembered, "but somehow I couldn't help thinking / His fighting must be wrong."[171]

Harper spent much of the poem discussing Aunt Chloe's understanding of politics, demonstrating that poor and uneducated people could have greater civic virtue than their supposed betters. Harper suggested that women—even without the vote—were the defenders of their communities. Chloe did not clamor for suffrage, but she had firm opinions on how she would vote "if [she] was a man." Chloe mentioned numerous instances where men who sold their votes were shamed by women. After a scolding by his wife, one man "just stood up and cried" as though he were a young child rather than an independent adult. Chloe insisted that not all black men were "shabby," but Harper's poem clearly suggested that the political future of the black community could not be staked on manhood alone.[172]

Though Chloe had the wisdom of experience, she also struggled to gain a formal education—one directed at deepening her faith. No lack of innate talent kept her and other slaves illiterate.

> Our masters always tried to hide
> Book learning from our eyes;
> Knowledge didn't agree with slavery—
> 'Twould make us all too wise.

Others told her,

> Chloe, you're too late;
> But as I was rising sixty,
> I had no time to wait.

Chloe went "straight to work" and learned to read.[173]

She also established her own economic independence. She got a little cabin and "felt as independent / As a queen upon her throne."[174] She succeeded in reuniting with her sons. Yet her goal remained the same: to achieve eternal life through her faith. Chloe was a matriarch—a "queen"—who had just learned her letters like a young child. Though she confounded normative expectations of development, it was clear that, with her faith in God, she would make a model citizen.

By construing aging freedwomen as the most morally mature of citizens, Harper urged other reformers to abandon claims to full citizenship that depended upon either manhood or education. Her argument fell on deaf ears as women's rights activists split into rival factions and continued to debate the relative maturity of black men and privileged white women. All participants in this debate continued to pay lip service to the idea that every American should gain the right to vote at age twenty-one regardless of race or sex, but they could no longer form effective coalitions as activists promoted irreconcilable measures of who most deserved recognition as an independent adult and who could continue to be classed with children. By the late 1870s, when the federal government began to roll back its effort to defend the rights of black men, women's rights activists protested white men's persistent tendency to classify black men as boys and all women as overgrown children, but rather than reuniting around a shared campaign to defend the equal rights of all adults, they continued to promote disparate measures of maturity and to infantilize each other.

CHAPTER SIX

PERPETUAL MINORITY AND
THE FAILURE OF RECONSTRUCTION

In the antebellum period, women's rights activists pursued competing political priorities but joined together at state and national conventions, where all participants agreed that every American, regardless of race or sex, should be free at age twenty-one to pursue his or her own journey of life. All struggled against other Americans, including many other reformers, who prescribed perpetual minority. Given this opposition, activists committed to equal adulthood looked to each other for ideas and strategies. This interracial alliance reached its peak in 1866, with the founding of the American Equal Rights Association as a national organization dedicated to winning universal rights for all adults.[1]

This alliance would not last long. As Radical Republicans in Congress revealed their determination to protect the equal rights of adult black men while classifying women with children in the U.S. Constitution, the most prominent advocates for equal adulthood split into rival camps. Though still paying lip service to the principle of equal rights for all adults, some focused on winning rights for black men as the best means of protecting black women and children, others argued that the most intellectually mature white women deserved the vote first, while still others supported black manhood suffrage while promoting the moral maturity of freedwomen.[2]

By the 1870s these activists no longer gathered together in conventions and spent more time criticizing than bolstering each other. Ironically, their divisions had become unbridgeable in part because they had been so successful in winning new recruits to their respective causes. Black male leaders gained an unprecedented influence within the Republican Party.[3] Woman suffragists could choose between two national organizations or take to the lecture circuit, where they found a larger audience than ever before.[4] Women who focused on moral maturity as the most important measure of adult citizenship could turn to the Women's Christian Temperance Union, founded in 1873 and soon the largest women's organization of the postwar period.[5]

As Reconstruction drew to a close, the former leaders of the AERA were scattered amid these separate organizations vying for national influence. Further, though they continued to agree that their ultimate goal was to convince state and federal governments to apply age qualifications equally to all Americans, thus freeing every individual to develop his or her capacities over the course of life, they had adopted competing measures of maturity that positioned some people as more deserving of adult citizenship and others as in need of guardianship. Republicans argued adult men had to protect women and children; woman suffragists stressed that educated women had a maternal duty to guide more childlike adults; and temperance activists insisted that those dedicated to Christian morality had to regulate the behavior of other citizens too immature to control themselves.[6]

The advantages and costs of pursuing these divergent strategies for achieving equal adulthood can be seen clearly by following the postwar commitments of veteran AERA leaders Frederick Douglass, Elizabeth Cady Stanton, and Frances Harper. During the late 1870s each made their boldest critique to date of most white men's tenacious contention that other adults could be treated like children. Further, each insisted that the federal government had gained the power to impose equal adulthood in every state, but Republican leaders and judges were not only refusing to do so but sanctioning the very laws and customs that prevented black men and all women from gaining rights or respect as fully realized adults. In short, these veteran leaders of the struggle for equal adulthood continued to identify a shared problem but did not ally with each other to innovate a shared solution. Through a bitter irony with profound implications for the course of American political development, white judges and politicians revealed their sustained commitment to classifying with children black men and all women at just the moment when black civil rights and women's rights leaders were most bitterly divided from each other.

The financial crisis that came to be known as the Panic of 1873 closed banks throughout the country, threw thousands out of work, and sparked strikes across the nation. Republican leaders tried to hold on to their electoral advantage by appealing to middle-class and elite voters throughout the North while taking the support of black men in the South for granted. Liberals within the party who equated equality and freedom with market competition and property rights gained an upper hand. Those who sustained their commitment to equal citizenship for freedmen saw their influence wane. The 1874 election was a turning point for Republicans; angry voters elected a Democratic majority to the House for the first time since 1861. Many white Republicans in the North came to see Reconstruction as a failure. They argued that freedmen had not yet developed the capacity for political leadership and should be placed under the political guardianship of white male leaders. Outraged by widespread evidence of political corruption, reformers began to equate good government with the rule of educated, propertied white men. Divided among themselves, Republicans failed to intervene as Democrats in the South used violence and fraud to "redeem" state governments from Republican control. If Frederick Douglass had won the short-term battle for black manhood rights, it began to look by 1876 like Elizabeth Cady Stanton's championing of social scientific hierarchies might carry the long-term war.[7]

Douglass found himself at the center of debates over how the federal government should respond to the economic crisis. In March 1874 he accepted the presidency of the Freedman's Savings and Trust Company, a national bank chartered by Congress in 1865. Though the bank was a private company, its employees worked hand in hand with Freedman's Bureau agents, and many of the freedmen and freedwomen who deposited small amounts of hard-earned cash assumed their savings had the backing of the federal government. By the time Douglass took the helm, the speculative investments made by trustees in the early 1870s were worthless, and the bank, like many around the country, was insolvent. Douglass hoped to save the institution by convincing depositors not to withdraw their funds, but in July 1874 he had to announce that the bank had failed. Black leaders and many white Republicans argued that Congress had a moral responsibility, though not a legal duty, to return the small deposits that were often the only savings that freedmen and freedwomen had to their name. Congress refused to act.[8]

Many attacked Douglass for his complicity in the bank's failure. He maintained that he did not know the bank was insolvent when he accepted its presidency. The situation was particularly painful for all involved because Douglass had for so long championed black people's right to pursue their own ambitions, which was precisely what the small depositors were trying to do. Those who lost their savings also lost their best hope for buying land, starting a business, or investing in a child's education. Douglass's insistence that the bank's failure was not his fault provided slim consolation for penniless depositors striving to navigate their own independent course of life.[9]

Douglass rededicated himself to ensuring that Republicans would retain control of the federal government, believing that this offered black people the best hope for sustaining their dreams of equal citizenship. He was, however, increasingly in a minority. In the fall of 1874 a reporter for the *New York Times* summed up declining support for federal intervention with the comment that men like Wendell Phillips and William Lloyd Garrison "represent ideas in regard to the South which the majority of Republicans have outgrown."[10] This new, more mature Republican Party would relegate immature radicals and blacks to the margins while championing the rule of the best men north and south.

In the 1876 presidential election, Douglass campaigned vigorously for the Republican candidate, Rutherford Hayes, against his Democratic rival, Samuel Tilden. In part because Congress and federal judges refused to intervene in the South, widespread reports of fraud and violence clouded the result of the election, leading to months of backroom dealing and public debate. While many details remain unclear, what came to be known as the Compromise of 1877 resulted in Hayes assuming the presidency and then withdrawing federal troops who had been guarding statehouses in Louisiana and South Carolina, thus enabling white southerners to regain political control of every state in the South. Douglass refrained from attacking this outcome, though it betrayed his deepest hopes for equal citizenship. Hayes, grateful for the support of the most famous black man in America, appointed Douglass marshal of the District of Columbia, the first office ever held by a black man that required Senate approval. Douglass used his position to try to defend the claims of black citizens and, perhaps most important, direct federal patronage to black people. Those who found work as civil servants during these years bought homes and sent their children to college. Douglass believed men such as these would finally prove to the nation that blacks as well as whites were capable of becoming equal adults.[11]

Douglass almost lost this opportunity, however, when he vented his frustrations in a May 1877 speech in Baltimore that harshly criticized former slave owners in the nation's capital for their continued refusal to recognize black men as men. "Slavery has left a residuum in Washington which, for the want of a better name, I call 'the black boy,'" Douglass contended, explaining that to be a black boy meant the perpetual obligation to serve and obey rather than to act independently. While white males might occupy servile positions for a short period of time—as children or apprentices—they eventually gained recognition as men, Douglass claimed, insisting that this was still not so for blacks. "The black boy may be old or young, large or small, tall or short, seven years or seventy years old, he is always, according to the parlance of slavery [persisting in Washington], the black boy," Douglass said.[12] White tradesmen denied black men the opportunity to learn skills. White clients refused to hire black men with professional skills. Perhaps most gallingly, white women, though subordinate to white men, claimed the authority to command black male servants. "When the wife of the humble mechanic in Washington goes to do her marketing . . . like all the rest she must have the black boy to walk behind her and carry the basket," Douglass reported. Focused on servitude as a barrier to equal manhood, Douglass never mentioned black women working as servants in the nation's capital. Nor did he acknowledge white women's rights activists who argued that white men also infantilized them.[13] This was Douglass's boldest and clearest protest against the infantilization of black men. But it was also entirely cut off from his earlier insistence that all adults, not just males, deserved rights and respect as adult citizens.

Offended white Washingtonians led a drive to have Douglass removed from his post as marshal. Douglass kept his appointment but over the next few years toned down his criticism of white prejudice.[14] In February 1878 he celebrated his sixtieth birthday and thereafter increasingly carved out a position for himself as the éminence grise of black America. For the rest of his life he would continue to support women's rights, but his central passions remained focused on enabling black men to pursue their own destiny despite the numerous barriers white people erected in their path.[15]

In June 1877 Douglass returned to the Eastern Shore of Maryland where as an enslaved boy he had, according to his 1845 *Narrative*, watched ships sail from the harbor and lamented his own inability to navigate the voyage of life. Still smarting from the backlash unleashed when he focused on the problem of the "black boy," he focused his homecoming speech on urging black men to pursue their own ambitions. According to a reporter from the *Baltimore Sun*, he "said to the colored people . . . 'We must not talk about equality until we can do what white people can do. As long as they can build vessels and we cannot, we are their inferiors; as long as they can build railroads and we cannot, we are their inferiors. . . . The question now is, will the black man do as much for his master (himself) as he used to do for his old master?'"[16] In other words, black men should not just dream of navigating the voyage of life but should build their own boats. This would remain Douglass's approach to black equality for the rest of his life.[17]

WOMEN AND MINORS

While Douglass fought for influence within the Republican Party, Stanton, Susan B. Anthony, and their allies began a bold campaign to test in the federal courts whether or not adult women had gained any new rights under the Fourteenth and Fifteenth Amendments. Known as the New Departure, this strategy presented their boldest claim to date that state governments needed to apply age qualifications equally to female and male citizens.[18] This strategy failed. Much to their frustration, they found that federal courts remained fully committed to the premise that adult women could be constitutionally classed with minors. As these activists fully realized, federal judges' refusal to protect the rights of adult women helped pave the way for states to deny rights to adult black men as well.[19]

The first important test case was brought by Myra Bradwell, editor of the *Chicago Legal News*, who in 1869 applied to the Illinois state supreme court for admittance to the bar and was denied on the grounds that as a married woman she was unable to sign contracts. The court justified this refusal by noting that "applications of the same character have occasionally been made by persons under twenty-one years of age, and have always been denied upon the same ground that they are not bound by their contracts."[20] The state thus explicitly classed married women with minors.

Bradwell challenged this decision, arguing that the right to practice law, if qualified by age and education, was one of the "privileges and immunities of citizens of the United States" protected from state interference under the Fourteenth Amendment. The U.S. Supreme Court heard her case in 1873. In his brief filed in her defense, Matthew Carpenter, a Republican senator from Wisconsin and women's rights supporter, tried his utmost to distinguish qualifications based on age or education, which he saw as legitimate because attainable by all, from a restriction based on sex, which he defined as unconstitutional in permanently barring "a whole class of citizens." Further, Carpenter warned that if the justices allowed

Illinois to exclude all adult women from the bar, "they may as well declare that no colored citizen shall practice law." In other words, to protect the civil rights of freedmen, the clear intent of the Fourteenth Amendment, the Court would have to interpret the Constitution as protecting adult white women's civil rights as well.[21]

The Supreme Court denied this logic, affirming its earlier decision in the *Slaughterhouse* cases that the Fourteenth Amendment did not create any new rights or elevate national over state citizenship but only offered enhanced protection for rights conferred by the federal government itself, a category that did not include admittance to the bar. A grown woman had no more right to practice law than a boy did.[22] In a concurring opinion, Justice Joseph Bradley went even further, arguing that the state had not only the right but the duty to prevent women from pursuing professional work that might set them at odds with men. He contended that "civil law, as well as nature herself, has always recognized a wide difference in the respective spheres and destinies of man and woman. Man is, or should be, woman's protector. . . . The harmony, not to say the identity of interests and views which belong, or should belong, to the family institution is repugnant to the idea of a woman adopting a distinct and independent career from that of her husband." He acknowledged that not all women were married, but single women were "exceptions to the general rule" and "the rules of civil society must be adopted to the general constitution of things."[23] According to Bradley, state and federal governments should ensure that women, married or single, remain perpetually dependent on men.

According to Stanton, Anthony, and Gage in *The History of Woman Suffrage*, "the result of this suit taught women . . . that the methods for earning their daily bread, in the trades and professions, the use of their powers of mind and body, could be defined, permitted or denied for the citizen by State authorities."[24] The ruling was particularly galling to activists who had struggled for equal adulthood, because it combined what they saw as the two major mechanisms by which white men infantilized all women. First of all, the decision allowed the State of Illinois to use the requirement that lawyers be twenty-one as a means of distinguishing boys from men while at the same time it classified all women with minors. Second, in Bradley's concurring opinion, the Court revealed that states would win only praise for maintaining laws that blocked women from determining their own course of life. The decision starkly revealed how judges' persistent refusal to recognize women's equal adulthood would hamper the ambitions of educated women in the postwar period. Despite women's success in winning some rights to marital property, their increasing access to higher education, their contributions to the union cause, and the newly enshrined constitutional principle of national citizenship, the State of Illinois could still class women with minors as dependent citizens incapable of signing contracts. According to Bradley this was nature's design, but to many women's rights advocates it appeared that nature had endowed Myra Bradwell with an exceptional capacity to practice law, a talent that men were determined to thwart at every turn.

While Bradwell pursued her civil rights through the courts, a number of black and white women attempted to vote throughout the country in the presidential election of 1872, arguing that the Fourteenth and Fifteenth Amendments together prevented states from denying any class of citizens their political rights.[25] Predictably, white men cited age qualifications as proof that voting was not a natural right but a privilege that states could regulate at will. When federal authorities arrested Susan B. Anthony in Rochester, New York, for "knowingly voting without a legal right to vote," her defense lawyer, Henry Selden, did all he could to put the analogy between sex and age to rest.[26] At Anthony's trial in federal circuit court in June 1873, Selden preemptively acknowledged that "it will doubtless be urged" that if all citizens have the right to vote, then "infants and lunatics" have that right as well. But, Selden argued, "this objection, which appears to have great weight with certain classes of persons, is entirely without force. It takes no note of the familiar fact, that every legislative provision, whether constitutional or statutory, which confers any *discretionary* power, is always confirmed in its operation to persons who are *compos mentis*" and therefore disqualified infants and lunatics from exercising rights guaranteed to other citizens. "But are women, *who are not infants*, ever included in this category? Does any such principle of exclusion apply to them? Not at all," Selden thundered.[27] In other words, the legal status of minors was irrelevant to the claims of adult women, who, in any case, *were not children*.

The presiding judge, U.S. Supreme Court justice Ward Hunt, thoroughly rejected these arguments, relying on the state's acknowledged power to set an age qualification for male electors as proof that voting was not a right guaranteed any citizen. As Hunt explained, "If the State of New York should provide that no person should vote until he had reached the age of 31 years, or after he had reached the age of 50, or that no person having gray hair [should vote] . . . I do not see how it could be held to be a violation of any right derived or held under the Constitution of the United States." Citing the recent *Slaughterhouse* and *Bradwell* decisions, Hunt told the jury that New York's requirement that all electors be male was "no violation of the letter or of the spirit of the 14th or of the 15th Amendment."[28] Hunt directed the jury that, as a matter of law, they must find Anthony guilty of illegal voting. Unable to appeal because of a technicality, Anthony protested the decision in speeches and articles while continuing to lecture around the country.[29]

The case that finally settled the question of women's voting rights was brought to the U.S. Supreme Court in 1875 by Virginia and Francis Minor, married leaders of the woman suffrage movement in Missouri.[30] When Virginia submitted her registration to vote in 1872, registrar Reese Happersett refused it because she was a woman. Her husband and two other attorneys urged the Supreme Court to rule that states could no longer deny any class of adult citizens the right to vote. As Selden had done at Anthony's trial, they argued for a distinction between age and sex. They contended that states could constitutionally require voters to be "of a certain age, be of sane mind, be free from crime, etc., because these are conditions for the good of the whole, and to which all citizens, sooner or later, may attain." This was, they argued, an entirely different legal principle than "to single out a class of citizens and say to them, 'Notwithstanding you possess all these qualifications, you shall never vote, or take part in your government.'"[31]

Chief Justice Morrison Waite refused to separate adult women from minors. He maintained that state constitutions, with the exception of New Jersey, had always limited the vote to males over twenty-one, a fact acknowledged in the second section of the Fourteenth Amendment itself, which reduced representation in Congress only for states that disenfranchised "male citizens twenty-one years of age." Women and children, Waite explained, were "persons" and citizens but not voters; state constitutions "which commit that important trust to men alone are not necessarily void."[32]

By 1875, when the Court handed down its decision in *Minor v. Happersett*, women's rights activists had to concede that federal judges were determined to defend laws that classified women with children, despite activists' many years of lobbying white male politicians to enfranchise all citizens at age twenty-one, regardless of women's many contributions during the crisis of the Civil War, and in the face of women's increased access to education, paid employment, and social welfare work.[33]

Stanton told the NWSA convention in May 1875 that the Supreme Court's decisions regarding women's rights under the Fourteenth Amendment had all been "decidedly retrogressive in their tendency, so much so, that in this strenuous effort, to prove that woman has no new guarantees of liberty by the amendments, there is a danger lest the rights of the black man be imperiled also."[34] Rather than calling for an alliance with black male leaders, however, Stanton continued to blame black men and Republicans for childishly pursuing their own self-interests at the expense of educated, native-born white women, "the mothers of the race," whose mature guidance was desperately needed to ensure the further progress of the nation.[35]

Throughout the 1870s Stanton and Anthony innovated new means by which elite women could gain influence and respect with age, increasingly offering themselves as examples of mature womanhood. Beginning in 1870, when Anthony turned fifty, members of the NWSA turned Anthony's and Stanton's birthdays into lavish celebrations aimed at recruiting new members while also promoting positive attitudes toward mature women. Stanton's seventieth birthday in 1885 was the occasion for her speech "The Pleasures of Age."[36] Her most memorable defense of female maturity, Stanton's speech turned on the assertion that "fifty not fifteen, is the heyday of a woman's life. Then the forces hitherto finding an outlet in flirtations, courtship, conjugal and maternal love, are garnered in the brain to find expression in intellectual achievements, in spiritual friendships and beautiful thoughts, in music, poetry and art."[37] At seventy, Stanton reported that a woman could continue to find pleasure in old age if she gives "her best hours and faculties to a higher world of thought . . . reads Buckle, Darwin, Spencer, John Stuart Mill . . . [and remains] interested in the reforms of the day." Such old women "will always be a charming companion to old and young."[38] As Stanton explained, offering herself as a model of successful aging, "I often hear women say, after their children are grown up and established in life, that they have nothing to live for. I would point them to the broad fields of philanthropic work . . . to the study of the useful sciences, to fine arts, to practical work in the trades and professions."[39]

Stanton's understanding of the "pleasures of age" was thoroughly rooted in her careful reading of Mary Wollstonecraft and Margaret Fuller. But, as Stanton was well aware, these women had died in the prime of life. She—endowed with vigorous health and boundless determination, confident in the power of her own mind, and flattered by the attention of younger women joining the ranks of the NWSA—resolved to spend her last years demonstrating what an old woman could do in the world.

COLORED WOMEN, YOUNG AND OLD

Frances Harper shared Stanton's concern with winning opportunities and respect for aging women but was painfully aware that freedwomen were not spending their time reading Buckle, Darwin, or Spencer; instead, they were struggling to survive with little education and few resources. She knew that championing the influence of the most educated women would do nothing to help those who grew up enslaved. Instead, she called on young black women to take full advantage of the new educational and occupational opportunities opening to them while forging intergenerational alliances with their aging relatives and interclass alliances with those who remained impoverished. True maturity, Harper insisted, was measured not by fancy degrees, material prosperity, or political power but by dedication to serving those with fewer advantages than oneself.[40]

Harper explored the question of what young black women owed their female elders in a short story, "Fancy Etchings," published serially between 1873 and 1874 in the *Christian Recorder*, a weekly publication of the AME Church. The story centered on a college-educated young girl, Jenny, and her relationship with her widowed, elderly aunt Jane. As the elder woman revealed to the younger when she returned home from school, "I feared that you might think Aunty too old fashioned for companionship, and that I should lose my loving, little girl in the accomplished woman." Instead, the aunt was "pleasantly surprised" that she "retained both." For her part, young Jenny aspired to achieve fame as a poet but also believed that "more valuable than the soarings of genius are the tender nestlings of love." Love of her elderly aunt sustained Jenny's broader belief in her Christian duty to "serve humanity."[41] These women were economically privileged, the daughter and granddaughter of free blacks who "had succeeded in acquiring wealth."[42] But Jenny did not mistake the trappings of formal education and material comfort for the development of inner talent. Unfolding faculties, Jenny said, required "looking within ourselves, and becoming acquainted with our powers and capacities."[43] This was a program of self-education available to the poor as well as to the rich.

The cause of greater humanity was not served, however, when Jenny's uncle refused to praise her poem and instead asked, "Can you cook a beef steak?" Within the story, the older man's refusal to acknowledge female talent and ambition was soothed by her aunt's encouragement. Harper thus presented an idealized vision of intergenerational relationships between black women, through which young women respected the mature wisdom of their elders while older women encouraged the advancement of the young.[44]

Jenny recognized that white women's rights activists shared her desire to open new occupations to female ambition, but she found them unwilling to aid black women in their particular struggles to transcend the legacy of slavery and racial discrimination. "If white women feel that they are limited by their sex," Jenny told her aunt, "how must it be with us who have the shadows of the past still projected on our lives? What they call limitation would be to us broad liberty." According to Jenny, black people would have to join together to improve opportunities for black women's employment. Nor could they look to electoral politics for solutions to their problems. Jenny argued that black people should no longer consider "what this party will do for us, or the other one against us," but rather ask, "What are we going to do for ourselves?"[45] In January 1874 Harper thus advised her black readers that they would receive little help from either white women's rights activists or black Republicans but could build a better future through intergenerational and interclass alliances among black women mutually dedicated to the advancement of the race.

In 1875, at the centennial anniversary of the Pennsylvania Society for Promoting the Abolition of Slavery, Harper explicitly engaged with new theories of evolution increasingly cited by Republican Party leaders to justify laissez-faire policies and withdrawal of federal troops from the South. "Ethnologists may differ about the origin of the human race," Harper said. "Huxley may search for it in protoplasms, and Darwin send for the missing links, but there is one thing of which we may rest assured,—that we all come from the living God and that He is the common Father."[46] Harper was not alone in invoking the idea of God as a "common Father" to justify the equal rights of black people. Many black leaders and sympathetic ministers made a similar argument.[47] For Harper, however, the central import of a divine father was not just racial equality but the need to respect the childlike qualities of adults—their weakness, feebleness, and dependence. What America needed, Harper argued, was not more "knowledge" or "material prosperity" but "a deeper and broader humanity, which will teach men to look upon their feeble breth[r]en not as vermin to be crushed out, or beasts of burden to be bridled and bitted, but as the children of the living God."[48] Harper thus countered the notion that human life should be a struggle for what Darwin, following Herbert Spencer, referred to as the "survival of the fittest."[49] If God valued all human beings because they were his children, Harper reasoned, then Americans had a duty to protect those who resembled children—those who were weaker, feebler, or more dependent than themselves—as well as those who could claim various forms of power.

As Americans prepared to celebrate the centennial of their independence from Great Britain, Harper looked forward to "what a noble work there is before our nation!" If the Civil War had been fought by young men, in the next great "battle" that would be waged for equal justice, "there is room for woman's work and woman's heart." To survive this coming war, which would be moral rather than military, black women with the most advantages would need to serve those with the least. "Let no magnificence of culture, or amplitude of fortune, or refinement of sensibilities, repel you from helping the weaker and less favored. If you have large gifts, hold them as larger opportunities with which you can benefit others," Harper advised.[50] This course of life would be difficult, she warned: "I do not promise you smooth sailing and unclouded skies." But, through imagery evoking Thomas Cole's *The Voyage of Life*, Harper promised that if men and women put their faith in God, they could weather rough seas and find a great reward "in eternity." Harper counseled that "for a life that is in harmony with God and sympathy for man there is no such word as fail."[51]

Fifty years old in 1875, Harper focused much of her energy on promoting the interests of black women within the Women's Christian Temperance Union, an organization that she hoped would enable the formation of a female community based on faith without regard to race. She supported woman suffrage but believed more could be accomplished by directing the resources of the largest and most influential women's organization toward the black community. She also hoped that a movement dedicated to the moral influence of women would recognize that freedwomen, even if they lacked education and property, had talents to offer. When white southern women insisted on racially segregated chapters, Harper urged black women to continue their work. In the wake of Reconstruction, she was convinced that the best resource black women had for navigating the journey of life was a shared commitment to each other and a steady promotion of their capacity for moral maturity.[52]

Frederick Douglass, Elizabeth Cady Stanton, Susan B. Anthony, and Frances Harper thus all adjusted their vision of equal adulthood to the political realities of the late 1870s. As Republicans abandoned the defense of black equality for the protection of private property and shifted from interventionist policies to laissez-faire liberalism, these veteran activists each called on their respective constituencies to continue the struggle to develop their full capacities over the course of life as the best hope for winning the guarantee of equal citizenship. Frustrated in their efforts to convince Congress or the federal courts that age qualifications for citizenship should extend to all adults equally and horrified by white southerners' violent suppression of the civil and political rights of freedmen, freedwomen, and white Republicans, Douglass, Stanton, Anthony, and Harper each dispensed remarkably similar advice—which is not surprising, given that all had developed their understanding of equal adulthood in conversation and debate with each other. The problem was that they spoke to different organizations with different concerns. They all agreed that every individual had to be free at age twenty-one to develop his or her capacity over the course of life, but Douglass focused on urging black men to compete with white, Stanton urged the most educated women to challenge their male peers for national leadership, and Harper counseled Christian reformers that the only true measure of maturity was service to others. Perhaps most tragically, each of these veteran activists recognized that as long as state and federal governments could deny equal rights to any adults, all adults remained vulnerable to infantilization, but their shared dismay was not enough to create an effective coalition.

While disappointing to all involved, this outcome was rooted in activists' commitment to hierarchical measures of adult citizenship. White women's assertion of their own maturity had long depended upon a contrast with other adults who remained more childlike, whether because of poverty, lack of education, or racial difference. Black men, meanwhile, had often fallen back on emphasizing their equal capacity as men to protect dependent women and children. Black women, because they could claim neither whiteness nor manhood and often struggled with poverty and lack of education as well, came closest to insisting upon equal adulthood for all Americans, but they too could infantilize others, as when Harper dismissed black men and white women for their childish pursuit of self-interest. In short, arguments for equal adulthood, when phrased in terms of comparative maturity, were more likely to divide than to unite the disenfranchised.

AGING AND INEQUALITY

As the nineteenth century wore on, champions of equal adulthood continued to promote hierarchical measures of maturity because they could be effective in winning specific opportunities. Black men, in some cases, were able to defend their legal and political rights as men. Advantaged white women gained new opportunities for higher education, professional advancement, and national influence by presenting themselves as maternal authorities who could guide and protect the childlike members of other races at home and abroad.[1] Black women found a toehold in the Women's Christian Temperance Union by emphasizing that they needed to be empowered as mothers to guide the moral development of their communities.[2] Despite these gains, however, many white men continued to claim rights and opportunities based on their status as independent adults while they treated others, in law and daily life, as though they were perpetual minors. Age certainly did not trump gender or race in nineteenth-century America.[3]

Indeed, I suggest that it is worth pondering whether or not the issues raised by Abigail Adams, Phillis Wheatley, and Mary Wollstonecraft during the American Revolution have ever been fully resolved. Granted, women won the right to vote on the same terms as men in 1920, black southerners finally won back their political rights in the 1960s, and eighteen-year-olds gained constitutional protection for their political rights in 1971. But did these reforms really settle the questions raised earlier? Every state still claims the power to disenfranchise citizens on the basis of age, even as many recognize the arbitrariness of allowing young people to drive at sixteen, vote at eighteen, and drink at twenty-one.[4] Does this power to impose age qualifications still underlie states' right to impose other qualifications as well? Can adult illegal immigrants and those with a criminal record be so easily denied a political voice because truly universal suffrage would mean admitting children to the polls? As scattered protests to enfranchise sixteen-year-olds suggest, the question of who counts as a mature citizen has not been resolved. The Twenty-Sixth Amendment merely shifted the boundary of contestation from twenty-one to eighteen.

What about nineteenth-century women's rights activists' radical claim that white men denied adult women equal rights because they found young girls, both black and white, sexually attractive and older women repellant? It is true that black and white women have won the legal right to compete with men in nearly every occupation, but middle-aged white men continue to occupy most of the positions of power within corporations, the professions, and electoral politics. Feminists continue to worry, as Wollstonecraft did so long ago, that young girls spend too much time cultivating their appearance and not enough time improving their talents and that middle-aged and old women focus more energy on looking young than on demanding respect for their experience and wisdom. Armed with numerous examples of the links between ageism and sexism in mass media, feminists continue to protest that many Americans have nothing but contempt for older women, especially those bold enough to lay a claim to political or economic power. But activists most committed to the needs of older women point out that many feminists are themselves prejudiced against the elderly.[5]

The trope of generational waves within the feminist movement does not help matters. In the antebellum period, women's rights activists, young and old, believed that all women had a stake in ensuring that every individual could develop their full potential over the course of life. Today, many feminists seek to carve out a particular voice for their generation, speaking for youth or old age, instead of building intergenerational alliances among women.[6] The tendency to see generational conflict is only reinforced by political commentary that posits a conflict between old baby boomers demanding more than their share of government resources and young taxpayers fearful for their own futures.[7] As more and more Americans live into advanced old age, it might make sense to reclaim the belief, championed by earlier women's rights activists, that young and old share an interest in ensuring that every individual can unfold his or her faculties over the entire life course.

Finally, today's feminists have yet to fully bridge the racial and class divisions inherited from the nineteenth century. By recovering the early struggle for equal adulthood, we can better understand how and why black civil rights and women's rights activists once reached across the color line to develop an analysis of a shared problem: white men's general refusal to recognize black men or any women as fully realized adults. From this perspective, so long as states denied rights to any adults, all were vulnerable. Holding on to this principle proved impossible. Various adults had too much to gain by emphasizing their maturity in relation to childlike others. It is worth asking, however, if this expediency has reached a dead end. Can career women ever compete equally with white men if they continue to pay other women low wages to care for their children and elderly relatives? Can we continue to describe adults who receive government assistance as "dependents" when many are full-time workers who don't receive an adequate wage? Can we congratulate ourselves on living in a color- and gender-blind society if white men continue to advance into higher-paying jobs in larger numbers than men of color or women of any race? In short, might it still be important to ask what counts as equal adulthood and who can achieve it?[8]

NOTES

INTRODUCTION

1. Fuller, *Woman*, 176; Capper, *Margaret Fuller*, vol. 2.

2. Fuller, *Woman*, 31, 33.

3. Leach, *True Love*. To date, the history of childhood and old age has received greater attention than the history of adulthood. See, for example, Mintz, *Huck's Raft*; Marten, *Children in Colonial America, Children and Youth in a New Nation*, and *Children and Youth during the Civil War Era*; Forman-Brunell and Paris, *Girls' History*; Premo, *Winter Friends*; Achenbaum, *Old Age*; and Fischer, *Growing Old*.

4. Stansell posits a distinction between "the politics of the mothers and the politics of the daughters." *Feminist Promise*, xv. I argue that nineteenth-century activists believed that mothers and daughters shared an interest in promoting female maturation over the course of life. Further, as Heineman points out, when talking about "mothers" it is important to distinguish between the older mothers of adult progeny and the younger mothers of small children. Heineman, "Whose Mothers?"

5. Wollstonecraft, *Vindication of the Rights of Woman* (hereafter cited as *VRW*), 74; Harper, "Aunt Chloe," in *Brighter Coming Day*, 196–208; [Stanton], "Editorial Correspondence," *Revolution*, 20 August 1868.

6. Brewer, *By Birth or Consent*.

7. On the intersections between what we today call sexism and ageism, see Sontag, "Double Standard"; Lorde, "Age, Race, Class"; Banner, *In Full Flower*; Friedan, *Fountain of Age*; Gullette, *Declining to Decline*; Rupp, "Is Feminism the Province?"; Calastani and Slevin, *Age Matters*; and Marshall, "Aging."

8. Many scholars have answered these questions by analyzing the links between public and private, for example, Kerber, *No Constitutional Right*; Norton, *Founding Mothers*; and Kessler-Harris, *In Pursuit of Equity*. I contend that Americans justified women's subordination in families, government, and workplaces by arguing that males outgrew childish dependence while females did not.

9. Recent histories analyzing life stages under slavery include Schwartz, *Born in Bondage*; and Jabour, *Scarlett's Sisters* and *Topsy-Turvy*.

10. Newman argues in *White Women's Rights* that white women's rights activists' ideas and strategies were fundamentally racist. While I agree with this analysis, I show that white activists were nonetheless profoundly influenced by black people's ideas about adulthood. On the contributions of African Americans to women's rights activism, see, for example, Parker, *Articulating Rights*; M. Jones, *All Bound Up*; Sklar, *Women's Rights*; and Painter, *Sojourner Truth*.

11. Kelley, *Learning to Stand*; Branson, *Fiery Frenchified Dames*; Schloesser, *Fair Sex*; Goodman, *Becoming a Woman*.

12. Some historians assert that the American women's rights movement was characterized by egalitarian influences, periodically sacrificed to racist expediency, as influentially argued by Kraditor, *Ideas*, and largely accepted by DuBois, *Feminism and Suffrage*. More recently, historians, including DuBois herself, have generally accepted Newman's argument that racism and elitism were fundamental. DuBois, *Woman Suffrage*; Sneider, *Suffragists*; M. Mitchell, "'Lower Orders.'"

13. Historians have explored how Americans used the dependence of children to understand the nature and limits of democracy. Sanchez-Eppler, *Dependent States*; Levander, *Cradle of Liberty*.

14. Hewitt, "Seneca Falls."

15. I chose to focus on many of the white foremothers who appear in Stanton, Anthony, and Gage, *History of Woman Suffrage* (hereafter cited as *HWS*), vol. 1. In expanding my frame, I owe much to Flexner, *Century of Struggle*, though to her credit, she pays greater attention to educators and trade unionists whose ideas about adulthood were too distinct to appear in this book. On black men and women in the suffrage movement, I drew upon Terborg-Penn, *African American Women*; and Gordon and Collier-Thomas, *African American Women*.

16. Many studies of adulthood take a male model for granted; see, for example, Modell, Furstenberg, and Hershberg, "Social Change"; and Winsborough, "Changes in the Transition." On the exclusion of women from the history of aging, see Feinson, "Where Are the Women?"; H. Smith, "'Age'"; and Maynes, "Age as a Category."

17. Latin writers distinguished between *pueritia* (childhood), *adolescentia* (adolescence), *juventus* (mature adulthood, the prime of life), and *senectus* (old age). Dove, *Perfect Age*, 14–17; *Oxford English Dictionary Online*, s.v. "youth" and "man," http://dictionary.oed.com (hereafter cited as *OED Online*).

18. Like the English word "adolescence," which had been in use since the fifteenth century, "adult" derived from the Latin *adolescere* and connoted a process of growing to maturity. *OED Online*, s.v. "adult," "adulthood," and "adolescence"; Brewer, *By Birth or Consent*; and chap. 1 in this volume.

19. *OED Online*, s.v. "manhood."

20. Modern social scientists carefully distinguish between life stages (phases of human development), the life course (the timing and sequence of transitions such as getting married or entering the workforce), and the family cycle (the changing composition of a family based on patterns of fertility, residence, and mortality). Mintz, "Life Stages"; Elder, "Life Course"; Riley, Johnson, and Foner, *Aging and Society*. Yet antebellum women's rights activists usually conflated all of these when they referred to manhood as a stage of life in which every white male could become the head of a family, a voting citizen, and an individual expected to chart his own course through life.

21. Brewer, *By Birth or Consent*; Herndon and Murray, *Children Bound to Labor*; Field and Syrett, *Politics of Age*.

22. Keyssar, *Right to Vote*; Grinspan, "Virgin Vote."

23. Horton and Horton, *Hope of Liberty*.

24. *New York Tribune*, 28 June 1867, p. 5. See also Stanton and Anthony, *Selected Papers of Stanton and Anthony* (hereafter cited as *SPSA*), 2:75–77. On women's rights activists' concern with age twenty-one, see Isenberg, *Sex and Citizenship*, 23–33

25. Chudacoff, *How Old?*; Kett, *Rites*; Schmidt, *Industrial Violence*; Mintz, "Reflections on Age."

26. See C. Field, "'Male Citizens.'"

27. Cole, *Journey of Life*, part 2.

28. Fuller, *Woman*, 37.

29. Qtd. in *Proceedings of the Woman's Rights Convention . . . 1851* (hereafter cited as *WRC 1851*), 29.

30. On the ideology of separate spheres, see Welter, "Cult of True Womanhood"; Sklar, *Catharine Beecher*; Cott, *Bonds of Womanhood*; Kelley, *Private Woman*; and Kerber, "Separate Spheres."

31. Harper, "Two Offers," 313.

32. These activists recognized middle age and old age as distinct phases within the broader stage of adulthood. I agree with Cohen in *In Our Prime* that Americans' concept of middle age became more refined in the late nineteenth century, but not with her argument that middle age was "invented" then.

33. Pateman, *Sexual Contract*. Pateman argues that social contract theorists challenged paternal rights (that is, fathers' rights to control sons) without challenging patriarchal rights (that is, men's rights to women's sexual and reproductive labor). I argue that boys had to become men before they could become either citizens or husbands/fathers. By denying females a stage of life equivalent to manhood, men ensured that women—whether married or single—would remain dependent in both public and private relations.

34. G. Brown, *Domestic Individualism*.

35. During the nineteenth and early twentieth centuries, the absolute and relative number of people over sixty in the U.S. population increased steadily. In 1850, nearly one million people were over sixty years old, 4.1 percent of the entire population. By 1920, nearly eight million had reached that age, 7.5 percent of the nation. See Achenbaum, *Old Age*, 1–3, 60; Klein, *Population History*; and Barbre, "'Goodwives.'"

36. J. Jones, *Labor of Love*, 92. The life expectancy at birth for black Americans in 1920 remained ten years fewer than for white: 47 compared to 57.4 years. Foner and Garraty, *Reader's Companion*, 104.

37. Douglass, *Terrible Honesty*; Scott, "Making the Invisible Woman"; Jensen, "Family, Career," 267–80.

38. These numbers express the "total number of births per woman if she experienced the current period age-specific fertility rates throughout her life." Foner and Garraty, *Reader's Companion*, 104.

39. Lock, *Encounters*; Brumberg, *Body Project*.

40. Birke, *Feminism*.

41. Gergen in "Finished at 40" argues that the "biologizing" of women's life course, by which she means the staging of female development around menarche and menopause, emphasizes women's reproductive capacities and overlooks other aspects of women's lives such as work, love, politics, and creativity. On the history of menarche

and menopause, see Smith-Rosenberg, "Puberty to Menopause"; Barbre, "'Good-wives'"; Banner, "Meaning of Menopause"; Perlmutter and Bart, "Changing Views"; and Formanek, "Continuity and Change."

42. Cruikshank, *Learning to Be Old*; Kenyon, Birren, and Schroots, *Metaphors of Aging;* Katz, *Disciplining Old Age;* A. Foner, *Aging and Old Age*, 1–9.

PROLOGUE

1. Hays, *Appeal to the Men*; Taylor, *Wollstonecraft*, 33–35; Myers, "Impeccable Governesses," 54, and "Reform or Ruin"; Zagarri, "Morals"; Popiel, *Rousseau's Daughters.*

2. Brewer, *By Birth or Consent.*

3. Fliegelman, *Prodigals and Pilgrims*; L. Hunt, *Inventing Human Rights*, chap. 1; Clarke, "'Cursed Barbauld Crew,'" 91–103.

4. DeLuzio, *Female Adolescence*, 24–28; Brewer, "Transformation."

5. Locke, *Second Treatise*, 290; Blackstone, *Commentaries*, 451; Rousseau, *Emile*, book 5.

6. Brewer, *By Birth or Consent.*

7. Locke, *Second Treatise*, 291.

8. Ibid., 298–99.

9. Ibid., 290; Brewer, "Transformation," 320. For an example of how this passage influenced American patriots during the Revolution, see the report from the citizens of Northampton in *Popular Sources*, 580.

10. Brewer, *By Birth or Consent*, 132, 232–338, 250–52.

11. Locke, *Second Treatise*, 290; Brewer, "Transformation," 320.

12. Brewer, *By Birth or Consent*, 2, 17–18, 26–28, 181–229; Mintz, *Huck's Raft*, 52; Banner, *In Full Flower*, pt. 3; John Gillis, "Life Course," http://www.faqs.org/childhood/Ke-Me/Life-Course-and-Transitions-to-Adulthood.html (accessed 10 October 2009); Norton, *Founding Mothers.*

13. Brewer, *By Birth or Consent*, 17.

14. Filmer, *Patriarcha*, 10; Brewer, *By Birth or Consent*, 24; Norton, *Founding Mothers*, 3–26, 281–92.

15. Locke, *Second Treatise*, 291; Brewer, "Transformation," 320; Norton, *Founding Mothers*, 5.

16. Locke, *Second Treatise*, 288.

17. Ibid., 291.

18. Ibid., 288.

19. Ibid.

20. A child did have a perpetual obligation to honor both his parents with "an inward esteem and reverence to be shown by all outward expressions." But, to honor was not necessarily to obey. Locke, *Second Treatise*, 293–94.

21. Ibid., 303.

22. Ibid., 290. On tests of ability and disability as a boundary of legal personhood, see Welke, *Law and the Borders of Belonging.*

23. Locke, *Second Treatise*, 288.

24. Others, most notably C. B. McPherson, have argued that Locke rooted individual personhood in ownership of one's own labor. For discussions of women's rights activists' engagement with issues of self-ownership, see Leach, *True Love*, 6–11. I shift the focus from possessive individualism to maturity, arguing that Locke defined maturity as the trait that enabled a man to own himself.

25. Locke, *Second Treatise*, 302.

26. Ibid., 300.

27. Ibid., 302.

28. Locke wrote that the "wife has, in many cases, a liberty separate" from her husband. His point was that when their wills directly conflicted, he did not have to obey her. Ibid.

29. Ibid., 288–89. By focusing on the son's maturation, I am adding to Pateman's argument in *Sexual Contract* that Locke's theory established a "fraternal" social contract in which sons became equal to fathers in the state by gaining control over women's sexuality within marriage. I am suggesting that sons had to outgrow their mothers before claiming either political or sexual power. Further, while I agree with Norton that Locke separated the private world of the family from the public world of the state, I am drawing attention to male maturation as the path between the two. Norton, *Founding Mothers*, 3–26.

30. Locke, *Essay Concerning Human Understanding*, 97.

31. Locke, *Second Treatise*, 272–73.

32. Mills, *Racial Contract*.

33. Ibid., 68.

34. Brewer, "Transformation," 312, 319; Welke, *Law and the Borders of Belonging*, 27.

35. Beard, *Woman as a Force*; Basch, *In the Eyes*; Grossberg, *Governing the Hearth*.

36. Brewer, "Transformation," 313.

37. Blackstone, *Commentaries*, 414.

38. Ibid., 165.

39. Ibid., 430.

40. Ibid., 441.

41. Ibid., 451.

42. Ibid., 123.

43. Ibid., 410.

44. Ibid., 441.

45. Brewer, "Transformation," 312, 319.

46. Okin, *Women*; Dent, *Rousseau Dictionary*; Weiss, *Gendered Community*; Wingrove, *Rousseau's Republican Romance*; Taylor, *Wollstonecraft*, especially chap. 2.

47. L. Hunt, *Inventing Human Rights*, 25. See also L. Hunt, *French Revolution*.

48. Rousseau, *Emile*, 118–19, 151, 167; Dent, *Rousseau Dictionary*, 101–11; Dent, *Rousseau: An Introduction*, chap. 1; Ogrodnick, *Instinct and Intimacy*.

49. Rousseau consciously rejected earlier divisions in the so-called Ages of Man as superstitious and based his upon the observation of nature. Shklar, *Men and Citizens*, chap. 2.

50. Rousseau, *Emile*, 211.

51. Ibid., 91.

52. Ibid., 480. Dent argues that Rousseau used chronological age merely as a device to illustrate the various aspects of human nature. *Rousseau Dictionary*, 107. In contrast, I argue that Rousseau emphasized precocious or delayed development as a source of personal and social corruption. He used the word "age"—along with "period" and "stage"—to refer to what modern sociologists would call "life stage." See, for example, Rousseau, *Emile*, 47, 48, 73, 74, 77, 84, 93, 120, 165–66, 208, 216, 221, 316–17, 418, 448, 471, 480.

53. Rousseau, *Emile*, 365.

54. Ibid.

55. Ibid., book 5.

56. Peabody, *There Are No Slaves*, 9, 96.

57. Rousseau, *Emile*, 460; Seeber, *Anti-Slavery Opinion in France*, 63–64.

58. Mills, *Racial Contract*, 68–69.

59. Trouille, *Sexual Politics*; Popiel, *Rousseau's Daughters*.

60. See, for example, Wollstonecraft, *VRW*, 151, 142–43, 160, 173.

61. Kant, "Answer to the Question," 54.

62. Pateman, *Sexual Contract*, 168–73; Mills, *Racial Contract*, 70–71.

CHAPTER 1

1. Gundersen, "Independence."

2. Mintz, *Huck's Raft*, chap. 3; Zagarri, *Revolutionary Backlash*; Bouton, *Taming Democracy*.

3. Holton, *Abigail Adams*; Sidbury, *Becoming African*, chap. 1; Taylor, *Wollstonecraft*.

4. Wollstonecraft, *VRW*, 186.

5. Ibid., 164.

6. Holton, *Abigail Adams*, 159.

7. Wheatley, "Thoughts on the Works of Providence" and "To Right Honourable WILLIAM Earl of DARTMOUTH," in *Complete Writings*, 28, 40; Adams and Pleck, *Love of Freedom*, 20.

8. For example, see Kelley, *Learning to Stand*; Branson, *Fiery Frenchified Dames*; Landes, *Women and the Public Sphere*; Hesse, *Other Enlightenment*; and Goodman, *Becoming a Woman*.

9. While I agree with Rosemarie Zagarri's warning that a definition of politics encompassing "almost every kind of relationship" can become so vague as to be useless, I argue that Adams's, Wheatley's, and especially Wollstonecraft's analyses of maturity provided a very precise understanding of the linkages between public and private power. Zagarri, *Revolutionary Backlash*, 7.

10. Fliegelman, *Prodigals and Pilgrims*; Yazawa, *Colonies to Commonwealth*.

11. Paine, *Common Sense*, 25; Mintz, *Huck's Raft*; Rosenfeld, *Common Sense*, chap. 4; E. Foner, *Tom Paine*.

12. Paine, *Complete Writings*, 78–79.

13. Yazawa, *Colonies to Commonwealth*, 87–95.

14. Holton, *Abigail Adams*, 46; W. Robinson, *Wheatley and Her Writings*, 3–13.

15. Holton, *Abigail Adams*, chap. 1; Crane, "Political Dialogue," 745–48.

16. Wheatley, *Complete Writings*, 7.

17. Adams and Pleck, *Love of Freedom*, 21; Sidbury, *Becoming African*, chap. 1; Grimsted, "Anglo-American Racism"; Piersen, *Black Yankees*, chap. 6; Gustafson, *Eloquence*, chap. 2.

18. Zagarri, "Morals"; Kelley, *Learning to Stand*, 17–18; Barker-Benfield, *Culture of Sensibility*; Guest, *Small Change*, chap. 12.

19. Holton, *Abigail Adams*, 44–46; Gustafson, *Eloquence*, 171–82; W. Robinson, *Wheatley*, 15–17, 455; Grimsted, "Anglo-American Racism," 383–84.

20. Abigail Adams to John Adams, 31 March 1776, *Adams Papers*, http://rotunda.upress.virginia.edu/founders/default.xqy?keys=ADMS-print-06-04-02-0091 (accessed 11 January 2010). This phrasing was a reference to Micah 4:4, a verse that American patriots and later women's rights activists would often invoke when discussing women's property rights.

21. Abigail Adams to John Adams, 31 March 1776, *Adams Papers*.

22. Schloesser, *Fair Sex*, 123–26; Crane, "Political Dialogue," 752–63; Holton, *Abigail Adams*, 99–102.

23. John Adams to Abigail Adams, 14 April 1776, *Adams Papers*.

24. Kann, *Republic of Men*, 25.

25. John Adams to Abigail Adams, 14 April 1776, *Adams Papers*.

26. Ibid.

27. Kerber, "Paradox"; Brewer, "Transformation."

28. Fraser and Gordon, "Genealogy." VanBurkleo in *"Belonging"* emphasizes how revolutionary leaders built a constitutional culture that denied equality to all women, not just to wives.

29. Sullivan wrote Elbridge Gerry on 6 May 1776. Gerry sent Sullivan's letter on to Adams. Kerber, "Paradox," 367.

30. John Adams to James Sullivan, 26 May 1776, *Adams Papers*.

31. Ibid. Keyssar notes that Blackstone's assertion that poor men had "no will of their own" echoed throughout revolutionary-era debates over suffrage. *Right to Vote*, 10.

32. John Adams to James Sullivan, 26 May 1776, *Adams Papers*.

33. Brewer, *By Birth or Consent*, especially chaps. 4 and 7.

34. John Adams to James Sullivan, 26 May 1776, *Adams Papers*. Massachusetts briefly classified slaves as taxable persons in the 1690s and again in the 1770s but generally taxed them as property. Einhorn, *American Taxation*, 66, 69, 72, 75, 76; Rabushka, *Taxation*, 169, 377, 583, 771; Brewer, *By Birth or Consent*, 138–39; Cox, "Boy Soldiers," 18. Free black males and slaves were sometimes required to serve in the militia with whites; other times they were barred. See Whisker, *American Colonial Militia*, 37, 49, 63, 79–80; and Malcolm, *Peter's War*, 27, 74–86, 95–108. On the importance of obligation, see Kerber, *No Constitutional Right*.

35. *Records of the Governor*, 173, 213.

36. *Acts and Resolves . . . of the Province of the Massachusetts Bay*, 445–48.

37. Zuckerman, "Social Context," 530–33.

38. Rorabaugh, *Craft Apprentice*, chap. 1.

39. Kett insightfully argued that from age ten to twenty-one, youth entered a stage of "semidependence." *Rites*, 29.

40. Einhorn, *American Taxation*, chap. 1; Rabushka, *Taxation*, 243–44, 252–53; K. Brown, *Good Wives*, chap. 4.

41. Brewer, *By Birth or Consent*, 138.

42. Gundersen, "Independence."

43. Keyssar, *Right to Vote*, 16; Brewer, *By Birth or Consent*, 139–40.

44. *Constitution . . . of Massachusetts-Bay . . . 1780*, 19, 25; Keyssar, *Right to Vote*, 19.

45. Keyssar, *Right to Vote*, 19; *Popular Sources*, 437.

46. Keyssar, *Right to Vote*, 20.

47. Ibid., 18.

48. *Federal and State Constitutions*, 2595; Keyssar, *Right to Vote*, 17, 55; Klinghoffer and Elkis, "'Petticoat Electors,'" 159.

49. Klinghoffer and Elkis, "'Petticoat Electors'"; Zagarri, *Revolutionary Backlash*, 30–37; Keyssar, *Right to Vote*, table A1, 340–41.

50. *Popular Sources*, 577, 580.

51. Ibid., 580.

52. Brewer, *By Birth or Consent*, 34–36.

53. For the censuses of 1800 and 1810, Congress divided the white population into five age categories for both sexes but did not divide black Americans by age or sex. Cohen, *Calculating People*, 159–60, 162–63; Dillon, *Shady Side*, chap. 2. Treas uses the census's age categories to track the "government's increasing desire for age exactitude" in the twentieth century. "Age in Standards," 76.

54. *Laws for Regulating and Governing the Militia*, n.p.; Malcolm, *Peter's War*, 74–86; Cox, "Boy Soldiers," 18.

55. Mintz, *Huck's Raft*, 62–63; Cox, "Boy Soldiers"; Rorabaugh, *Craft Apprentice*, chap. 1.

56. *Laws for Regulating and Governing the Militia*, 4.

57. *Records of the Governor*, 174.

58. Ibid. Einhorn emphasizes that estimating the age of those being taxed was an easier administrative task than valuing property. *American Taxation*, 39. For discussions of how officials determined ages in later periods, see Bensel, *American Ballot Box*, chap. 2; and Schmidt, *Industrial Violence*.

59. Gutman, "Birth and Death Registration" and "Birth and Death Registration II"; Shapiro, "Development of Birth Registration," 86–111; Klein, *Population History*, 69–72.

60. Kelley, *Learning to Stand*; Kerber, *Women of the Republic*; Norton, *Liberty's Daughters*.

61. Holton, *Abigail Adams*, 159; for Wollstonecraft's reaction to this same passage, see Gubar, "Feminist Misogyny," 459; on Warren's response to Chesterfield, see Zagarri, *Woman's Dilemma*, 110–11; Hayes, "Mercy Otis Warren."

62. Abigail Adams to Mercy Otis Warren, 28 February 1780, in *Adams Papers*; Holton, *Abigail Adams*, 159.

63. The boy was bound to Adams until he was twenty-one. Abigail Adams to Mary Smith Cranch, 12 March 1791, in *Adams Papers*; Schloesser, *Fair Sex*, 128, 145; Holton, *Abigail Adams*, 195.

64. Grimsted, "Anglo-American Racism," 371–94; Carretta, introduction, xiv, xvi; Sidbury, *Becoming African*, chap. 1.

65. Wheatley, "To the Publick," in *Complete Writings*, 8; Gates, *Trials*, 5–16.

66. Arlette Frund points out (in "Phillis Wheatley") that Wheatley knew many of Boston's leading citizens who may have testified to her talent without holding any formal examination.

67. Wheatley, *Complete Writings*, 11–12.

68. O'Neale, "Slave's Subtle War," 148, 154; Grimsted, "Anglo-American Racism," 350–51, 359.

69. Critics have long wrestled with Wheatley's stated preference for European over African culture. See Sidbury, *Becoming African*, 27–33; and Gates, *Trials*.

70. Wheatley, *Complete Writings*, 12.

71. Ibid., 16; Sidbury, *Becoming African*, 33.

72. Gates, *Trials*, 35–44; Carretta, introduction, xvi.

73. Qtd. in Gates, *Trials*, 40–41; Grimsted, "Anglo-American Racism," 414–26; Sweet, *Bodies Politic*, 295–311.

74. Jefferson, *Notes*, 147.

75. Ibid., 150–51.

76. Ibid., 144–45.

77. Onuf, "Every Generation."

78. Melish, *Disowning Slavery*.

79. Waldstreicher, *Slavery's Constitution*; Lewis, "'Of Every Age.'"

80. Melish, *Disowning Slavery*, 110–18; White, *Somewhat More Independent*, 66–75.

81. Herndon and Murray, *Children Bound to Labor*, 1.

82. White, *Somewhat More Independent*, 38.

83. One of the first proposals for gradual emancipation based on age was made in 1774 by Levie Hart, a Congregational minister in Connecticut, who carefully calculated the value of male and female slaves based on age. Saillant, "'Some Thoughts.'"

84. *Constitution or Frame . . . of Massachusetts-Bay . . . 1780*, 32.

85. Brewer, *By Birth or Consent*, 145.

86. Ibid., chap. 7.

87. *Revised Statutes of the Commonwealth of Massachusetts*, 494; Brewer, *By Birth or Consent*, 278–79.

88. *Revised Statutes of the Commonwealth of Massachusetts*, 477; Brewer, *By Birth or Consent*, 324.

89. Syrett, "'I Did.'"

90. Saillant, "'Some Thoughts'"; Melish, *Disowning Slavery*, 57–64; Sundue, *Industrious*.

91. Allen and Jones, "Narrative of the Proceedings," 41; Nash, *Forging Freedom*, 185–86.

92. W. Robinson, *Wheatley*, 43.

93. Holton, *Abigail Adams*, 294; L. Gordon, *Life of Mary Wollstonecraft*, 53–54.

94. Poovey, *Proper Lady*, 70; Sapiro, *Vindication*; and Taylor, *Wollstonecraft*.

95. L. Gordon, *Life of Mary Wollstonecraft*; Kelly, *Revolutionary Feminism*; Tomalin, *Life and Death*.

96. Taylor, "Religious Foundations"; Taylor, *Wollstonecraft*, 40–44, 103–8, 145–46, 205. On Price's theology, see Labboucheix, *Richard Price*; and Zebrowski, "Richard Price."

97. A. Richardson, "Mary Wollstonecraft"; Myers, "Reform or Ruin."

98. Wollstonecraft, *Thoughts on the Education*, 32; C. Field, "'Made Women.'"

99. Taylor, *Wollstonecraft*, 6, 31–38, 178–202; Braithwaite, *Romanticism*.

100. L. Hunt, *French Revolution*, 77–79.

101. Qtd. in L. Gordon, *Life of Mary Wollstonecraft*, 139.

102. Taylor, *Wollstonecraft*, 67–70, 145. On Price, see Spadåfora, *Idea of Progress*, 249; and Laboucheix, *Richard Price*, 128, 133, 136.

103. Popiel, *Rousseau's Daughters*, 144–47; McPhee, *French Revolution*, chap. 5.

104. Wollstonecraft, "Advertisement," in *VRW*, 70.

105. Wollstonecraft, *VRW*, 70, 74.

106. Ibid., 125, 116, 160, 264.

107. Ibid., 76, 138. She claimed not to "recollect his name." She may actually have had in mind a fictional character in a novel by Fanny Burney. In *Evelina*, the rake Lord Merton asks, "I don't know what the devil a woman lives for after thirty; she is only in other folks' way." See Wollstonecraft, *Vindication*, ed. Poston, 11n8. Wollstonecraft may have refused to make a specific reference precisely because she found this attitude typical of so many people, or she may have needed a straw man to make her argument about maturity more explicit.

108. Wollstonecraft, *VRW*, 66.

109. Ibid., 76.

110. Ibid.

111. Ibid., 125. Taylor, "Feminists versus Gallants"; Poovey, *Proper Lady*, 73.

112. Wollstonecraft, *VRW*, 73.

113. Rousseau, *Letters on the Elements of Botany*, qtd. in George, "Cultivation of the Female Mind," 220. See also Bewell, "'Jacobean Plants,'" 135–36; and Shteir, *Cultivating Women*.

114. Wollstonecraft, *VRW*, 73.

115. Schiebinger, *Nature's Body*, chap. 1; Bewell, "'Jacobean Plants'"; V. Jones, "Advice and Enlightenment," 150–52; Shteir, *Cultivating Women*, 25–27; George, "Cultivation of the Female Mind"; Spadafora, *Idea of Progress*, 171–73; Moran, "Between the Savage"; Sapiro, *Vindication*, 13, 27.

116. Wollstonecraft, *VRW*, 151, 142–43; Taylor, *Wollstonecraft*, especially 108–13; Poovey, *Proper Lady*, 72–73; Weiss, *Gendered Community*, chap. 3; Sapiro, *Vindication*, 185.

117. Wollstonecraft, *VRW*, 160, 173.

118. Ibid., 150 (emphasis in original).

119. Ibid., 164; Taylor, "Feminists versus Gallants," 126–27.

120. Wollstonecraft, *VRW*, 164, 76. See also O'Neill, "Shifting the Scottish Paradigm," 100; Taylor, "Feminists versus Gallants"; Bowles, "John Millar"; Olson, "Sex and Status"; Moran, "Between the Savage," 8–25; Sapiro, *Vindication*, 97.

121. C. Field, "Breast-Feeding," 25–44; Schiebinger, *Nature's Body*, chap. 2.

122. Wollstonecraft, *VRW*, 213.

123. Burke, *Philosophical Enquiry*, 105.

124. Wollstonecraft, *VRW*, 212–13.

125. Ibid., 138, 76.

126. Ibid., 95, 74. Taylor, "Religious Foundations," 110; Taylor, *Wollstonecraft*, 103–7; Spadafora, *Idea of Progress*, 247–52; Richey, "'A More Godlike Portion'"; D. Robinson, "Theodicy," 195–99; E. Hunt, "Family as Cave," 103–4. On changing ideas about the sexlessness of the soul, see Riley, *"Am I That Name?,"* chap. 2.

127. Wollstonecraft, *VRW*, 74. Wollstonecraft likely adopted this strategy from Catharine Macaulay; see Taylor, *Wollstonecraft*, 15, 49–51, 91–93, 87; and Titone, *Gender Equality*, 11. In an early review Wollstonecraft described Macaulay as a "masculine writer" but in the later *Vindication* described her achievements as "the matured fruit of profound thinking." Taylor, *Wollstonecraft*, 93; Sapiro, *Vindication*, 222; Wollstonecraft, *VRW*, 175. Where Adams disparaged Macaulay's marriage to a man twenty-six years younger, Wollstonecraft did not comment on this. Holton, *Abigail Adams*, 47–50, 232.

128. On this paradox, see Scott, *Only Paradoxes to Offer*; Riley, *"Am I That Name?"*; and Taylor, *Wollstonecraft*, 106–7.

129. Wollstonecraft, *VRW*, 170. Wollstonecraft wrote, "To subject a rational being to the mere will of another, after he is of age to answer to society for his own conduct, is a most cruel and undue stretch of power." *VRW*, 224. See also Sapiro, *Vindication*, 74.

130. Taylor, *Wollstonecraft*, 21; Poovey, *Proper Lady*, 65.

131. Wollstonecraft, *VRW*, 266; Taylor, *Wollstonecraft*, 110; Sapiro, *Vindication*, 53–55; Poovey, *Proper Lady*, 60–61; Spadafora, *Idea of Progress*, chap. 4.

132. Wollstonecraft, *VRW*, 114; O'Neill, "Shifting the Scottish Paradigm," 100; Taylor, "Feminists versus Gallants"; Sapiro, *Vindication*, 83–85, 177. See also Taylor, *Wollstonecraft*, 110, 145.

133. Wollstonecraft, *VRW*, 217–20; Sapiro, *Vindication*, chaps. 5 and 6; Taylor, *Wollstonecraft*, chap. 8

134. Wollstonecraft, *VRW*, 138. In 1790 Wollstonecraft worked on a translation of *Physiognomy*, by Johann Kaspar Lavater, who had been a friend of Fuseli's in Zurich. Sapiro, *Vindication*, 20–21, 69. Black women would not fare so well, as Lavater's reading of facial angles linked beauty and intelligence to typical European features. Sweet, *Bodies Politic*, 298–99.

135. Wollstonecraft, *VRW*, 239–40; Sapiro, *Vindication*, 237–49.

136. Wollstonecraft, *VRW*, 240.

137. Ibid., 241.

138. Ibid., 105.

139. Ibid., 96, 99, 199–200; Sapiro, *Vindication*, 141; Taylor, *Wollstonecraft*, 117–21; Poovey, *Proper Lady*, 74; Kaplan, "Wild Nights," 32.

140. Wollstonecraft, *VRW*, 213, 211; Taylor, *Wollstonecraft*, 219–21; Sapiro, *Vindication*, 74.

141. Wollstonecraft, *VRW*, 120; Taylor, *Wollstonecraft*, 221; Sapiro, *Vindication*, 178–79; E. Hunt, "Family as Cave."

142. Wollstonecraft, *VRW*, 217.

143. Ibid., 213. In her last unfinished novel, Wollstonecraft explored in depth both the way in which maid service distorted female development and how servitude could

be reconfigured so as to be mutually improving for both mistress and maid. Taylor, *Wollstonecraft*, chap. 9; Sapiro, *Vindication*, 100–108.

144. Focused on adult independence, Wollstonecraft paid little attention to the problem of old age decline and dependence. This is particularly striking given that her mentor Richard Price was an innovator of annuity-based life insurance and an early advocate for state support of the elderly. Laboucheix, *Richard Price*, 16–18

145. Wollstonecraft, *VRW*, 228; Sapiro, *Vindication*, 246.

146. Qtd. in Mintz, *Huck's Raft*, 54; Novak, *Rights of Youth*.

147. Zagarri, *Revolutionary Backlash*, 40–45; Kelley, "'Need of Their Genius,'" 21–22.

148. W. Robinson, *Critical Essays*, 36.

149. Shuffelton, "On Her Own Footing"; Carretta, introduction, xxiii–xxvii; W. Robinson, *Wheatley*, 53–60.

150. W. Robinson, *Critical Essays*, 47; L. Gordon, *Life of Mary Wollstonecraft*, 202–13. See also Furniss, "Mary Wollstonecraft's French Revolution."

151. O'Neill, "John Adams versus Mary Wollstonecraft," 462, 467, 469, 472; Holton, *Abigail Adams*, 302–7.

152. Elizabeth Smith Shaw to Abigail Adams, 29 December 1793, *Adams Papers*; Holton, *Abigail Adams*, 293–94, 307.

153. Holton, *Abigail Adams*; Bouton, *Taming Democracy*.

154. Zagarri, *Revolutionary Backlash*, chap. 2; Boydston, "Making Gender."

155. Thiebaux, "Mary Wollstonecraft"; Botting and Carey, "Wollstonecraft's Philosophical Impact"; Zagarri, *Revolutionary Backlash*, 40–45; Zagarri, "The Rights of Man."

156. For a discussion of how a shared printed culture sustained women's rights claims among rural farm women in the 1840s, see Ginzberg, *Untidy Origins*.

157. Wollstonecraft, *VRW*, 76.

158. Boydston, "Making Gender."

159. Keyssar, *Right to Vote*, chaps. 2–3; for the effect on women, see Zagarri, *Revolutionary Backlash*; and Boydston, "Making Gender."

CHAPTER 2

1. Chudacoff, *How Old?*, chaps. 1–2; Rotundo, *American Manhood*; Cole, *Journey of Life*, part 2; Kett, *Rites*, chaps. 1–4; Mintz, *Huck's Raft*, chaps. 4–5.

2. *Reports of the Proceedings . . . 1821* (hereafter cited as *NY 1821*), 235; Cogan, "Look Within"; Ryan, "Competency Within."

3. Keyssar, *Right to Vote*; Brewer, *By Birth or Consent*, 41–43.

4. Keyssar, *Right to Vote*, tables A2 and A4.

5. Furstenberg, "Beyond Freedom"; Watson, *Liberty and Power*; Roediger, *Wages of Whiteness*; Berthoff, "Conventional Mentality"; Stanley, *Bondage to Contract*.

6. Fraser and Gordon, "Genealogy"; *Journal of Debates . . . Massachusetts* (hereafter cited as *MA 1820*), 252; *NY 1821*, 251, 281.

7. I am arguing that age was essential to what Walter Johnson calls "slavery reduced to the simplicity of pure form: a person with a price." *Soul by Soul*, 144, 2, 5–7, 19,

45. Schwartz argues that slaves' valuation was determined more by size, skill, and, for women, beauty than by chronological age, but she also notes that slaves brought the highest prices between ages fifteen and twenty-five. Schwartz, *Born in Bondage*, chap. 6.

8. Chudacoff, *How Old?*, chaps. 1–2; Kett, *Rites*, chaps. 1–4; Mintz, *Huck's Raft*, chaps. 4–5.

9. Keyssar, *Right to Vote*, chaps. 2–3.

10. Ibid., 41–42; Pole, "Suffrage."

11. *MA 1820*, 246; Pole, "Suffrage," 575.

12. *MA 1820*, 252.

13. Ibid., 377–78; *Constitution . . . of Massachusetts-Bay . . . 1780*, 32.

14. Wellman, *Road to Seneca Falls*, chap. 6; P. Field, *Politics of Race*; Parkinson, "Antebellum State Constitution-Making"; Williamson, *American Suffrage*.

15. *NY 1821*, 235; Wellman, *Road to Seneca Falls*, 141; Casais, "New York State."

16. *NY 1821*, 274.

17. Ibid., 239, 197, 251, 281; Kann, *Republic of Men*, chap. 3.

18. *NY 1821*, 191; Wellman, *Road to Seneca Falls*, 139–44; P. Field, *Politics of Race*, 35–37.

19. *NY 1821*, 180; Wellman, *Road to Seneca Falls*, 141; P. Field, *Politics of Race*.

20. *NY 1821*, 661.

21. Ibid., 364.

22. Ibid., 359. Cultice argues that "the idea that a man who was old enough to fight was old enough to vote received serious debate in the New York Convention of 1821." *Youth's Battle*, 7. I have not found any evidence for this. The proposed amendment specified every voter must be a "male citizen of the age of twenty-one years," three years after males were old enough to fight. *NY 1821*, 202, 210–12, 214, 359–60.

23. *NY 1821*, 359–60.

24. Ibid., 252.

25. Ibid., 195.

26. Keyssar, *Right to Vote*, 61–63.

27. Klinghoffer and Elkis, "'Petticoat Electors,'" 191.

28. Miskolcze, *Women and Children*.

29. Keyssar, *Right to Vote*, 175; see, for example, *Report of the Debates . . . New York, 1846* (hereafter cited as *NY 1846*), 1027.

30. Grinspan, "Virgin Vote," chap. 3.

31. Bensel, *American Ballot Box*, 20, 22–24, 93–106.

32. Grinspan, "Virgin Vote."

33. Schmidt, "'Restless Movements,'" 328–38.

34. Rotundo, *American Manhood*.

35. Holt, *Rise and Fall*.

36. Varon, *We Mean to Be Counted*; Zaeske, *Signatures of Citizenship*.

37. Keyssar, *Right to Vote*, chaps. 2–3; Forten, "Series of Letters"; Horton and Horton, *Hope of Liberty*.

38. Bay, *White Image*, 22.

39. Hinks, introduction, xi–xliv; Hinks, *To Awaken*, 113–15; Horton and Horton, *Hope of Liberty*, 172–73; Bay, *White Image*, 32–37.

40. Walker, *Walker's Appeal*, 30; Bay, *White Image*, 41.

41. Walker, *Walker's Appeal*, 7.

42. Ibid., 2, 32; Horton and Horton, *Hope of Liberty*, 173.

43. Walker, *Walker's Appeal*, 28, 31.

44. Ibid., 7.

45. Furstenberg, "Beyond Freedom."

46. Walker, *Walker's Appeal*, 28.

47. Ibid., 12.

48. Ibid.

49. W. Stanton, *Leopard's Spots*; Bay, *White Image*, chap. 1.

50. Horton and Horton, *Hope of Liberty*, 174–76; M. Richardson, introduction, 3–9; M. Jones, *All Bound Up*, 23–26; Coleman, "Architects of a Vision," 27; Giddings, *When and Where*, 49–54; Yellin, *Women and Sisters*, 46–48; Peterson, *"Doers of the Word,"* chap. 3.

51. Walker, *Walker's Appeal*, 173.

52. Stewart, "Religion," 29.

53. Ibid., 29.

54. Ibid., 40, 31.

55. Ibid., 40.

56. Ibid., 29; M. Jones, *All Bound Up*, chap. 1; Coleman, "Architects of a Vision."

57. Stewart, "Lecture," 46, 48.

58. Ibid., 49.

59. Stewart, "Address," 59.

60. Ibid., 57.

61. Ibid., 60.

62. M. Jones, *All Bound Up*; Coleman, "Architects of a Vision"; Bogin and Yellin, introduction, 10–12; Yellin, *Women and Sisters*; Yee, *Black Women*; Jeffrey, *Great Silent Army*.

63. Purvis, "Appeal of Forty Thousand," 142.

64. Keyssar, *Right to Vote*, table A4.

65. M. Jones, *All Bound Up*, chap. 1.

66. Welter, "Cult of True Womanhood," 21–41; Lerner, "Lady and the Mill Girl," 15–30; Cott, *Bonds of Womanhood*; Kelley, *Private Woman*; Hewitt, *Women's Activism*; Stansell, *City of Women*; Blackmar, *Manhattan for Rent*; Boydston, *Home and Work*; G. Brown, *Domestic Individualism*; Kerber, "Separate Spheres"; Hewitt, "Taking the True Woman."

67. Beecher, "Essay on Slavery," 127.

68. Sklar, *Catharine Beecher*.

69. Beecher, "Suggestions," 42.

70. Beecher, "Essay on Slavery," 129.

71. Sarah Grimké briefly noted that woman should not be treated like "a spoiled child" and that God never set man up as her "guardian, or teacher." *Letters*, 102, 35. Lerner, *Grimké Sisters*; Botting and Carey, "Wollstonecraft's Philosophical Impact," 715.

72. Fuller, *Woman*, 176.

73. Capper, *Fuller*, 2:xiii–xiv, 38–39, 107–8.

74. Ibid., 1:30.

75. Fuller, *Woman*, 74; Wach, "Boston Vindication."

76. Fuller, *Woman*, 31.

77. Ibid., 33.

78. Ibid., 36.

79. Ibid., 121; DeLuzio, *Female Adolescence*, chap. 1.

80. Fuller, *Woman*, 170.

81. Ibid., 49–50.

82. Ibid., 172.

83. Ibid., 122–24.

84. Ibid., 36; Banner, *In Full Flower*, 242.

85. Fuller, *Woman*, 96–97.

86. Ibid., 99.

87. Ibid., 100.

88. Ibid., 165.

89. Mintz, *Huck's Raft*, chap. 4; Kincaid, *Erotic Innocence* and *Child-Loving*.

90. Fuller, *Woman*, 107.

91. Ibid., 137.

92. Ibid., 177. On Swedenborg's idea that angels advance toward youth, see Harper, "Youth in Heaven," in *Brighter Coming Day*, 87.

93. Fuller, *Woman*, 174; Capper, *Fuller*, 2:185.

94. Fuller, *Woman*, 174.

95. Ibid.

96. Capper, *Fuller*, 2:191–93.

97. Ibid., 34–39.

98. Stanton, "Solitude of Self," 248.

99. Capper, *Fuller*, 2:191–93.

100. Ibid.

101. Fuller, *New York Tribune*, 10 June 1845, qtd. in Chevigny, *Woman and the Myth*, 342.

102. McFeely, *Frederick Douglass*, 95.

103. W. Martin, *Mind of Frederick Douglass*; and McFeely, *Frederick Douglass*.

104. McFeely, *Frederick Douglass*, chaps. 1–7; W. Martin, *Mind of Frederick Douglass*, chap. 1; McDowell, "In the First Place."

105. W. Martin, *Mind of Frederick Douglass*, 3–25; McFeely, *Frederick Douglass*, chaps. 8–10.

106. Mintz, *Huck's Raft*, 76.

107. Douglass, *Narrative*, 13. Sojourner Truth, the only other slave to rise to prominence in the women's rights movement, also did not know the date of her birth. In contrast, she carefully recorded the date when she took the same Sojourner Truth, thus crafting a second birth on her own terms. Painter, *Sojourner Truth*, 5.

108. Douglass, *Narrative*, 213.

109. Dickson Preston's research reveals that Aaron Anthony kept a careful inventory of his slaves in which someone recorded the birth of Frederick Augustus in February 1818. In his autobiography, Douglass calculated his own birth as occurring in 1817.

Evidence suggests that late in Douglass's life, Anthony's great-granddaughter shared the evidence in her family's slave inventory that Douglass was born in 1818, but he did not publicly correct the mistaken impression that he was a year older. He continued to search for more evidence. Less than a year before he died, he wrote an Auld descendant asking for information that would allow him to determine his "exact age." Preston, *Young Frederick Douglass*, 31–34. Douglass may have retained the public impression of being a year older as this provided a dramatic narrative in which he reached freedom on the brink of manhood, defined as age twenty-one. Further, he may not have wanted to appear younger at a time when his advanced age was winning him praise as the "sage of Anacostia."

110. Douglass, *Narrative*, 34–35 (emphasis in original).

111. Blassingame, introduction, xxxix–xl.

112. Cole, *Journey of Life*, 121–27.

113. Douglass, *Narrative*, 49–50.

114. It is important to remember that Douglass wrote this passage in 1845 after seven years of freedom in the North. We will never know whether, while still enslaved, he was so acutely aware of metaphors describing manhood as a voyage. Douglass, *Narrative*, 50.

115. Schwartz, *Born in Bondage*, chap. 5.

116. Douglass, *Narrative*, 45.

117. Ibid., 50.

118. On Douglass's recruitment efforts during the war, see Blight, *Douglass's Civil War*; and chap. 5 in this volume.

119. Franchot, "Punishment"; Wallace, *Constructing the Black Masculine*, 87–88, 91–94.

120. Gibson, "Christianity and Individualism."

121. Douglass, *Narrative*, 60.

122. Ibid., 61–66; Douglass, "Slavery and the Slave Power," in *Frederick Douglass Papers* (hereafter cited as *FDP*), 2:253; see also in the same work Douglass, "A Call for the British Nation to Testify Against Slavery," 28 August 1846, 1:362; Douglass, "American Slavery . . . and the Free Church of Scotland," 22 May 1846, 1:270; and Douglass, "*Cambria* Riot," 1:86.

123. Douglass, "American Prejudice Against Color," 23 October 1845, ibid., 1:66. Interestingly, Douglass remembered the quote slightly inaccurately when he mentioned it in another speech, recalling that the paper had called him "an excellent specimen of the Negro." Though this appears age-neutral, Douglass compared it to an advertisement for Negroes "in prime condition," a phrase that suggests vigorous adulthood. See Douglass, "Slavery Corrupts American Society and Religion," 17 October 1845, ibid., 1:50. The reporter had in fact called Douglass "young." *Cork Constitution* (Ireland), 16 October 1845, qtd. in ibid., 1:50n10. On Douglass and British reform networks, see Rice and Crawford, *Liberating Sojourn*.

124. See Douglass, "Slavery Corrupts," *FDP*, 1:50 (emphasis in original).

125. Douglass, "Farewell to the British People," ibid., 2:21, 24; Douglass, "Slavery and the American Churches," 2 September 1846, ibid., 1:387.

126. Douglass, *Narrative*, 14.

127. Douglass, "Horrors of Slavery," *FDP*, 1:372.

128. See, for example, the *Waterford Freeman* (Ireland), 10 September 1845, qtd. in ibid., 1:77n1.

129. Douglass, "International Moral Force," ibid., 1:183–84.

130. Douglass, preface to the second Dublin edition of *Narrative of the Life of Frederick Douglass*, reprinted in *Narrative*, 153.

131. W. Martin, *Mind of Frederick Douglass*, chap. 6; Douglass, *Douglass on Women's Rights*.

CHAPTER 3

1. Wellman, "Seneca Falls"; Wellman, *Road to Seneca Falls*; Ginzberg, *Elizabeth Cady Stanton*, 52–70; Hoffert, *When Hens Crow*; DuBois, *Feminism and Suffrage*, 23–24, 40–47; Flexner, *Century of Struggle*, chap. 5; Isenberg, *Sex and Citizenship*, 1–6.

2. Sklar, *Women's Rights*, 34; Jeffrey, *Great Silent Army*, 94–95; Wellman, "Women's Rights."

3. Isenberg, *Sex and Citizenship*; Leach, *True Love*, chaps. 1–3. Isolated individuals, including Stanton's cousin Gerrit Smith at the Liberty Party convention in June 1848, had already proposed extending suffrage to all adults. Wellman, *Road to Seneca Falls*, 177; Isenberg, *Sex and Citizenship*, 19–20.

4. *Proceedings of the Woman's Rights Convention . . . 1850* (hereafter cited as *WRC 1850*), 32.

5. *Proceedings of the National Women's Rights Convention . . . 1853* (hereafter cited as *WRC 1853*), 110; Stanley, *Bondage to Contract*.

6. Grossberg, *Governing the Hearth*, 105–8; Syrett, "'I Did,'" 314–31.

7. Chudacoff, *How Old?*, chap. 2; DeLuzio, *Female Adolescence*, chap. 1; Mintz, *Huck's Raft*, chap. 4.

8. See, for example, *Proceedings of the Woman's Rights Convention . . . 1852* (hereafter cited as *WRC 1852*), 26.

9. I culled biographical information on participants from a variety of standard reference sources. See, for example, James, James, and Boyer, *Notable American Women*; Wilson and Fiske, *Appletons' Cyclopedia of American Biography*; and Willard and Livermore, *Woman of the Century*. Judith Wellman found that signers of the 1848 Seneca Falls "Declaration of Sentiments" ranged in age from 14 to 68, with a mean age of 38.7 years. "Seneca Falls," 15–17.

10. Painter, *Sojourner Truth*, chaps. 14 and 18; M. Jones, *All Bound Up*; Gordon, introduction; Coleman, "Architects of a Vision."

11. On black participants in antebellum women's rights conventions, see M. Jones, *All Bound Up*, chaps. 2–3; Terborg-Penn, *African American Women*, chap. 2; and W. Martin, *Mind of Frederick Douglass*, chap. 6. Though few female factory workers participated in women's rights conventions, they espoused women's rights ideas in the 1840s; see Murphy, *Ten Hours' Labor*, chap. 8. Suffragists first made a concerted appeal to working-class women in the late 1860s; DuBois, *Feminism and Suffrage*, chap. 5.

12. Hoffert, *When Hens Crow*; DuBois, *Feminism and Suffrage*, 47–52.

13. Berthoff, "Conventional Mentality"; Rotundo, *American Manhood*.

14. Wellman, *Road to Seneca Falls*, chap. 6; Doress-Worters, *Mistress of Herself*, 11; Banner, *Elizabeth Cady Stanton*, 27–29; Ginzberg, *Elizabeth Cady Stanton*, 47.

15. Wellman, *Road to Seneca Falls*, 148–50; Wellman, "Women's Rights."

16. *NY 1846*, 272.

17. Ibid., 1027, 1018; see Wellman, *Road to Seneca Falls*, 150–51.

18. *NY 1846*, 540; Ginzberg, *Untidy Origins*; P. Field, *Politics of Race*, 62.

19. DuBois, *Stanton–Anthony Reader*, 32.

20. *NY 1821*, 16, 86, 173, 687–90.

21. *NY 1846*, 3–6, 193–94, 235–38, 249–50, 265.

22. Ibid., 246.

23. Ibid., 190. For a strikingly similar debate in a western state, see *Report of the Debates . . . Ohio, 1850–51*, 217–18, 226–28, 302–6.

24. *NY 1846*, 187.

25. Ibid., 182, 277, 210. Although less defined by precise chronological boundaries than it would later become, middle age was regarded as a distinct phase of life by participants in antebellum constitutional and women's rights conventions. This finding challenges the idea that middle age was an invention of the late nineteenth or twentieth century. See Neugarten and Datan, "Middle Years," 137–40; and Cohen, *In Our Prime*.

26. *NY 1846*, 179, 187, 190–98, 204, 247.

27. Ibid., 214 (quotation), 210, 275. On old age, see Fischer, *Growing Old*; and Achenbaum, *Old Age*.

28. *NY 1846*, 206.

29. Ibid., 192.

30. Ibid., 1057–58; Wellman, *Road to Seneca Falls*, 149; Basch, *In the Eyes*, chap. 5; Berthoff, "Conventional Mentality," 773–74.

31. Wellman, *Road to Seneca Falls*; Ginzberg, *Elizabeth Cady Stanton*; *NY 1846*, 272.

32. *Woman's Rights Conventions, Seneca Falls and Rochester* (hereafter cited as *WRC 1848*), 3.

33. Wellman, "Seneca Falls."

34. *WRC 1848*, 5–8; Wellman, *Road to Seneca Falls*, 192; Hoffert, *When Hens Crow*, chap. 5.

35. *WRC 1848*, 6–7.

36. *WRC 1852*, 26. See also *WRC 1853*, 69.

37. Chudacoff, *How Old?*, 36–37.

38. Ibid., chap. 2; DeLuzio, *Female Adolescence*, chap. 1; Blackwell, *Laws of Life*.

39. *WRC 1852*, 59–60; *WRC 1853*, 49–53; *WRC 1851*, 88–89; *Proceedings of the Ninth National Woman's Rights Convention . . . 1859*, 7.

40. *HWS*, 1:73.

41. *Report of the Proceedings of the Colored National Convention . . . 1848*, reprinted in *Minutes of the Proceedings of the National Negro Conventions*, 12, 17; M. Jones, *All Bound Up*, 59–60.

42. Sterling, *Ahead of Her Time*, 273–75; Diedrich, *Love across the Color Lines*, 182–83; "Frederick Douglass," *National Anti-Slavery Standard*, 24 September 1853.

43. *WRC 1853*, 109–10.

44. Sterling, *Ahead of Her Time.*

45. Bay, *White Image*, 56–63.

46. M. Jones, *All Bound Up*, chaps. 2–3; Terborg-Penn, *African American Women*, chap. 2; Painter, *Sojourner Truth.*

47. Swisshelm, "The Worcester Convention"; Painter, *Sojourner Truth*, chap. 14; M. Jones, *All Bound Up*, 91–93.

48. Hoffert, *Jane Grey Swisshelm.*

49. Swisshelm, "Woman's Rights."

50. Ibid.

51. Pillsbury, "Women's Rights Convention."

52. Douglass, "Too Much Religion, Too Little Humanity," 9 May 1849, *FDP*, 2:192; see also Douglass, "Colonization Revival," 31 May 1849, ibid., 2:206.

53. Henry Clay to Richard Pindell, 17 February 1849, in Clay, *Works of Henry Clay*, 3:346–52; Eaton, *Henry Clay*, 120–36; A. Martin, "Anti-Slavery Movement," 124–37.

54. Clay, *Works of Henry Clay*, 3:348.

55. A. Martin, "Anti-Slavery Movement," 127–29.

56. Douglass mistakenly thought that Clay granted masters the right to sell slaves during the first twenty-five years of their life. In fact, Clay's rather convoluted proposal allowed masters the right to sell slaves only until "the commencement of the system" in either 1855 or 1860. Clay, *Works of Henry Clay*, 3:348–49, 351.

57. Douglass, "Too Much Religion, Too Little Humanity," 192; see also Douglass, "Colonization Revival," 206.

58. Painter, *Sojourner Truth*, chaps. 1–2.

59. Ibid., chap. 3.

60. Ibid., chap. 5; White, *Somewhat More Independent*, chap. 2.

61. Painter, *Sojourner Truth*, chap. 12.

62. Ibid., 13.

63. Truth, *Narrative*, 18–19.

64. Melish, *Disowning Slavery*, 240–41.

65. Jacobs, *Incidents*, 191.

66. M. Jones, *All Bound Up*, chap. 3; Dudden, *Fighting Chance*, 18.

67. Douglass, "What to the Slave Is the Fourth of July?," 5 July 1852, *FDP*, 2:360–61. On the importance of this speech, see E. Foner, *Story of American Freedom*, 87–94.

68. Douglass, "What to the Slave Is the Fourth of July?," 371.

69. Ibid., 369.

70. Ibid., 373.

71. Ibid., 375.

72. Ibid., 360.

73. W. Martin, *Mind of Frederick Douglass*, chap. 9; Blight, *Douglass's Civil War*, chaps. 1 and 5; Rael, "A Common Nature."

74. Douglass, "What to the Slave Is the Fourth of July?," 383.

75. Douglass, "The Anti-Slavery Movement," 19 March 1855, *FDP*, 3:39–40.

76. Grossberg, *Governing the Hearth*, 105–8.

77. Ibid.; Leach, *True Love*, chap. 3. Anthony, "Address by SBA on Educating the Sexes Together," 2 February 1857, *SPSA*, 1:334–38.

78. E. Smith, "Woman and Her Needs"; Wyman, *Selections*, 43–45.

79. Stanton, "Address by ECS to the Legislature of New York," *SPSA*, 1:245–46; see also speech of Henry Blackwell, *WRC 1853*, 51.

80. Syrett, "'I Did.'"

81. Grossberg, *Governing the Hearth*, 105–8. New York briefly raised the age of consent to seventeen for males and fourteen for females but then reverted to the common-law standard again in 1830. See *SPSA*, 1:257n11.

82. Blackwell, *Laws of Life*, 113; Kett, *Rites*, 133–37; Deluzia, *Female Adolescence*, chap. 1.

83. Blackwell, *Laws of Life*, 48.

84. Ibid., 33.

85. Ibid., 135, 71. Blackwell acknowledged variation in the completion of physical growth—"Each human body . . . may reach its maturity at different ages, 15, 20, 25, no matter"—yet still recommended postponing marriage until the midtwenties. Ibid., 39.

86. Ibid., 136.

87. Ibid., 141.

88. *WRC 1851*, 88, 89; see also *WRC 1852*, 59.

89. Stanton, "Our Young Girls."

90. *WRC 1848*, 7; *WRC 1850*, 34, 46.

91. Stanton, "Our Young Girls."

92. Older activists alternately referred to the rising generation of women as daughters and younger sisters. *WRC 1851*, 100; *WRC 1853*, 103, 188.

93. *WRC 1848*, 6.

94. Activists did identify a clear generational difference between women who were adults at the time of the American Revolution and those who were of full age in the 1840s and 1850s. See *WRC 1850*, 29; and *WRC 1853*, 65–66.

95. *WRC 1852*, 18.

96. Ibid., 36, 48.

97. Elizabeth Cady Stanton to Susan B. Anthony, 10 February 1856, qtd. in Griffith, *In Her Own Right*, 89.

98. Elizabeth Cady Stanton to Susan B. Anthony, [20 August 1857?], *SPSA*, 1:351–52.

99. Jabour, *Scarlett's Sisters*; Yellin, *Harriet Jacobs*.

100. Sanchez-Eppler, *Touching Liberty*, chap. 3; King, *Stolen Childhood*, 109–10. As both Douglass and Jacobs hint in their narratives, enslaved boys were also vulnerable to rape by white men; Wallace, *Constructing the Black Masculine*, 88–90.

101. DeLuzio, *Female Adolescence*, chap. 1; Kincaid, *Child-Loving*; Zelizer, *Pricing the Priceless Child*.

102. Jacobs, *Incidents*, 27. For a discussion of the historical timing of menarche, see Brumberg, *Body Project*, chaps. 1 and 2.

103. Jacobs, *Incidents*, 51.

104. Ibid., 27.

105. Ibid., 51.

106. Ibid., 28.

107. Jabour, *Scarlett's Sisters*, chap. 7.

108. In 1826, Child began editing the *Juvenile Miscellany*, one of the earliest and most popular magazines aimed at American children. Mintz, *Huck's Raft*, 92–93; Karcher, *First Woman*, chaps. 3 and 7; Sanchez-Eppler, *Dependent States*, chap. 1.

CHAPTER 4

1. Sigourney, *Past Meridian*; Cole, *Journey of Life*, 145–51; Haight, *Mrs. Sigourney*; Karcher, *First Woman*, 728; Premo, *Winter Friends*, 93–97.

2. I am focusing here on ideas about younger and older women, ideas held by women who were themselves various ages. This approach differs from those who emphasize the divergent goals and leadership styles of younger and older women, including Rupp, "Is Feminism the Province?"; and Stansell, *Feminist Promise*.

3. Leach, *True Love*. Stanton provided a powerful restatement of this argument in her well-known 1892 speech "Solitude of Self."

4. I am arguing that antebellum women's rights activists recognized middle age as a distinct phase of life, a finding that differs from sociologists who see middle age as an invention of the twentieth century (see Neugarten and Datan, "Middle Years," 137–40, and Cohen, who dates the "invention" of middle age to the late nineteenth century [*In Our Prime*]).

5. Graebner, "Age and Retirement"; Achenbaum, "Delineating Old Age."

6. Cole, *Journey of Life*, part 2.

7. Bensel, *American Ballot Box*, 107–13.

8. In 1814, Congress raised the recruitment age to fifty. *Military Laws of the United States*, 42, 135, 178.

9. Graebner, *History of Retirement*, 10.

10. Cole, *Journey of Life*, part 2; Haber and Gratton, *Old Age*, 144–50; Achenbaum, *Old Age*; Haber, *Beyond Sixty-Five*, chap. 1. Fischer emphasizes a more negative view of old age in *Growing Old*.

11. Cole, *Journey of Life*, chap. 1.

12. Le Beau, *Currier and Ives*, 188–89.

13. Cole, *Journey of Life*, 118–19; Ariès, *Centuries*, 24; Sears, *Ages of Man*, 153; Day, "Representing Aging," 708–13.

14. The same imagery and text were used in a set of 1850 prints by Currier and Ives. Perry, *Young America*, 41–43.

15. Le Beau, *Currier and Ives*, 195–97.

16. *WRC 1852*, 60–61.

17. Ceniza, *Walt Whitman*, chap. 3; Tyler, "Paulina Kellogg Wright Davis"; Wellman, *Road to Seneca Falls*, 148. On true womanhood, see Welter, "Cult of True Womanhood," 21–41.

18. *WRC 1852*, 60–61.

19. Ibid.

20. Abbot, introduction, 2; Cole, *Journey of Life*, 120–21; Wallach, "Voyage of Life"; Kasson, "Voyage of Life."

21. Cole's written description is qtd. in Parry, *Art of Thomas Cole*, figs. 190, 205, 210; pl. 15.

22. Ibid., 227.

23. Kasson, "Voyage of Life," 45–46.

24. Cole, *Journey of Life*, chap. 4; Kett, *Rites*, chap. 3; P. Johnson, *Shopkeeper's Millennium*; Ryan, *Cradle*; A. Douglass, *Feminization*.

25. Qtd. in Parry, *Art of Thomas Cole*, fig. 205.

26. On patriarchs as models of longevity, see Cole, *Journey of Life*, 100–102. On Ham, see Jordan, *White over Black*, 17–20; and Haynes, *Noah's Curse*.

27. In his written description, Cole was careful not to identify the gender of this "Angelic Form," but the flowing hair and rounded form evoke femininity. Parry, *Art of Thomas Cole*, figs. 190, 205, 210; pl. 15.

28. Kerber, *Women of the Republic*.

29. Cole qtd. in Parry, *Art of Thomas Cole*, fig. 190, pl. 15; Ryan, *Empire of the Mother*.

30. *WRC 1852*, 61.

31. Nautical imagery permeated American literature and sermons at a time when boats were still a major means of transportation. Cole, *Journey of Life*, 118–24. Stanton began her comparison of a woman's life to a "ship wreck" by noting the strong emotions she felt when reading of an actual shipwreck in the morning paper. Stanton, "Fashionable Women Shipwreck," 1–3. The contrasting images of shipwreck and safe harbor date back to the classical period. See Eyben, "Roman Notes," 217.

32. Stanton, "Fashionable Women Shipwreck," 1–3.

33. Ibid., 4, 10.

34. Her most famous statement of this principle was her 1892 speech "The Solitude of Self," reprinted in DuBois, *Stanton–Anthony Reader*, 247–54.

35. Late romantics like Cole, Poe, Hawthorne, and Melville all wrote about coming of age through disillusionment. Kasson, "Voyage of Life."

36. In 1849, James Smillie made an engraving of *Youth* that was offered as a premium by the American Art-Union; 16,000 copies were distributed. Parry, *Art of Thomas Cole*, 364; Kasson, "Voyage of Life," 54. For example, Jared Bell Waterbury, an author of popular advice books, argued that Cole's dark picture of manhood was a "just reflection" but that sometimes manhood brought "an uninterrupted flow of prosperity." Waterbury, *Voyage of Life*, 70.

37. *WRC 1851*, 29.

38. *NY 1821*, 235, 274. Delegates also used nautical imagery to compare democratic government to a ship that they must safely captain. See ibid., 220, 281, 284, 286.

39. *WRC 1851*, 29.

40. *WRC 1850*, 11.

41. *WRC 1851*, 53; *WRC 1850*, 46; *WRC 1852*, 31; *WRC 1853*, 8, 11–12, 49–52, 91.

42. *WRC 1850*, 27–28; see also Price qtd. in *WRC 1851*, 19–20; and Ceniza, *Walt Whitman*, 63–66.

43. Ceniza, *Walt Whitman*, chap. 2; *WRC 1850*, 20–36.

44. *WRC 1853*, 23–24. See also *WRC 1848*, 6.

45. *WRC 1851*, 20. See also *WRC 1853*, 105–6.

46. *WRC 1850*, 23; Ceniza, *Walt Whitman*, 63–66.

47. *WRC 1850*, 46. See also *WRC 1851*, 9, 53.

48. Qtd. in *WRC 1853*, 53–54; Leach, *True Love*.

49. Kerr, *Lucy Stone*.

50. Doress-Worters, *Mistress of Herself*; Kolmerten, *American Life*.

51. Siegel, "Home as Work," 1073–1217, esp. 1086–91; Basch, *In the Eyes*.

52. *WRC 1851*, 40. See also *WRC 1851*, 37; and *WRC 1850*, 28.

53. *NY 1846*, 1057.

54. *WRC 1853*, 44. See also *WRC 1853*, 10, 59, 108; *WRC 1851*, 56, 67–68; and *WRC 1852*, 23.

55. *WRC 1851*, 30.

56. Eickhoff, *Revolutionary Heart*; Blackwell and Oertel, *Frontier Feminist*.

57. *WRC 1851*, 68.

58. Siegel, "Home as Work," 1120, 1086–91.

59. *WRC 1853*, 59.

60. *WRC 1850*, 11; *WRC 1851*, 15; *WRC 1852*, 38–40.

61. *WRC 1850*, 33.

62. *WRC 1853*, 51.

63. *WRC 1850*, 22.

64. *WRC 1852*, 27.

65. Stanton qtd. in Stanton and Blatch, *Elizabeth Cady Stanton*, 19–20.

66. *WRC 1850*, 53.

67. *WRC 1851*, 67–68; *WRC 1853*, 82–83.

68. *WRC 1853*, 49.

69. Ryan, "Competency Within."

70. Fee, "Sexual Politics," 86–102; Eller, *Myth*.

71. *WRC 1850*, 33.

72. *WRC 1852*, 19.

73. Russett, *Sexual Science*, 27; Gould, *Mismeasure*, 62; Fraser and Gordon, "Genealogy."

74. W. Stanton, *Leopard's Spots*; Fredrickson, *Black Image*, chaps. 2–3; Gould, *Mismeasure*, chap. 2; Bay, *White Image*, chap. 2; Carson, *Measure of Merit*, chap. 3.

75. [Agassiz], "Diversity," 145.

76. Ibid., 142–43.

77. Gould, *Mismeasure*, 50–69; W. Stanton, *Leopard's Spots*, 33.

78. For a particularly lucid analysis of these developmental metaphors, see W. Martin, *Mind of Frederick Douglass*, chap. 9.

79. Combe qtd. in W. Stanton, *Leopard's Spots*, 36. For Combe's view of individual development, see Combe, *Constitution of Man*; for his influence on Stanton and Mott, see *SPSA*, 1:23, and *FDP*, 2:510.

80. Bay, *White Image*, 43.

81. Qtd. in Gould, *Mismeasure*, 70; W. Stanton, *Leopard's Spots*, 63.

82. Fitzhugh, *Sociology for the South*, 83, qtd. in Sklansky, *Soul's Economy*, 101; Fredrickson, *Black Image*, 84–86. Fredrickson aptly identifies the "the perennial racist dichotomy between the Negro as child and the Negro as beast," 285.

83. Stowe, *Uncle Tom's Cabin*, 235, 192; Frederickson, *Black Image*, 111.

84. Stowe explained, "What God asks of the soul more than anything else is faith and simplicity, the affection and reliance of the little child." Stowe, *Key*, 25; Frederickson, *Black Image*, 111.

85. Stowe, *Uncle Tom's Cabin*, 580; Frederickson, *Black Image*, 115.

86. On black intellectuals' engagement with racial science, see Bay, *White Image*.

87. Douglass, "Claims of the Negro," *FDP*, 2:500.

88. Ibid., 525.

89. Bay, *White Image*.

90. Douglass, "Claims of the Negro," 507.

91. Bay, *White Image*, 69–71; Rael, "Common Nature," 194–95.

92. Douglass, "Claims of the Negro," 514, 511–12.

93. W. Martin, *Mind of Frederick Douglass*, chap. 9.

94. Douglass, "Trials and Triumphs of Self-Made Men," 4 January 1860, *FDP*, 3:289.

95. Blassingame, editor's introduction to Douglass, "Claims of the Negro," 497.

96. Douglass, "Trials and Triumphs," 291.

97. Ibid., 300.

98. McDowell, "In the First Place"; Blight, *Douglass's Civil War*, 20; Stauffer, *Black Hearts*, 228–34; Franchot, "Punishment," 149; Diedrich, *Love across the Color Lines*.

99. Douglass, "The Property Rights of Women," 1 December 1853, *FDP*, 2:451.

100. Painter, *Sojourner Truth*, chaps. 14, 18. The Akron speech is quoted on pp. 125–26.

101. Painter points out that Truth's metaphor was "virtually craniometric." *Sojourner Truth*, 127.

102. Qtd. in ibid., 126.

103. Ibid.

104. Ibid.

105. Qtd. in *HWS*, 1:568; Terborg-Penn, *African American Women*, 16.

106. Qtd. in Painter, *Sojourner Truth*, 139. Painter aptly notes that "Truth's counterattack turned on the tensions between infancy and adulthood, black motherhood and white motherhood, and the Madonna-whore imagery of the bare female breast" and that she "infantilized" and "unmanned" the hecklers. *Sojourner Truth*, 139–40.

107. Boyd, *Discarded Legacy*, 37–38, 60; Foster, introduction, 5–8; Foster, "Frances Ellen Watkins Harper."

108. Boyd, *Discarded Legacy*, 37–38; Foster, introduction.

109. Boyd, *Discarded Legacy*, 38; Foster, introduction, 9–10.

110. Boyd, *Discarded Legacy*, 42–51, 57–59; Foster, introduction, 11–18; Harper, *Complete Poems*.

111. Harper, "Colored People," in *Brighter Coming Day*, 99–100.

112. Harper, "Christianity," in *Brighter Coming Day*, 96–98. First published in *Christian Recorder* in 1853. Reprinted in *Provincial Freeman* and *Frederick Douglass's Paper*. Included in 1854 edition of *Poems on Miscellaneous Subjects*.

113. Harper, "Christianity," 98.

114. Ibid., 97–98. In the 1871 poem "Youth in Heaven," Harper explored Swedenborg's comment that angels in heaven advance toward youth, in *Brighter Coming Day*, 172.

115. Harper, "The Dying Christian," in *Brighter Coming Day*, 66–67. Along with theologians like Horace Bushnell, Harper suggested that infants were particularly—if unconsciously—susceptible to religious impressions. See "To a Babe Smiling in Her Sleep," in ibid., 187–88. On Bushnell, see Sklansky, *Soul's Economy*, 48.

116. Bouwsma, "Christian Adulthood."

117. *HWS*, 1:568; Brewer, *By Birth or Consent*; Mintz, *Huck's Raft*; Bunge, *Child in the Bible* and *Child in Christian Thought*.

118. On the participation of black children in political meetings during Reconstruction, see E. Brown, "Negotiating and Transforming."

119. M. N. Mitchell, *Raising Freedom's Child*; Riggs, "African American Children," 365–85; Mitchell, *Righteous Propagation*.

120. Harper, "Our Greatest Want."

121. Ibid., 160.

122. Harper, "I Am Able to Give Something," in *Brighter Coming Day*, 52.

123. Harper, "I Have a Right to Do My Share," in ibid., 47.

124. Boyd, *Discarded Legacy*. See also Harper's 1886 allegory "Shalmanezer, Prince of Cosman," in *Brighter Coming Day*, 295–98.

125. Harper, "Bible Defense of Slavery," in *Brighter Coming Day*, 60.

126. Harper, "Two Offers."

127. Ibid., 289.

128. Ibid. On women's rights activists' relationship to romanticism, see Leach, *True Love*.

129. Harper, "Two Offers," 289.

130. Ibid., 290.

131. Ibid.

132. Ibid., 311.

133. Ibid., 291.

134. Ibid.

135. Ibid., 313.

136. Ibid.

CHAPTER 5

1. E. Foner, *Short History*, 114–17.

2. Dudden, *Fighting Chance*.

3. See, for example, Douglass, "What the Black Man Wants," 26 January 1865, *FDP*, 4:63–66; *HWS*, 2:382–83.

4. Stanton to the editor of the *National Anti-Slavery Standard*, 26 December 1865, and Stanton and Anthony, "Appeal," *SPSA*, 1:564, 566.

5. Stanton, "Manhood Suffrage," *Revolution*, 24 December 1868; *SPSA*, 2:194–98; Stanton, *Revolution*, 8 January 1868; Mitchell, "'Lower Orders,'" 111–27.

6. Bouwsma, "Christian Adulthood."

7. Harper, "Great Problem," in *Brighter Coming Day*, 219–22.

8. Douglass, "Hope and Despair in These Cowardly Times," 28 April 1861, *FDP*, 3:427; Douglass, "Revolutions Never Go Backward," 5 May 1861, ibid., 3:435.

9. Blight, *Douglass's Civil War*, chap. 7; McFeely, *Frederick Douglass*, 212–13; Berlin, Reidy, and Rowland, *Freedom's Soldiers*, 7.

10. See, for example, Douglass, "Revolutions Never Go Backward," 435; McFeely, *Frederick Douglass*, 212–13.

11. Douglass, "Fighting the Rebels with One Hand," 14 January 1862, *FDP*, 3:483; Blight, *Douglass's Civil War*, 99.

12. Douglass, "William the Silent," 8 February 1869, *FDP*, 4:192.

13. Douglass, "Proclamation," 6 February 1863, ibid., 3:559; Stauffer, *Black Hearts*, 224–25.

14. Douglass, "Slaveholder's Rebellion," 4 July 1862, *FDP*, 3:522.

15. Walker, *Walker's Appeal*, 28.

16. McFeely, *Frederick Douglass*, 214–15, 223; McPherson, *Struggle for Equality*, 202–7; Blight, *Douglass's Civil War*, 157; Berlin, Reidy, and Rowland, *Freedom's Soldiers*, 11–12.

17. Douglass, "Let the Negro Alone," 11 May 1869, *FDP*, 4:212; Douglass, "There Was a Right Side in the Late War," 30 May 1878, ibid., 4:483. In 1861 the Union army allowed seventeen-year-olds to enlist with parental consent. In 1862 Lincoln barred the enlistment of boys under eighteen. As during the Revolutionary War, recruiting agents were complicit in enabling younger boys to lie about their ages in order to enlist. Approximately 5 percent of Union soldiers were under eighteen. Mintz, *Huck's Raft*, 120–21.

18. Douglass, "Proclamation," 564.

19. Berlin, Reidy, and Rowland, *Freedom's Soldiers*, 32, 28–30.

20. McPherson, *Struggle for Equality*, 212–17; Blight, *Douglass's Civil War*, 161–69.

21. Douglass, "Proclamation," 565.

22. Douglass, "Negroes and the National War Effort," *FDP*, 3:597.

23. Douglass, "What the Black Man Wants," 63, 66.

24. Ibid., 66.

25. See for example, Douglass, "Emancipation, Racism, and the Work before Us," 4 December 1863, *FDP*, 3:604.

26. Stanton to Caroline Healey Dall, 7 May 1864, *SPSA*, 1:520. See also ibid., 1:507, 525.

27. Anthony to Wendell Phillips, 29 April 1861, ibid., 1:464–65.

28. *SPSA*, 1:480, 487–98; Dudden, *Fighting Chance*, chap. 2; Silber, *Daughters of the Union*, 153–56; Ginzberg, *Elizabeth Cady Stanton*, 108–15.

29. *HWS*, 2:67.

30. *SPSA*, 2:498.

31. Ginzberg, *Elizabeth Cady Stanton*, 108.

32. Stanton, Anthony, and Gage compared women in the league to soldiers on the battlefield. *HWS*, 2:79–80, 89.

33. Surgeon General's Office, Circular No. 8, 14 July 1862, National Archives.

34. Massey, *Bonnet Brigades*, 46.

35. Bucklin qtd. in Leonard, *Yankee Women*, 17.

36. Leonard, *Yankee Women*, 18–22; Silber, *Daughters of the Union*, 213.

37. Silber, *Daughters of the Union*, 203–21; Fahs, introduction, 37.

38. *HWS*, 2:13.

39. Gordon, "Stanton on the Right to Vote," 114–15.

40. *SPSA*, 1:566. Stanton and Anthony were also upset because Wendell Phillips took funds that could have been used for woman suffrage and directed them toward black manhood suffrage. Dudden, *Fighting Chance*, chap. 3.

41. M. Mitchell, "'Lower Orders,'" 128–35.

42. *SPSA*, 1:564.

43. Ibid.

44. Stanton to Gerrit Smith, 1 January 1866, ibid., 1:569.

45. *Proceedings of the . . . Women's Rights Convention . . . 1866* (hereafter cited as *WRC 1866*), 45–48.

46. Ibid., 45; Boyd, *Discarded Legacy*, 51–54; Foster, introduction, 18.

47. *WRC 1866*, 46.

48. Ibid., 7, 11.

49. Ibid., 46.

50. Ibid., 46–47.

51. Ibid., 48.

52. Stanton and Anthony, "Appeal," *SPSA*, 1:566.

53. Boyd, *Discarded Legacy*, 119–20.

54. Harper, "A Private Meeting with Women," [29 March 1870?], in *Brighter Coming Day*, 127.

55. Other African Americans prominent in the AERA were Harriet Purvis, Sarah Remond, and Sojourner Truth. Terborg-Penn, *African American Women*, 24–26.

56. *WRC 1866*, 49. On the importance of this campaign as a high point of cooperation across race and gender lines, see Dudden, *Fighting Chance*, chap. 4.

57. Quigley, *Second Founding*, chap. 4.

58. *New York Tribune*, 28 June 1867, 5. See also *SPSA*, 2:75–77; and Dudden, *Fighting Chance*, 100–103.

59. Greeley's committee report advocated enfranchising black men but not women or "boys above the age of eighteen years." *Documents of the Convention of the State of New York, 1867-68*. Delegates repeatedly invoked the disenfranchisement of women and children to prove that voting was not a natural right but a privilege. *Proceedings . . . of the Constitutional Convention of the State of New York . . . 1867 and 1868* (hereafter cited as *NY 1867*), 200, 213, 237, 243, 245, 260, 336–39, 347, 427, 432. See also Keyssar, *Right to Vote*, 44.

60. Cultice argues that there was real support for enfranchising teen militiamen in antebellum New York, but his conclusions are marred by a tendency to misinterpret the broader context of debate. *Youth's Battle*, 7.

61. *NY 1867*, 101, 102, 489–91, 541. On Bickford, see Haddock, *Growth of a Century*, 314–15. On Robertson, see Jones and Spencer, *Reports of Cases Argued . . . Superior Court of the City of New York*, vol. 61, xxvii–xxviii; and "A New Political Club," *New York Times*, 13 November 1865.

62. For the debate over woman suffrage, see *NY 1867*, 207, 215, 364–76, 393, 427–469. On 25 July the convention met for a roll call vote on both these measures.

Twenty-six delegates supported substituting eighteen for twenty-one in the constitution; the majority of these (eighteen) were Democrats. Two of these Democrats were also the only members of their party to support woman suffrage. Of the eight Republicans who supported enfranchising minors, five also supported woman suffrage. For the partisan breakdown of these two votes, see *New York Tribune*, 26 July 1867, 5. The committee of the whole voted on the proposal to enfranchise women on 23 July and eighteen-year-olds on 24 July. The woman suffrage proposal lost by a vote of 63 to 24. Bickford's resolution enfranchising eighteen-year-olds was defeated by a vote of 82 to 33. More delegates were present the second day. There was no roll call. *NY 1867*, 469, 490.

63. He also noted that many women had aided the war effort, but because he viewed women as naturally destined to occupy a more noble sphere than politics, he regarded sex as less arbitrary than age. *NY 1867*, 260.

64. Ibid., 261.

65. Ibid., 214. On Hand, see *SPSA* 2:77n1. For other delegates of both parties invoking age twenty-one as arbitrary but necessary, see *NY 1867*, 426, 428, 432.

66. Quigley, *Second Founding*.

67. *Documents of the Convention of the State of New York, 1867–68*, 7; *HWS*, 2:285. See DuBois, *Feminism and Suffrage*, 87–88.

68. *HWS*, 2:287; Kerr, *Lucy Stone*, 125–26.

69. Terborg-Penn, *African American Women*, 30; Dudden, *Fighting Chance*, chap. 5.

70. Dudden, *Fighting Chance*, chap. 5; DuBois, *Feminism and Suffrage*, 82–87; Kerr, *Lucy Stone*, 123–27; McFeely, *Frederick Douglass*, 267–69.

71. DuBois, *Feminism and Suffrage*, 89; Eickhoff, *Revolutionary Heart*, 177–79. The *Fort Scott (Kansas) Weekly Monitor* poked fun at Stanton as "a jolly looking woman, fat and probably forty," qtd. in McFeely, *Frederick Douglass*, 267.

72. Dudden, *Fighting Chance*, chap. 5.

73. M. Mitchell, "'Lower Orders,'" 134; *SPSA*, 2:94–95n11.

74. DuBois, *Feminism and Suffrage*, 94–96; Kerr, *Lucy Stone*, 127–29. On disputes over funding, see Dudden, *Fighting Chance*, 138–41.

75. The word "white" would not be struck from the Kansas state constitution until the 1870 passage of the Fifteenth Amendment; the word "male" not until 1912. DuBois, *Feminism and Suffrage*, 96–98. Terborg-Penn argues that Stanton and Anthony scapegoated black men for the defeat of female enfranchisement. *African American Women*, 28–30.

76. Garrison to Anthony, 4 January 1868, *SPSA*, 2:124.

77. DuBois, *Feminism and Suffrage*, 99; Kerr, *Lucy Stone*, 130–32.

78. DuBois, *Feminism and Suffrage*, 103; Dudden, *Fighting Chance*, chap. 6.

79. *Revolution*, 8 January 1868.

80. Most of the money Train promised never materialized. Dudden, *Fighting Chance*, 137; Griffith, *In Her Own Right*, 131–32; DuBois, *Feminism and Suffrage*, 103–4; Ginzberg, *Elizabeth Cady Stanton*, 135–40.

81. *SPSA*, 2:183n3.

82. Elizabeth Cady Stanton, "Manhood Suffrage," 24 December 1868, *SPSA*, 2:195. The second issue of the *Revolution* noted the number of women present at the meeting

of the Social Science Association, in clear contrast to women's exclusion from political parties. "Social Science," *Revolution*, 15 January 1868. See also Leach, *True Love*, chaps. 6, 11–12; Sklansky, *Soul's Economy*; and Harp, *Positivist Republic*.

83. Leach, *True Love*, 142–52; Kern, *Mrs. Stanton's Bible*, 54–60; Banner, *Elizabeth Cady Stanton*, 86; *SPSA*, 2:183. In her autobiography, Stanton said she read Harriet Martineau's translation of Comte while traveling in England in 1886 and found his views "unsatisfactory." Stanton, *Eighty Years and More*, 395. This statement elides her earlier engagement with Comtean ideas in the 1860s.

84. *Revolution*, 16 April 1868; 30 April 1868.

85. Ibid., 16 April 1868. For a modern translation of Comte's views on women, see Comte, *Auguste Comte and Positivism*, 372–89.

86. *Revolution*, 13 August 1868; see also "Rev. Henry Edgar [*sic*]," ibid., 10 June 1869. His correct name is Edger.

87. Wollstonecraft, "The Rights of Woman," ibid., 13 August 1868.

88. Stanton, "Advice to the Strong-Minded," ibid., 21 May 1868.

89. Comte, *Introduction*, 1.

90. [Stanton], "Miss Becker on the Difference in Sex," *Revolution*, 24 September 1868. By the 1880s, Stanton would critique male bias in science but continue to champion science itself as a progressive force. See Kern, *Mrs. Stanton's Bible*, 106–16.

91. "Man the Usurper," *Revolution*, 12 March 1868.

92. "Editorial Correspondence," ibid., 13 August 1868; see also "Rev. Henry Edgar."

93. [Stanton], "Miss Becker on the Difference in Sex."

94. "Positivism," *Revolution*, 19 November 1868; see also an excerpt from *Saturday Review*, reprinted in "The Goose and the Gander," ibid., 19 February 1868.

95. "New Books," ibid., 5 February 1868; ibid., 2 April 1868; and "Woman as Mendicant," ibid., 23 April 1868, in which Willard recommended her own book, *Sexology as the Philosophy of Life*.

96. Willard, *Sexology*.

97. *Revolution*, 3 September 1868.

98. "Anniversary of the American Equal Rights Association, Address of Elizabeth Cady Stanton," ibid., 13 May 1869; see also "William Lloyd Garrison," ibid., 29 January 1868.

99. Caine, "Elizabeth Cady Stanton." Stanton was also influenced by Mill's argument that disenfranchisement was more degrading in proportion to the number of people holding political power. "The Fifteenth Amendment," *Revolution*, 3 June 1869.

100. Sklansky, *Soul's Economy*, 75.

101. On Stanton's likely familiarity with racial science, see M. Mitchell, "'Lower Orders,'" 132.

102. Stanton, "Advice to the Strong-Minded," *Revolution*, 21 May 1868; on Croly, see Harp, *Positivist Republic*, 30–48.

103. Stanton, "Our Young Girls," *Revolution*, 29 January 1868; Stanton, "Our Young Girls," ibid., 25 June 1868; H. M. H. P., "A Mother to a Daughter," ibid., 22 January 1868; H. M. H. P., "A Mother to a Daughter," ibid., 12 March 1868; Paulina Wright Davis, "Our Daughters," ibid., 2 December 1869.

104. Stanton, "Marriages and Mistresses," ibid., 15 October 1868; Stanton, "Marriage and Divorce," ibid., 22 October 1868; Stanton, "Hester Vaughan," ibid., 19 November

1868. Stanton also noted the attempted rape of a fifty-five-year-old woman, implying that age was no protection against male violence. "Woman's Protectors," ibid., 21 January 1869. Stanton pointed to the popular young orator Anna Dickinson as an example of a "noble girl" displaying youthful womanhood in its fully realized glory. Stanton, "Anna Dickinson," ibid., 8 October 1868. On the importance of Dickinson's youth, see Gallman, *America's Joan of Arc*.

105. Stanton noted that "'Dame Partingtons,' 'Miss Nancys,' and 'Old Grannys'" were invariably the names applied to incompetent men. "The Degradation of Woman," *Revolution*, 15 January 1868. Parker Pillsbury printed a long editorial characterizing witch trials in Europe and America as persecution of old women sanctioned by Christianity — a critique Stanton would later adopt. "Woman as Witch," ibid., 25 June 1868.

106. "Editorial Correspondence," ibid., 20 August 1868; Cora Barey, "A Woman's Age," ibid., 1 April 1869.

107. "The Modern Old Maid," ibid., 2 September 1869; Banner, *In Full Flower*, 280.

108. E. M. H., "Old Maids," *Revolution*, 20 August 1868; [anon.], "Old Maids," ibid., 16 December 1869.

109. "Rev. Joseph Thompson on Woman's Suffrage," ibid., 22 April 1869.

110. "Maternity," ibid., 10 February 1870; see also "Editorial Correspondence," ibid., 14 April 1870.

111. "Editorial Correspondence," ibid., 6 August 1868.

112. "National Suffrage Convention," ibid., 28 January 1869; "Editorial Correspondence," ibid., 24 September 1868.

113. "Flabby Old Woman — Cause and Effect," ibid., 29 October 1868.

114. Douglass, "Equal Rights for All," 14 May 1868, *FDP*, 4:173, 177.

115. *SPSA*, 2:135.

116. "Infanticide," *Revolution*, 6 August 1868.

117. "The Rights of Woman," ibid.

118. Stanton, "Manhood Suffrage," 24 December 1868, *SPSA*, 2:195.

119. Ibid.

120. Ibid., 196. On Nast's racial types, see Painter, *History of White People*, 142, 203–4. In 1868 Stanton also endorsed false rumors that black men were raping white women throughout the South. Dudden, *Fighting Chance*, 151–60.

121. *SPSA*, 2:194; *Revolution*, 29 April 1869.

122. *SPSA*, 2:194.

123. Ibid., 197.

124. Stanton, "Rev. Henry Edgar [*sic*]."

125. Leach, *True Love*, chap. 6.

126. Stanton was probably influenced by John Stuart Mill, who published Comte in England but later argued that Comte was promoting society's despotism over individual liberty. See Lenzer introduction to Comte, *Auguste Comte and Positivism*, xxvi–xxx.

127. On the 1869 AERA convention, see Dudden, *Fighting Chance*, chap. 7.

128. *Revolution*, 8 January 1868.

129. *HWS*, 2:381.

130. Ibid., 382.

131. "Remarks by SBA to the American Equal Rights Association," 12 May 1869, *SPSA*, 2:238–40. Ann Gordon points out that this version, based on a phonographic report, is more accurate than the report in *HWS*. See *HWS*, 2:383.

132. *HWS*, 2:384.

133. Ibid., 2:387; see also Paulina Wright Davis qtd. in ibid., 2:391.

134. Ibid., 2:390.

135. Ibid.

136. DuBois, *Feminism and Suffrage*, chap. 5.

137. Parker, *Articulating Rights*, chap. 3.

138. *HWS*, 2:391–92.

139. Dudden, *Fighting Chance*, chap. 7; Flexner, *Century of Struggle*, chap. 10; DuBois, *Feminism and Suffrage*, chap. 6; Kerr, *Lucy Stone*, 146–50. More black women were active in the AWSA than in the NWSA. Terborg-Penn, *African American Women*, chap. 3.

140. "National Woman's Suffrage Association," *Revolution*, 10 June 1869.

141. Stanton, "Time to Rest," ibid., 5 May 1870; "Anniversary of the National Woman Suffrage Association," ibid., 19 May 1870.

142. "Who Shall Fill Our Places," ibid., 26 May 1870.

143. "Anniversary of the National Woman Suffrage Association."

144. Stanton responded to O. B. Frothingham's argument that men protected women, "The Subjection of Women," *SPSA*, 2:622.

145. Tetrault, "Incorporation," 1036–38, 1046; *SPSA*, 2:282; Banner, *In Full Flower*, 250.

146. Tetrault, "Incorporation." Stanton and Douglass both signed with James Redpath's Boston Lyceum Bureau, *SPSA*, 2:282; *FDP*, 4:xvi.

147. Stanton, "Subjection of Women," 631.

148. Ginzberg, *Elizabeth Cady Stanton*, 127–31; Stansell, "Missed Connections."

149. DuBois, *Feminism and Suffrage*, 125.

150. "Meeting of the Working Woman's Association," 17 September 1868, *SPSA*, 2:163.

151. "Working Women's Association, No. 2," *Revolution*, 1 October 1868. Lara Vapnek argues this attitude was typical of feminist labor reformers in the late nineteenth century. *Breadwinners*, 3, 11–33.

152. The *Revolution* frequently held up educated black women as qualified voters. See, for example, "Why Not?," an article on Ellen Frances Watkins Harper touring in Virginia, *Revolution*, 29 January 1868; and "Convention of the Universal Peace Association" and "What Shall be Done with the Negroes?," ibid., 12 February 1868. Stanton also pointed to Frederick Douglass as an example of leadership, ibid., 17 December 1868.

153. Stanton, "Gerrit Smith on Petitions," ibid., 14 January 1869, reprinted in DuBois, *Stanton–Anthony Reader*, 123. On Stanton's use of the myth of black men as rapists, see Dudden, *Fighting Chance*, 155–60; and Mitchell, "'Lower Orders.'"

154. Stanton, "Gerrit Smith on Petitions," 124.

155. Harper, *Minnie's Sacrifice*, 72.

156. Ibid., 48.

157. Ibid., 65.

158. Ibid., 68.

159. Ibid., 79.

160. Carby, *Reconstructing Womanhood*, chap. 4.

161. The only extant copy of "Moses" is the 1869 "second" edition. Foster argues that the poem was most likely first published in 1868; *Brighter Coming Day*, 135. Boyd points out that Harper construed the self-sacrifice of Moses and Christ as models that could empower black women to assert a specifically feminine form of moral leadership, *Discarded Legacy*, chaps. 3–5; see also Grohsmeyer, "Frances Harper."

162. Harper, "Moses," in *Complete Poems*, 64.

163. Ibid., 62; Stancliff, *Frances Ellen Watkins Harper*, chap. 5.

164. Harper, "Moses," 61–62.

165. For a discussion of how other black leaders used the trope of God's children, see Blum, *Reforging the White Republic*, 43–48.

166. Boyd, *Discarded Legacy*, chaps. 3–5; Petrino, "'We are Rising.'"

167. Harper, "Aunt Chloe," 196.

168. Ibid., 196–98.

169. Harper, "The Deliverance," in *Brighter Coming Day*, 200.

170. Ibid., 201.

171. Ibid., 198–99.

172. Ibid., 202–4.

173. Harper, "Learning to Read," in *Brighter Coming Day*, 205–6.

174. Ibid., 206.

CHAPTER 6

1. M. Jones, *All Bound Up*, 88, 92–93, 140–42.

2. Dudden, *Fighting Chance*; Gordon, "Stanton on the Right to Vote."

3. E. Foner, *Short History*.

4. DuBois, *Feminism and Suffrage*, chap. 6; Kerr, *Lucy Stone*, chaps. 11 and 12; Tetrault, "Incorporation."

5. Parker, *Articulating Rights*, chaps. 3–4; Bordin, *Woman and Temperance*.

6. M. Mitchell, "'Lower Orders'"; Stansell, *Feminist Promise*, chap. 4.

7. E. Foner, *Short History*, 219–23; Leach, *True Love*, chap. 11.

8. E. Foner, *Short History*, 225–27; McFeely, *Frederick Douglass*, 280–85.

9. McFeely, *Frederick Douglass*, 280–85; W. Martin, *Mind of Frederick Douglass*, 104.

10. E. Foner, *Short History*, 234.

11. Ibid., 245–47; McFeely, *Frederick Douglass*, 289, 291; W. Martin, *Mind of Frederick Douglass*, 132.

12. Douglass, "Our National Capital," 8 May 1877, *FDP*, 4:466.

13. Ibid.

14. Editor's note, Douglass, "Our National Capital," 443; McFeely, *Frederick Douglass*, 291.

15. W. Martin, *Mind of Frederick Douglass*, 65–67; McFeely, *Frederick Douglass*, 296.

16. Douglass, "Coming Home: An Address Delivered in St. Michael's, Maryland, on 17 June 1877," *FDP*, 4:479.

17. W. Martin, *Mind of Frederick Douglass*, chap. 10.

18. DuBois, "Outgrowing."

19. Stansell, *Feminist Promise*, 100–105; DuBois, "Taking the Law."

20. *HWS*, 2:601–3; VanBurkleo, *"Belonging,"* 156–59.

21. *Bradwell v. The State*; *HWS*, 2:620; DuBois, "Outgrowing," 105.

22. DuBois, "Outgrowing," 105.

23. *HWS*, 2:625–26.

24. Ibid., 626.

25. Terborg-Penn, *African American Women*, chap. 3.

26. Anthony, *Account*, v.

27. Ibid., 46–47.

28. Qtd. in ibid., 62–64; VanBurkleo, *"Belonging,"* 160.

29. DuBois, "Outgrowing."

30. DuBois, "Taking the Law"; *SPSA*, 3:75n.

31. *HWS*, 2:721.

32. *Minor v. Happersett*; *HWS*, 2:234–42; DuBois, *Stanton-Anthony Reader*, 107; DuBois, "Outgrowing"; DuBois "Taking the Law."

33. DuBois, "Outgrowing," 860.

34. *SPSA*, 3:188.

35. Ibid., 179.

36. Griffith, *In Her Own Right*, 187.

37. Stanton, "Pleasures," *SPSA*, 4:457.

38. Ibid., 454.

39. Ibid., 457.

40. Carby, *Reconstructing Womanhood*, chap. 4; Petrino, "'We are Rising'"; Stancliff, *Frances Ellen Watkins Harper*, chap. 5

41. Harper, "Fancy Etchings," in *Brighter Coming Day*, 224.

42. Ibid., 227.

43. Ibid., 225.

44. Ibid., 226.

45. Ibid., 230.

46. Harper, "Great Problem," in *Brighter Coming Day*, 220.

47. Blum, *Reforging the White Republic*, 43–48.

48. Harper, "Great Problem," 220.

49. Hofstadter, *Social Darwinism*; Werth, *Banquet at Delmonicos*.

50. Harper, "Great Problem," 221.

51. Ibid.

52. Harper began work with the Philadelphia Women's Christian Temperance Union sometime in the 1870s. Parker, *Articulating Rights*, 124–28, 167; Terborg-Penn, *African American Women*, 85; Fulton, "Sowing Seeds," 207–24.

EPILOGUE

1. Sneider, *Suffragists*; Newman, *White Women's Rights*.

2. Parker, *Articulating Rights*, chap. 4; Terborg-Penn, *African American Women*, chap. 5.

3. C. Field, "Woman's Rights," chaps. 7–9.

4. De Schweinitz, "'The Proper Age for Suffrage'"; Zimring, *Changing Legal World.*

5. Frederickson and Roberts, "Objectification Theory"; Calastani and Slevin, *Age Matters*; Marshall, "Aging"; Macdonald and Rich, *Look Me in the Eye.*

6. MacDonald and Rich argue for intergenerational alliances in *Look Me in the Eye.*

7. Graebner, "Age and Retirement"; Achenbaum, "Delineating Old Age."

8. Fraser and Gordon, "Genealogy"; Hondagneu-Sotelo, *Doméstica.*

BIBLIOGRAPHY

PRIMARY SOURCES

Published Manuscript and Archival Collections

The Adams Papers Digital Edition. Edited by C. James Taylor. Charlottesville, University of Virginia Press, Rotunda, 2008. http://rotunda.upress.virginia.edu/founders/ADMS.html. 15 January 2012.

Clay, Henry. *The Works of Henry Clay.* 10 vols. Edited by Calvin Colton. New York: G. P. Putnam's Sons, 1904.

Douglass, Frederick. *Frederick Douglass on Women's Rights.* Edited by Philip S. Foner. Westport, Conn.: Greenwood Press, 1976.

———. *The Frederick Douglass Papers.* Ser. 1. *Speeches, Debates, and Interviews,* 5 vols. Edited by John Blassingame and John McKivigan. New Haven: Yale University Press, 1979–92.

Stanton, Elizabeth Cady, and Susan B. Anthony. *Papers of Elizabeth Cady Stanton and Susan B. Anthony.* Ser. 3. Edited by Patricia G. Holland and Ann D. Gordon. Wilmington, Del.: Scholarly Resources, 1991. Microfilm.

———. *The Selected Papers of Elizabeth Cady Stanton and Susan B. Anthony.* 4 vols. Edited by Ann D. Gordon. New Brunswick, N.J.: Rutgers University Press, 1997–2006.

Court Cases

Bradwell v. The State, 83 U.S. 130 (1873). http://www.law.cornell.edu/supremecourt/text/83/130. 5 October 2013.

Minor v. Happersett, 88 U.S. 162 (1875). http://www.law.cornell.edu/supct/html/historics/USSC_CR_0088_0162_ZS.html. 5 October 2013.

Government Documents

The Acts and Resolves, Public and Private, of the Province of the Massachusetts Bay: To which are Prefixed the Charters of the Province, with Historical and Explanatory Notes, and an Appendix. Vol. 5, *1775–1776.* Boston: Wright and Potter, 1918.

A Constitution or Frame of Government, Agreed upon by the Delegates of the People of the State of Massachusetts-Bay, in Convention, Begun and Held at Cambridge on the First of September, 1779, and Continued by Adjournments to the Second of March, 1780. Boston: Benjamin Edes and Sons, 1780.

The Federal and State Constitutions, Colonial Charters, and Other Organic Laws of the States, Territories, and Colonies, Now or Heretofore Forming the United States of America. Vol. 5. Washington: Government Printing Office, 1909.

Laws for Regulating and Governing the Militia of the Commonwealth of Massachusetts, with an Index, to which is added, in an Appendix, the United States Militia Acts, Passed in Congress, May 8, 1792, and March 2, 1803. Boston: Tomas and Andrews, 1803.

Military Laws of the United States: Including those relating to the Marine Corps, to Which is Prefixed the Constitution of the United States. 2nd ed. Compiled by Colonel Trueman Cross. Washington: George Templeman, 1838.

Records of the Governor and Company of the Massachusetts Bay in New England. Vol. 11, *1642–49.* Edited by Nathaniel Shurtleff. Boston: William White, 1853.

The Revised Statutes of the Commonwealth of Massachusetts, Passed November 4, 1835; to Which are Subjoined, an Act in Amendment Thereof, and an Act Expressly to Repeal the Acts Which are Consolidated Therein, both Passed in February 1836; and to Which are Prefixed the Constitution of the United States and the Commonwealth of Massachusetts. Boston: Dutton and Wentworth, 1836.

Surgeon General's Office, Circular No. 8, July 14, 1862, National Archives, Washington, D.C. http://docsteach.org/documents/3819334/detail?menu=closed &page=29&sortBy=era. 7 June 2013.

Proceedings of Conventions

Documents of the Convention of the State of New York, 1867–68. Vol. 1. Albany: Weed, Parsons, and Company, 1868, No. 15.

Journal of Debates and Proceedings in the Convention of Delegates Chosen to Revise the Constitution of Massachusetts, Begun and holden at Boston, November 15, 1820, and continued by Adjournment to January 9, 1821. Boston: Daily Advertiser, 1853.

Minutes of the Proceedings of the National Negro Conventions, 1830–1864. Edited by Howard Holman Bell. New York: Arno, 1969.

The Popular Sources of Political Authority: Documents on the Massachusetts Constitution of 1780. Edited by Oscar Handlin and Mary F. Handlin. Cambridge, Mass.: Belknap Press of Harvard University Press, 1966.

Proceedings and Debates of the Constitutional Convention of the State of New York, Held in 1867 and 1868, in the City of Albany. Vol. 1. Albany: Weed, Parsons, and Company, 1868.

Proceedings of the Black State Conventions, 1840–1865. Edited by Phillip S. Foner and George E. Walker. Philadelphia: Temple University Press, 1980.

The Proceedings of the Woman's Rights Convention Held at Worcester, October 23rd and 24th, 1850. Boston: Prentiss and Sawyer, 1851.

Proceedings of the Woman's Rights Convention, Held at Worcester, October 15th and 16th, 1851. New York: Fowlers and Wells, 1852.

The Proceedings of the Woman's Rights Convention, Held at Syracuse, September 8th, 9th, and 10th, 1852. Syracuse: J. E. Masters, 1852.

Proceedings of the National Women's Rights Convention, Held at Cleveland, Ohio, Wednesday, Thursday, and Friday, October 5th, 6th, and 7th, 1853. Cleveland: Gray, Beardsley, Spear, and Co., 1854.

Proceedings of the Ninth National Woman's Rights Convention, Held in New York City, Thursday, May 12, 1859. Rochester: A. Strong and Co., 1859.

Proceedings of the Eleventh National Woman's Rights Convention, Held at the Church of the Puritan, New York, May 10, 1866. New York: Robert J. Johnston, 1866.

Report of the Debates and Proceedings of the Convention for the Revision of the Constitution of the State of New York, 1846. Albany: Evening Atlas, 1846.

Report of the Debates and Proceedings of the Convention for the Revision of the Constitution of the State of Ohio, 1850-51. Vol. 1. Columbus, Ohio: S. Medary, 1851.

Reports of the Proceedings and Debates of the Convention of 1821, Assembled for the Purpose of Amending the Constitution of the State of New York. Albany: E. and E. Hosford, 1821.

Woman's Rights Conventions, Seneca Falls and Rochester, 1848. New York: Arno Press/New York Times, 1969.

Books, Articles, and Pamphlets

Abbot, Gorham. Introduction to *The Voyage of Life: A Series of Allegorical Pictures.* Engravings by James Smillie. New York: Spingler Institute, 1856. 1–4.

[Agassiz, Louis]. "The Diversity of the Origin of the Human Races." *Christian Examiner and Religious Miscellany,* July 1850, 110–45.

Allen, Richard, and Absalom Jones. "A Narrative of the Proceedings of the Black People During the Late Awful Calamity in Philadelphia (1794)." In *Pamphlets of Protest: An Anthology of Early African-American Protest Literature, 1790–1860,* edited by Richard Newman, Patrick Rael, and Philip Lapsansky, 33–42. New York: Routledge, 2001.

Anthony, Susan B. *An Account of the Proceedings of the Trial of Susan B. Anthony, on the Charge of Illegal Voting, at the Presidential Election of Nov., 1872.* Rochester, N.Y.: Daily Democrat and Chronicle, 1874.

Beecher, Catharine. "Essay on Slavery and Abolitionism." In *The Limits of Sisterhood: The Beecher Sisters on Women's Rights and Woman's Sphere.* Edited by Jeanne Boydston, Mary Kelley, and Anne Margolis, 125–29. Chapel Hill: University of North Carolina Press, 1988.

———. "Suggestions Respecting Improvements in Education." In *The Limits of Sisterhood: The Beecher Sisters on Women's Rights and Woman's Sphere.* Edited by Jeanne Boydston, Mary Kelley, and Anne Margolis, 42–46. Chapel Hill: University of North Carolina Press, 1988.

Blackstone, William. *Commentaries on the Laws of England.* 1765. Vol. 1. Reprint of the 1st ed. London: Dawsons of Pall Mall, 1966.

Blackwell, Elizabeth. *The Laws of Life, with Special Reference to the Physical Education of Girls.* 1852; London: Sampson Low, Son, and Co., 1859.

Burke, Edmund. *A Philosophical Enquiry into the Origin of Our Ideas of the Sublime and the Beautiful.* 1757. Edited by Adam Phillips. New York: Oxford University Press, 1998.

Combe, George. *The Constitution of Man.* Boston: Marsh, Capen, Lyon, and Webb, 1841.

Comte, Auguste. *Auguste Comte and Positivism: The Essential Writings.* Edited by Gertrude Lenzer. Chicago: University of Chicago Press, 1975.

———. *Introduction to Positivist Philosophy.* Edited by Frederick Ferré. Indianapolis: Hackett, 1988.

Douglass, Frederick. *Narrative of the Life of Frederick Douglass, an American Slave.* 1845. In *The Frederick Douglass Papers,* ser. 2. *Autobiographical Writings,* vol. 1. Edited by John Blassingame, John McKivigan, and Peter Hinks, 1–86. New Haven: Yale University Press, 1999.

Eaton, Clement. *Henry Clay and the Art of American Politics.* Boston: Little, Brown, 1957.

Filmer, Robert. *Patriarcha and Other Writings.* Edited by Johann P. Sommerville. New York: Cambridge University Press, 1991.

Forten, James. "Series of Letters by a Man of Color" (1813). In *Pamphlets of Protest: An Anthology of Early African-American Protest Literature, 1790–1860,* edited by Richard Newman, Patrick Rael, and Philip Lapsansky, 67–72. New York: Routledge, 2001.

Fuller, Margaret. *Woman in the Nineteenth Century.* Edited by Bernard Rosenthal. 1845; New York: W. W. Norton, 1971.

Grimké, Sarah. *Letters on the Equality of the Sexes, and Other Essays.* 1838. Edited by Elizabeth Ann Bartlett. New Haven: Yale University Press, 1988.

Haddock, John A. *The Growth of a Century: As Illustrated in the History of Jefferson County, New York, from 1793 to 1894.* Albany: Weed-Parsons, 1895.

Harper, Frances Ellen Watkins. *A Brighter Coming Day: A Frances Ellen Watkins Harper Reader,* edited by Frances Smith Foster. New York: Feminist Press at the City University of New York, 1990.

———. *Complete Poems.* Edited by Maryemma Graham. New York: Oxford University Press, 1988.

———. *Minnie's Sacrifice, Sowing and Reaping, Trial and Triumph.* 1869. Edited by Frances Smith Foster. Boston: Beacon Press, 1994.

———. "Our Greatest Want." *Anglo-African* 1 (May 1859): 160.

———. "The Two Offers." *Anglo-African* 1 (September 1859): 288–91; 1 (October 1859): 311–13.

Hays, Mary. *Appeal to the Men of Great Britain on Behalf of Women.* 1798; New York: Garland, 1974.

Jacobs, Harriet. *Incidents in the Life of a Slave Girl.* 1861; Cambridge, Mass.: Harvard University Press, 1987.

Jefferson, Thomas. *Notes on the State of Virginia.* 1785. Edited by Frank Shuffleton. New York: Penguin Books, 1999.

Jones, Samuel, and James C. Spencer. *Reports of Cases Argued and Determined in the Superior Court of the City of New York,* v. 61. New York: Banks and Brothers Law Publishers, 1893.

Kant, Immanuel. "An Answer to the Question: 'What is Enlightenment?'" In *Kant: Political Writings*, edited by Hans Reiss, 54–60. 1970; New York: Cambridge University Press, 1991.

Locke, John. *An Essay Concerning Human Understanding*. 1689. Edited by Roger Woolhouse. New York: Penguin Books, 1997.

———. *The Second Treatise of Government*. 1689. In *Political Writings of John Locke*, edited by David Wootton, 261–387. New York: Mentor, 1993.

Paine, Thomas. *Common Sense*. 1776. New York: Bantam, 2004.

———. *The Complete Writings of Thomas Paine*. Vol. 1. Edited by Philip S. Foner. New York: Citadel Press, 1945.

Pillsbury, Parker. "Women's Rights Convention and the People of Color." *National Anti-Slavery Standard*, 5 December 1850.

Purvis, Robert. "Appeal of Forty Thousand Citizens, Threatened with Disenfranchisement, to the People of Pennsylvania" (1837). In *Pamphlets of Protest: An Anthology of Early African-American Protest Literature, 1790–1860*, edited by Richard Newman, Patrick Rael, and Philip Lapsansky, 132–42. New York: Routledge, 2001.

Rousseau, Jean-Jacques. *Emile, or On Education*. 1762. Translated by Allan Bloom. New York: Basic Books, 1979.

Sigourney, Lydia. *Past Meridian*. 2nd ed. Hartford, Conn.: F. A. Brown, 1856.

Smith, Elizabeth Oakes. "Woman and Her Needs." *New York Tribune*, 23 January 1851, 4 March 1851, and 24 April 1851. http://www.neiu.edu/~thscherm/eos/w&n. htm. 20 July 2011.

Stanton, Elizabeth Cady. *Eighty Years and More*. 1898. Boston: Northeastern University Press, 1993.

———. "Fashionable Women Shipwreck." Lecture [1861?]. In *Papers of Elizabeth Cady Stanton and Susan B. Anthony*, ser. 3, edited by Patricia G. Holland and Ann D. Gordon. Wilmington, Del.: Scholarly Resources, 1991. Microfilm, reel 10, frames 105–29.

———. "Our Young Girls." *Lily*, 1 Mar 1853. In *Papers of Elizabeth Cady Stanton and Susan B. Anthony*, ser. 3, edited by Patricia G. Holland and Ann D. Gordon. Wilmington, Del.: Scholarly Resources, 1991. Microfilm, reel 7, frames 562–63.

———. "The Pleasures of Age." In *The Selected Papers of Elizabeth Cady Stanton and Susan B. Anthony*, vol. 4, edited by Ann D. Gordon, 451–63. New Brunswick, N.J.: Rutgers University Press, 1997–2006.

———. "The Solitude of Self." 1892. In *The Elizabeth Cady Stanton–Susan B. Anthony Reader: Correspondence, Writings, Speeches*, edited by Ellen Carol DuBois, 246–54. 1981; Boston: Northeastern University Press, 1992.

Stanton, Elizabeth Cady, Susan B. Anthony, and Matilda Joslyn Gage, eds. *History of Woman Suffrage*. 3 vols. 1881–86; New York: Arno Press, 1969.

Stanton, Theodore, and Harriot Stanton Blatch, eds. *Elizabeth Cady Stanton as Revealed in Her Letters, Diary and Reminiscences*. Vol. 2. New York: Harper and Brothers, 1922.

Stewart, Maria. "An Address Delivered at the African Masonic Hall" (1833). In *Maria Stewart: America's First Black Woman Political Writer*, edited by Marilyn Richardson, 56–64. Bloomington: Indiana University Press, 1987.

———. "Lecture Delivered at the Franklin Hall" (1832). In *Maria Stewart: America's First Black Woman Political Writer,* edited by Marilyn Richardson, 45–49. Bloomington: Indiana University Press, 1987.

———. "Religion and the Pure Principles of Morality" (1831). In *Maria Stewart: America's First Black Woman Political Writer,* edited by Marilyn Richardson, 28–42. Bloomington: Indiana University Press, 1987.

Stowe, Harriet Beecher. *A Key to "Uncle Tom's Cabin."* Boston: Jewett, 1854.

———. *Uncle Tom's Cabin: Or, Life among the Lowly.* 1852; Cambridge, Mass.: Harvard University Press, 2009.

Swisshelm, Jane. "Woman's Rights and the Color Question." *Pittsburgh Saturday Visiter,* 23 November 1850.

———. "The Worcester Convention." *Pittsburgh Saturday Visiter,* 2 November 1850.

Truth, Sojourner. *Narrative of Sojourner Truth: A Bondswoman of Olden Time, with a History of Her Labors and Correspondence Drawn from her "Book of Life."* 1850. Introduction by Jeffrey C. Stewart. New York: Oxford University Press, 1991.

Walker, David. *David Walker's Appeal to the Colored Citizens of the World, but in particular and very expressly, to those of the United States of America.* 1829. Edited by Peter Hinks. University Park: Pennsylvania State University Press, 2000.

Waterbury, Jared Bell. *The Voyage of Life, Suggested by Cole's Celebrated Allegorical Paintings.* Boston: Massachusetts Sabbath School Society, 1852.

Wheatley, Phillis. *Complete Writings.* Edited by Vincent Carretta. New York: Penguin Books, 2001.

Willard, Elizabeth Osgood Goodrich. *Sexology as the Philosophy of Life: Implying Social Organization and Government.* Chicago: J. R. Walsh, 1867.

Willard, Frances, and Mary Livermore, eds. *A Woman of the Century.* New York: Moulton, 1893.

Wilson, James Grant, and John Fiske, eds. *Appletons' Cyclopedia of American Biography.* 7 vols. New York: D. Appleton and Co., 1894–1900.

Wollstonecraft, Mary. *Thoughts on the Education of Daughters: With Reflections on Female Conduct, in the More Important Duties of Life.* 1787. Vol. 4 of *The Works of Mary Wollstonecraft,* edited by Janet Todd and Marilyn Butler. London: William Pickering, 1989.

———. *A Vindication of the Rights of Woman.* 1792. 2nd ed. Edited by Carol H. Poston. New York: W. W. Norton, 1988.

———. *A Vindication of the Rights of Woman, with Strictures on Moral and Political Subjects.* 1792. Vol. 5 of *The Works of Mary Wollstonecraft,* edited by Janet Todd and Marilyn Butler. London: William Pickering, 1989.

SECONDARY SOURCES

Books and Dissertations

Achenbaum, W. Andrew. *Old Age in the New Land: The American Experience since 1790.* Baltimore: Johns Hopkins University Press, 1978.

Adams, Catherine, and Elizabeth Pleck. *Love of Freedom: Black Women in Colonial and Revolutionary New England*. New York: Oxford University Press, 2010.

Anderson, Bonnie S. *Joyous Greetings: The First International Women's Movement, 1830–1860*. New York: Oxford University Press, 2000.

Ariès, Philippe. *Centuries of Childhood: A Social History of Family Life*. Trans. Robert Baldick. 1960; New York, Vintage, 1962.

Banner, Lois W. *Elizabeth Cady Stanton: A Radical for Woman's Rights*. New York: Addison Wesley Longman, 1980.

———. *In Full Flower: Aging Women, Power and Sexuality: A History*. New York: Alfred Knopf, 1992.

Barbre, Joy Webster. "From 'Goodwives' to Menoboomers: Reinventing Menopause in American History." Ph.D. diss., University of Minnesota, 1994.

Barker-Benfield, G. J. *The Culture of Sensibility: Sex and Society in Eighteenth-Century Britain*. Chicago: University of Chicago Press, 1992.

Basch, Norma. *In the Eyes of the Law: Women, Marriage, and Property in Nineteenth-Century New York*. Ithaca: Cornell University Press, 1982.

Bay, Mia. *The White Image in the Black Mind: African American Ideas about White People, 1830–1925*. New York: Oxford University Press, 2000.

Beard, Mary R. *Woman as a Force in History: A Study in Traditions and Realities*. 1946. New York: Persea Books, 1987.

Bensel, Richard Franklin. *The American Ballot Box in the Mid-Nineteenth Century*. New York: Cambridge University Press, 2004.

Berlin, Ira, Joseph P. Reidy, and Leslie S. Rowland, eds. *Freedom's Soldiers: Black Military Experience in the Civil War*. New York: Cambridge University Press, 1998.

Birke, Lynda. *Feminism and the Biological Body*. New Brunswick, N.J.: Rutgers University Press, 1999.

Blackmar, Elizabeth. *Manhattan for Rent, 1785–1850*. Ithaca: Cornell University Press, 1989.

Blackwell, Marilyn S., and Kristen T. Oertel, eds. *Frontier Feminist: Clarina Howard Nichols and the Politics of Motherhood*. Lawrence: University of Kansas Press, 2010.

Blight, David W. *Frederick Douglass's Civil War: Keeping Faith in Jubilee*. Baton Rouge: Louisiana State University Press, 1989.

Blum, Edward J. *Reforging the White Republic: Race, Religion, and American Nationalism, 1865–1898*. Baton Rouge: Louisiana State University Press, 2007.

Bordin, Ruth. *Woman and Temperance: The Quest for Power and Liberty, 1873–1900*. 1981; New Brunswick, N.J.: Rutgers University Press, 1990.

Bouton, Terry. *Taming Democracy: "The People," the Founders, and the Troubled Ending of the American Revolution*. New York: Oxford University Press, 2007.

Boyd, Melba Joyce. *Discarded Legacy: Politics and Poetics in the Life of Frances E. W. Harper, 1825–1911*. Detroit: Wayne State University Press, 1994.

Boydston, Jeanne. *Home and Work: Housework, Wages, and the Ideology of Labor in the Early Republic*. New York: Oxford University Press, 1990.

Braithwaite, Helen. *Romanticism, Publishing, and Dissent: Joseph Johnson and the Cause of Liberty*. New York: Palgrave Macmillan, 2003.

Branson, Susan. *These Fiery Frenchified Dames: Women and Political Culture in Early National Philadelphia*. Philadelphia: University of Pennsylvania Press, 2001.

Brewer, Holly. *By Birth or Consent: Children, Law, and the Anglo-American Revolution in Authority*. Chapel Hill: University of North Carolina Press, 2005.

Brown, Gillian. *Domestic Individualism: Imagining Self in Nineteenth-Century America*. Berkeley: University of California Press, 1990.

Brown, Kathleen M. *Good Wives, Nasty Wenches, and Anxious Patriarchs: Gender, Race, and Power in Colonial Virginia*. Chapel Hill: University of North Carolina Press, 1996.

Brumberg, Joan Jacobs. *The Body Project: An Intimate History of American Girls*. New York: Vintage Books, 1997.

Bunge, Marcia J., ed. *The Child in Christian Thought*. Grand Rapids, Mich.: William B. Eerdmans, 2001.

————, ed. *The Child in the Bible*. Grand Rapids, Mich.: William B. Eerdmans, 2008.

Calastani, Toni M., and Kathleen Slevin. *Age Matters: Re-aligning Feminist Thinking*. New York: Routledge: 2006.

Capper, Charles. *Margaret Fuller: An American Romantic Life*. Vol. 1, *The Private Years*. New York: Oxford University Press, 1992.

————. *Margaret Fuller: An American Romantic Life*. Vol. 2, *The Public Years*. New York: Oxford University Press, 2007.

Carby, Hazel. *Reconstructing Womanhood: The Emergence of the Afro-American Woman Novelist*. New York: Oxford, 1987.

Carson, John. *The Measure of Merit: Talents, Intelligence, and Inequality in the French and American Republics, 1750–1940*. Princeton: Princeton University Press, 2007.

Casais, John Anthony. "The New York State Constitutional Convention of 1821 and Its Aftermath." Ph.D. diss., Columbia University, 1967.

Ceniza, Sherry. *Walt Whitman and Nineteenth-Century Women Reformers*. Tuscaloosa: University of Alabama Press, 1998.

Chevigny, Bell Gale. *The Woman and the Myth: Margaret Fuller's Life and Writings*. Rev. ed. Boston: Northeastern University Press, 1994.

Chudacoff, Howard P. *How Old Are You? Age Consciousness in American Culture*. Princeton: Princeton University Press, 1989.

Cohen, Patricia. *In Our Prime: The Invention of Middle Age*. New York: Scribner, 2012.

Cohen, Patricia Cline. *A Calculating People: The Spread of Numeracy in Early America*. Chicago: University of Chicago Press, 1982.

Cole, Thomas. *The Journey of Life: A Cultural History of Aging in America*. New York: Cambridge University Press, 1992.

Cott, Nancy. *The Bonds of Womanhood: 'Woman's Sphere' in New England, 1780–1835*. New Haven: Yale University Press, 1977.

————. *The Grounding of Modern Feminism*. New Haven: Yale University Press, 1987.

Cruikshank, Margaret. *Learning to Be Old: Gender, Culture, and Aging*. 2nd ed. New York: Rowman and Littlefield, 2009.

Cultice, Wendell W. *Youth's Battle for the Ballot: A History of Voting Age in America.* New York: Greenwood Press, 1992.

DeLuzio, Crista. *Female Adolescence in American Scientific Thought, 1830–1930.* Baltimore: Johns Hopkins University Press, 2007.

Dent, N. J. H. *Rousseau: An Introduction to His Psychological, Social, and Political Theory.* New York: Basil Blackwell, 1989.

———. *A Rousseau Dictionary.* Cambridge, Mass.: Blackwell, 1992.

Diedrich, Maria. *Love across the Color Lines: Ottilie Assing and Frederick Douglass.* New York: Hill and Wang, 1999.

Dillon, Lisa. *The Shady Side of Fifty: Age and Old Age in Late Victorian Canada and the United States.* Montreal: McGill-Queen's University Press, 2008.

Doress-Worters, Paula, ed. *Mistress of Herself: Speeches and Letters of Ernestine L. Rose, Early Women's Rights Leader.* New York: Feminist Press at the City University of New York, 2007.

Douglass, Ann. *The Feminization of American Culture.* New York: Anchor Books, 1977.

———. *Terrible Honesty: Mongrel Manhattan in the 1920s.* New York: Farrar, Straus and Giroux, 1995.

Dove, Mary. *The Perfect Age of Man's Life.* Cambridge: Cambridge University Press, 1986.

DuBois, Ellen Carol. *Feminism and Suffrage: The Emergence of an Independent Women's Movement in America, 1848–1869.* Ithaca: Cornell University Press, 1978.

———, ed. *The Elizabeth Cady Stanton–Susan B. Anthony Reader: Correspondence, Writings, Speeches.* Boston: Northeastern University Press, 1992.

———, ed. *Woman Suffrage and Women's Rights.* New York: New York University Press, 1998.

Dudden, Faye E. *Fighting Chance: The Struggle over Woman Suffrage and Black Suffrage in Reconstruction America.* New York: Oxford University Press, 2011.

Eickhoff, Diane. *Revolutionary Heart: The Life of Clarina Nichols and the Pioneering Crusade for Women's Rights.* Kansas City, Kans.: Quindaro Press, 2006.

Einhorn, Robin L. *American Taxation, American Slavery.* Chicago: University of Chicago Press, 2006.

Eller, Cynthia. *The Myth of Matriarchal Prehistory: Why an Invented Past Won't Give Women a Future.* Boston: Beacon Press, 2000.

Field, Corinne T. "Woman's Rights and the Politics of Adulthood in the United States, 1792–1939." Ph.D. diss., Columbia University, 2008.

Field, Corinne T., and Nicholas L. Syrett. *The Politics of Age in America: Colonial Era to the Present.* New York: New York University Press, forthcoming.

Field, Phyllis. *The Politics of Race in New York: The Struggle for Black Suffrage in the Civil War Era.* Ithaca: Cornell University Press, 1982.

Fischer, David Hackett. *Growing Old in America.* New York: Oxford University Press, 1977.

Flexner, Eleanor. *Century of Struggle: The Woman's Rights Movement in the United States.* Rev. ed. Cambridge, Mass.: Harvard University Press, 1975.

Fliegelman, Jay. *Prodigals and Pilgrims: The American Revolution against Patriarchal Authority, 1750–1800*. New York: Cambridge University Press, 1982.

Foner, Anne. *Aging and Old Age: New Perspectives*. Englewood Cliffs, N.J.: Prentice-Hall, 1986.

Foner, Eric. *A Short History of Reconstruction*. New York: Harper and Row, 1990.

———. *The Story of American Freedom*. New York: W. W. Norton, 1998.

———. *Tom Paine and Revolutionary America*. New York: Oxford University Press, 1976.

Foner, Eric, and John A. Garraty, eds. *The Reader's Companion to American History*. Boston: Houghton Mifflin, 1991.

Forman-Brunell, Miriam, and Leslie Paris, eds. *The Girls' History and Culture Reader: The Nineteenth Century*. Urbana: University of Illinois Press, 2011.

Fredrickson, George M. *The Black Image in the White Mind: The Debate on Afro-American Character and Destiny, 1817–1914*. 1971; Hanover, N.H.: Wesleyan University Press, 1987.

Friedan, Betty. *The Fountain of Age*. New York: Simon and Schuster, 1993.

Gallman, J. Matthew. *America's Joan of Arc: The Life of Anna Elizabeth Dickinson*. New York: Oxford University Press, 2006.

Gates, Henry Louis, Jr. *The Trials of Phillis Wheatley: America's First Black Poet and Her Encounters with the Founding Fathers*. New York: Basic Books, 2003.

Giddings, Paula. *When and Where I Enter: The Impact of Black Women on Race and Sex in America*. New York: Bantam Books, 1984.

Ginzberg, Lori D. *Elizabeth Cady Stanton: An American Life*. New York: Hill and Wang, 2010.

———. *Untidy Origins: A Story of Woman's Rights in Antebellum New York*. Chapel Hill: University of North Carolina Press, 2005.

Goodman, Dena. *Becoming a Woman in the Age of Letters*. Ithaca: Cornell University Press, 2009.

Gordon, Ann D., and Bettye Collier-Thomas, eds. *African American Women and the Vote, 1837–1965*. Amherst: University of Massachusetts Press, 1997.

Gordon, Lyndall. *A Life of Mary Wollstonecraft*. New York: Harper Perennial, 2005.

Gould, Stephen Jay. *The Mismeasure of Man*. New York: W. W. Norton, 1981.

Graebner, William. *A History of Retirement: The Meaning and Function of an American Institution, 1885–1978*. New Haven: Yale University Press, 1980.

Griffith, Elizabeth. *In Her Own Right: The Life of Elizabeth Cady Stanton*. New York: Oxford University Press, 1984.

Grinspan, Jon. "The Virgin Vote: Young Americans in the Age of Popular Politics." Ph.D. diss., University of Virginia, 2013.

Grossberg, Michael. *Governing the Hearth: Law and the Family in Nineteenth-Century America*. Chapel Hill: University of North Carolina Press, 1985.

Guest, Harriet. *Small Change: Women, Learning, Patriotism*. Chicago: University of Chicago Press, 2000.

Gullette, Margaret Morganroth. *Declining to Decline: Cultural Combat and the Politics of the Midlife*. Charlottesville: University of Virginia Press, 1997.

Gustafson, Sandra M. *Eloquence Is Power: Oratory and Performance in Early America*. Chapel Hill: University of North Carolina Press in association with the Omohundro Institute of Early American History and Culture, 2000.

Haber, Carole. *Beyond Sixty-Five: The Dilemma of Old Age in America's Past*. New York: Cambridge University Press, 1983.

Haber, Carole, and Brian Gratton. *Old Age and the Search for Security: An American Social History*. Bloomington: Indiana University Press, 1994.

Haight, Gordon S. *Mrs. Sigourney, the Sweet Singer of Hartford*. New Haven: Yale University Press, 1930.

Harp, Gillis J. *Positivist Republic: Auguste Comte and the Reconstruction of American Liberalism, 1865–1920*. University Park: Pennsylvania State University Press, 1995.

Haynes, Stephen. *Noah's Curse: The Biblical Justification of American Slavery*. New York: Oxford University Press, 2002.

Herndon, Ruth Wallis, and John E. Murray, eds. *Children Bound to Labor: The Pauper Apprentice System in Early America*. Ithaca: Cornell University Press, 2009.

Hesse, Carla. *The Other Enlightenment: How French Women Became Modern*. Princeton: Princeton University Press, 2001.

Hewitt, Nancy. *Women's Activism and Social Change: Rochester, New York, 1822–1872*. Ithaca: Cornell University Press, 1984.

Hinks, Peter P. *To Awaken My Afflicted Brethren: David Walker and the Problem of Antebellum Slave Resistance*. University Park: Pennsylvania State University Press, 1997.

Hoffert, Sylvia D. *Jane Grey Swisshelm: An Unconventional Life, 1815–1884*. Chapel Hill: University of North Carolina Press, 2004.

———. *When Hens Crow: The Woman's Rights Movement in Antebellum America*. Bloomington: University of Indiana Press, 1995.

Hofstadter, Richard. *Social Darwinism in American Thought*. 1944. Boston: Beacon Press, 1992.

Holt, Michael. *The Rise and Fall of the American Whig Party: Jacksonian Politics and the Onset of the Civil War*. New York: Oxford University Press, 2003.

Holton, Woody. *Abigail Adams*. New York: Free Press, 2009.

Hondagneu-Sotelo, Pierette. *Doméstica: Immigrant Workers Cleaning and Caring in the Shadows of Affluence*. Berkeley: University of California Press, 2007.

Horton, James Oliver, and Lois E. Horton. *In Hope of Liberty: Culture, Community, and Protest among Northern Free Blacks, 1700–1860*. New York: Oxford University Press, 1997.

Hunt, Lynn. *The French Revolution and Human Rights: A Brief Documentary History*. New York: Bedford/St. Martin's, 1996.

———. *Inventing Human Rights: A History*. New York: W. W. Norton, 2007.

Isenberg, Nancy. *Sex and Citizenship in Antebellum America*. Chapel Hill: University of North Carolina Press, 1998.

Jabour, Anya. *Scarlett's Sisters: Young Women in the Old South*. Chapel Hill: University of North Carolina Press, 2007.

————. *Topsy-Turvy: How the Civil War Turned the World Upside Down for Southern Children*. Chicago: Ivan R. Dee, 2010.

James, Edward T., Janet Wilson James, and Paul S. Boyer, eds. *Notable American Women: A Biographical Dictionary*. 3 vols. Cambridge, Mass.: Harvard University Press, Belknap Press, 1971.

Jeffrey, Julie Roy. *The Great Silent Army of Abolitionism: Ordinary Women in the Antislavery Movement*. Chapel Hill: University of North Carolina Press, 1998.

Johnson, Paul E. *A Shopkeeper's Millennium: Society and Revivals in Rochester, New York, 1815–1837*. New York: Hill and Wang, 1978.

Johnson, Walter. *Soul by Soul: Life inside the Antebellum Slave Market*. Cambridge, Mass.: Harvard University Press, 1999.

Jones, Jacqueline. *Labor of Love, Labor of Sorrow: Black Women, Work, and the Family, from Slavery to the Present*. New York: Vintage Books, 1985.

Jones, Martha S. *All Bound Up Together: The Woman Question in African American Public Culture, 1830–1900*. Chapel Hill: University of North Carolina Press, 2007.

Jordan, Winthrop. *White over Black: American Attitudes toward the Negro, 1550–1812*. New York: W. W. Norton, 1968.

Kann, Mark. *A Republic of Men: The American Founders, Gendered Language, and Patriarchal Politics*. New York: New York University Press, 1998.

Karcher, Carolyn L. *The First Woman in the Republic: A Cultural Biography of Lydia Maria Child*. Durham: Duke University Press, 1994.

Katz, Stephen. *Disciplining Old Age: The Formation of Gerontological Knowledge*. Charlottesville: University of Virginia Press, 1996.

Kelley, Mary. *Learning to Stand and Speak: Women, Education, and Public Life in America's Republic*. Chapel Hill: University of North Carolina Press in association with the Omohundro Institute of Early American History and Culture, 2006.

————. *Private Woman, Public Stage: Literary Domesticity in Nineteenth-Century America*. Chapel Hill: University of North Carolina Press, 2001.

Kelly, Gary. *Revolutionary Feminism: The Mind and Career of Mary Wollstonecraft*. London: Macmillan, 1992.

Kenyon, Gary M., James E. Birren, and Johannes J. F. Schroots, eds. *Metaphors of Aging in Science and the Humanities*. New York: Springer, 1991.

Kerber, Linda. *No Constitutional Right to Be Ladies: Women and the Obligations of Citizenship*. New York: Hill and Wang, 1998.

————. *Women of the Republic: Intellect and Ideology in Revolutionary America*. 1980; New York: W. W. Norton, 1986.

Kern, Kathi. *Mrs. Stanton's Bible*. Ithaca: Cornell University Press, 2001.

Kerr, Andrea Moore. *Lucy Stone: Speaking Out for Equality*. New Brunswick, N.J.: Rutgers University Press, 1992.

Kessler-Harris, Alice. *In Pursuit of Equity: Women, Men, and the Quest for Economic Citizenship in 20th-Century America*. New York: Oxford University Press, 2001.

Kett, Joseph. *Rites of Passage: Adolescence in America, 1790 to the Present*. New York: Basic Books, 1977.

Keyssar, Alexander. *The Right to Vote: The Contested History of Democracy in the United States.* New York: Basic Books, 2000.

Kincaid, James R. *Child-Loving: The Erotic Child and Victorian Culture.* New York: Routledge, 1992.

———. *Erotic Innocence: The Culture of Child Molesting.* Durham: Duke University Press, 1998.

King, Wilma. *Stolen Childhood: Slave Youth in Nineteenth-Century America.* Bloomington: Indiana University Press, 1998.

Klein, Herbert S. *A Population History of the United States.* Cambridge: Cambridge University Press, 2004.

Kolmerten, Carol. *The American Life of Ernestine L. Rose.* Syracuse: Syracuse University Press, 1999.

Kraditor, Aileen. *The Ideas of the Woman Suffrage Movement, 1890–1920.* New York: Columbia University Press, 1965; Garden City, N.Y.: Anchor Books, 1971.

Laboucheix, Henri. *Richard Price as Moral Philosopher and Political Theorist.* Trans. by Sylvia and David Raphael. Oxford: Voltaire Foundation, 1982.

Landes, Joan B. *Women and the Public Sphere in the Age of the French Revolution.* Ithaca: Cornell University Press, 1988.

Leach, William. *True Love and Perfect Union: The Feminist Reform of Sex and Society.* New York: Basic Books, 1980.

Le Beau, Bryan F. *Currier and Ives: America Imagined.* Washington, D.C.: Smithsonian Institution Press, 2001.

Leonard, Elizabeth D. *Yankee Women: Gender Battles in the Civil War.* New York: W. W. Norton, 1997.

Lerner, Gerda. *The Grimké Sisters from South Carolina: Pioneers for Women's Rights and Abolition.* Rev. and expanded ed. Chapel Hill: University of North Carolina Press, 1998.

Levander, Caroline F. *Cradle of Liberty: Race, the Child, and National Belonging from Thomas Jefferson to W. E. B. Du Bois.* Durham: Duke University Press, 2006.

Lock, Margaret. *Encounters with Aging: Mythologies of Menopause in Japan and North America.* Berkeley: University of California Press, 1993.

MacDonald, Barbara, and Cynthia Rich. *Look Me in the Eye: Old Women, Aging, and Ageism.* Expanded ed. San Francisco: Spinsters Book Company, 1991.

Malcolm, Joyce Lee. *Peter's War: A New England Slave Boy and the American Revolution.* New Haven: Yale University Press, 2009.

Marten, James, ed. *Children and Youth during the Civil War Era.* New York: New York University Press, 2012.

———, ed. *Children and Youth in a New Nation.* New York: New York University Press, 2009.

———, ed. *Children in Colonial America.* New York: New York University Press, 2007.

Martin, Asa Earl. "The Anti-Slavery Movement in Kentucky Prior to 1850." Ph.D. diss., Cornell University, 1918.

Martin, Waldo E., Jr. *The Mind of Frederick Douglass.* Chapel Hill: University of North Carolina Press, 1985.

Massey, Mary Elizabeth. *Bonnet Brigades.* New York: Alfred Knopf, 1966.

McFadden, Margaret. *Golden Cables of Sympathy: The Transatlantic Sources of Nineteenth-Century Feminism.* Lexington: University Press of Kentucky, 1999.

McFeely, William S. *Frederick Douglass.* New York: W. W. Norton, 1991.

McPhee, Peter. *The French Revolution, 1789–1799.* New York: Oxford University Press, 2002.

McPherson, James. *The Struggle for Equality: Abolitionists and the Negro in the Civil War and Reconstruction.* Princeton: Princeton University Press, 1964.

Melish, Joanne Pope. *Disowning Slavery: Gradual Emancipation and "Race" in New England.* Ithaca: Cornell University Press, 1998.

Mills, Charles. *The Racial Contract.* Ithaca: Cornell University Press, 1997.

Mintz, Steven. *Huck's Raft: A History of American Childhood.* Cambridge, Mass.: Harvard University Press, Belknap Press, 2004.

Miskolcze, Robin. *Women and Children First: Nineteenth-Century Sea Narratives and American Identity.* Lincoln: University of Nebraska Press, 2007.

Mitchell, Mary Niall. *Raising Freedom's Child: Black Children and Visions of the Future after Slavery.* New York: New York University Press, 2008.

Mitchell, Michele. *Righteous Propagation: African Americans and the Politics of Racial Destiny after Reconstruction.* Chapel Hill: University of North Carolina Press, 2004.

Murphy, Teresa Anne. *Ten Hours' Labor: Religion, Reform, and Gender in Early New England.* Ithaca: Cornell University Press, 1992.

Nash, Gary. *Forging Freedom: The Formation of Philadelphia's Black Community, 1720–1840.* Cambridge: Harvard University Press, 1991.

Newman, Louise Michele. *White Women's Rights: The Racial Origins of Feminism in the United States.* New York: Oxford University Press, 1999.

Norton, Mary Beth. *Founding Mothers and Fathers: Gendered Power and the Forming of American Society.* New York: Vintage Books, 1997.

———. *Liberty's Daughters: The Revolutionary Experience of American Women, 1750–1800.* Boston: Little, Brown, 1980.

Novak, Steven J. *The Rights of Youth: American Colleges and Student Revolt, 1798–1815.* Cambridge, Mass.: Harvard University Press, 1977.

Ogrodnick, Margaret. *Instinct and Intimacy: Political Philosophy and Autobiography in Rousseau.* Toronto: University of Toronto Press, 1999.

Okin, Susan Moller. *Women in Western Political Thought.* Princeton: Princeton University Press, 1979.

Painter, Nell Irvin. *The History of White People.* New York: W. W. Norton, 2010.

———. *Sojourner Truth: A Life, a Symbol.* New York: W. W. Norton, 1996.

Parker, Alison M. *Articulating Rights: Nineteenth-Century American Women on Race, Reform, and the State.* DeKalb: Northern Illinois University Press, 2010.

Parkinson, George P., Jr. "Antebellum State Constitution-Making: Retention, Circumvention, Revision." Ph.D. diss., University of Wisconsin, 1972.

Parry, Ellwood C., III. *The Art of Thomas Cole: Ambition and Imagination.* Newark: University of Delaware Press, 1988.

Pateman, Carole. *The Sexual Contract.* Stanford: Stanford University Press, 1988.

Peabody, Sue. *There Are No Slaves in France: The Political Culture of Race and Slavery in the Ancien Régime.* New York: Oxford University Press, 1996.

Perry, Claire. *Young America: Childhood in Nineteenth-Century Art and Culture*. New Haven: Yale University Press, 2006.

Peterson, Carla L. *"Doers of the Word": African-American Women Speakers and Writers in the North (1830–1880)*. New York: Oxford University Press, 1995.

Piersen, William D. *Black Yankees: The Development of an Afro-American Subculture in Eighteenth-Century New England*. Amherst: University of Massachusetts Press, 1988.

Poovey, Mary. *The Proper Lady and the Woman Writer: Ideology as Style in the Works of Mary Wollstonecraft, Mary Shelley, and Jane Austen*. Chicago: University of Chicago Press, 1984.

Popiel, Jennifer. *Rousseau's Daughters: Domesticity, Education, and Autonomy in Modern France*. Durham: University of New Hampshire Press, 2008.

Premo, Terri. *Winter Friends: Women Growing Old in the New Republic, 1785–1835*. Urbana: University of Illinois Press, 1990.

Preston, Dickson J. *Young Frederick Douglass: The Maryland Years*. Baltimore: Johns Hopkins University Press, 1980.

Quigley, David. *Second Founding: New York City, Reconstruction, and the Making of American Democracy*. New York: Hill and Wang, 2004.

Rabushka, Alvin. *Taxation in Colonial America*. Princeton: Princeton University Press, 2008.

Rice, Alan J., and Martin Crawford, eds. *Liberating Sojourn: Frederick Douglass and Transatlantic Reform*. Athens: University of Georgia Press, 1999.

Riley, Denise. *"Am I That Name?": Feminism and the Category of "Women" in History*. Minneapolis: University of Minnesota Press, 1988.

Riley, Matilda White, Marilyn Johnson, and Anne Foner. *Aging and Society*. Vol. 3, *A Sociology of Age Stratification*. New York: Russell Sage Foundation, 1968.

Robinson, William. *Phillis Wheatley and Her Writings*. New York: Garland, 1984.

———, ed. *Critical Essays on Phillis Wheatley*. Boston: G. K. Hall, 1982.

Roediger, David. *The Wages of Whiteness: Race and the Making of the American Working Class*. New York: Verso, 1991.

Rorabaugh, W. J. *The Craft Apprentice: From Franklin to the Machine Age in America*. New York: Oxford University Press, 1986.

Rosenfeld, Sophie. *Common Sense: A Political History*. Cambridge, Mass.: Harvard University Press, 2011.

Rotundo, E. Anthony. *American Manhood: Transformations in Masculinity from the Revolution to the Modern Era*. New York: Basic Books, 1993.

Russett, Cynthia Eagle. *Sexual Science: The Victorian Construction of Womanhood*. Cambridge, Mass.: Harvard University Press, 1989.

Ryan, Mary. *The Cradle of the Middle Class: The Family in Oneida County, New York, 1790–1865*. New York: Cambridge University Press, 1981.

———. *The Empire of the Mother: American Writing about Domesticity*. New York: Harrington Park Press, 1985.

Sanchez-Eppler, Karen. *Dependent States: The Child's Part in Nineteenth-Century American Culture*. Chicago: University of Chicago Press, 2005.

———. *Touching Liberty: Abolition, Feminism, and the Politics of the Body*. Berkeley: University of California Press, 1993.

Sapiro, Virginia. *A Vindication of Political Virtue: The Political Theory of Mary Wollstonecraft*. Chicago: University of Chicago Press, 1992.

Schiebinger, Londa. *Nature's Body: Gender in the Making of Modern Science*. Boston: Beacon Press, 1993.

Schloesser, Pauline E. *The Fair Sex: White Women and Racial Patriarchy in the Early American Republic*. New York: New York University Press, 2005.

Schmidt, James. *Industrial Violence and the Legal Origins of Child Labor*. New York: Cambridge University Press, 2010.

Schwartz, Marie Jenkins. *Born in Bondage: Growing Up Enslaved in the Antebellum South*. Cambridge, Mass.: Harvard University Press, 2000.

Scott, Joan Wallach. *Only Paradoxes to Offer: French Feminists and the Rights of Man*. Cambridge, Mass.: Harvard University Press, 1996.

Sears, Elizabeth. *The Ages of Man: Medieval Interpretations of the Life Cycle*. Princeton: Princeton University Press, 1986.

Seeber, Edward. *Anti-Slavery Opinion in France during the Second Half of the Eighteenth Century*. Baltimore: Johns Hopkins University Press, 1937.

Shklar, Judith. *Men and Citizens: A Study of Rousseau's Social Theory*. New York: Cambridge University Press, 1969.

Shteir, Ann B. *Cultivating Women, Cultivating Science: Flora's Daughters and Botany in England, 1760 to 1860*. Baltimore: Johns Hopkins University Press, 1996.

Sidbury, James. *Becoming African in America: Race and Nation in the Early Black Atlantic*. New York: Oxford University Press, 2007.

Silber, Nina. *Daughters of the Union: Northern Women Fight the Civil War*. Cambridge, Mass.: Harvard University Press, 2005.

Sklansky, Jeffrey. *The Soul's Economy: Market Society and Selfhood in American Thought, 1820–1920*. Chapel Hill: University of North Carolina Press, 2002.

Sklar, Kathryn Kish. *Catharine Beecher: A Study in American Domesticity*. New York: W. W. Norton, 1976.

———. *Women's Rights Emerges within the Anti-slavery Movement, 1830–1870: A Brief History with Documents*. Boston: Bedford/St. Martin's, 2000.

Sneider, Allison L. *Suffragists in an Imperial Age: U.S. Expansion and the Woman Question, 1870–1929*. New York: Oxford University Press, 2008.

Spadafora, David. *The Idea of Progress in Eighteenth-Century Britain*. New Haven: Yale University Press, 1990.

Stancliff, Michael. *Frances Ellen Watkins Harper: African American Reform Rhetoric and the Rise of the Modern Nation State*. New York: Routledge, 2011.

Stanley, Amy Dru. *From Bondage to Contract: Wage Labor, Marriage, and the Market in the Age of Slave Emancipation*. New York: Cambridge University Press, 1998.

Stansell, Christine. *City of Women: Sex and Class in New York, 1789–1860*. Urbana: University of Illinois Press, 1987.

———. *The Feminist Promise: 1792 to the Present*. New York: Modern Library, 2010.

Stanton, William. *The Leopard's Spots: Scientific Attitudes towards Race in America, 1815–1859*. Chicago: University of Chicago Press, 1960.

Stauffer, John. *The Black Hearts of Men: Radical Abolitionists and the Transformation of Race*. Cambridge, Mass.: Harvard University Press, 2002.

Sterling, Dorothy, ed. *Ahead of Her Time: Abby Kelley and the Politics of Antislavery*. New York: W. W. Norton, 1991.

Sundue, Sharon Braslaw. *Industrious in Their Stations: Young People at Work in Urban America, 1720–1810*. Charlottesville: University of Virginia Press, 2009.

Sweet, John Wood. *Bodies Politic: Negotiating Race in the American North, 1730–1830*. Philadelphia: University of Pennsylvania Press, 2003.

Taylor, Barbara. *Mary Wollstonecraft and the Feminist Imagination*. New York: Cambridge University Press, 2003.

Terborg-Penn, Rosalyn. *African American Women in the Struggle for the Vote, 1850–1920*. Bloomington: Indiana University Press, 1998.

Titone, Connie. *Gender Equality in the Philosophy of Education: Catherine Macaulay's Forgotten Contribution*. New York: Peter Lang, 2004.

Tomalin, Claire. *The Life and Death of Mary Wollstonecraft*. Rev. ed. New York: Penguin Books, 1992.

Trouille, Mary Seidman. *Sexual Politics in the Enlightenment: Women Writers Read Rousseau*. Albany: State University of New York Press, 1997.

VanBurkleo, Sandra. *"Belonging to the World": Women's Rights and American Constitutional Culture*. New York: Oxford University Press, 2001.

Vapnek, Lara. *Breadwinners: Working Women and Economic Independence, 1865–1920*. Urbana: University of Illinois Press, 2009.

Varon, Elizabeth. *We Mean to Be Counted: White Women and Politics in Antebellum Virginia*. Chapel Hill: University of North Carolina Press, 1998.

Wagner, Sally Roesch. *Sisters in Spirit: Haudenosaunee (Iroquois) Influence on Early American Feminists*. Summertown, Tenn.: Native Voices, 2001.

Waldstreicher, David. *Slavery's Constitution: From Revolution to Ratification*. New York: Hill and Wang, 2009.

Wallace, Maurice. *Constructing the Black Masculine: Identity and Ideality in African American Men's Literature and Culture, 1775–1995*. Durham: Duke University Press, 2002.

Watson, Harry. *Liberty and Power: The Politics of Jacksonian America*. New York: Hill and Wang, 1990.

Weiss, Penny. *Gendered Community: Rousseau, Sex, and Politics*. New York: New York University Press, 1993.

Welke, Barbara. *Law and the Borders of Belonging in the Long Nineteenth Century United States*. New York: Cambridge University Press, 2010.

Wellman, Judith. *The Road to Seneca Falls: Elizabeth Cady Stanton and the First Woman's Rights Convention*. Urbana: University of Illinois Press, 2004.

Werth, Barry. *Banquet at Delmonicos: Great Minds, the Gilded Age, and the Triumph of Evolution in America*. New York: Random House, 2009.

Whisker, James B. *The American Colonial Militia*. Vol. 2, *The New England Militia, 1606–1785*. Lewiston, N.Y.: Edwin Mellen Press, 1997.

White, Shane. *Somewhat More Independent: The End of Slavery in New York City, 1770–1810*. Athens: University of Georgia Press, 1991.

Williamson, Chilton. *American Suffrage: From Property to Democracy, 1760–1860*. Princeton: Princeton University Press, 1960.

Wingrove, Elizabeth Rose. *Rousseau's Republican Romance*. Princeton: Princeton University Press, 2000.

Wyman, Mary Alice. *Selections from the Autobiography of Elizabeth Oakes Smith*. Lewiston, Maine: Lewiston Journal Company, 1924.

Yazawa, Melvin. *From Colonies to Commonwealth: Familial Ideology and the Beginnings of the American Republic*. Baltimore: Johns Hopkins University Press, 1985.

Yee, Shirley J. *Black Women Abolitionists: A Study in Activism, 1828–1860*. Knoxville: University of Tennessee Press, 1992.

Yellin, Jean Fagan. *Harriet Jacobs: A Life*. New York: Basic Books, 2004.

———. *Women and Sisters: Antislavery Feminists in American Culture*. New Haven: Yale University Press, 1989.

Zaeske, Susan. *Signatures of Citizenship: Petitioning, Antislavery, and Women's Political Identity*. Chapel Hill: University of North Carolina Press, 2003.

Zagarri, Rosemarie. *Revolutionary Backlash: Women and Politics in the Early American Republic*. Philadelphia: University of Pennsylvania Press, 2007.

———. *A Woman's Dilemma: Mercy Otis Warren and the American Revolution*. Wheeling, Ill.: Harlan Davidson, 1995.

Zelizer, Vivianna. *Pricing the Priceless Child: The Changing Social Value of Children*. New York: Basic Books, 1985.

Zimring, Franklin. *The Changing Legal World of Adolescence*. New York: Free Press, 1982.

Articles, Chapters, and Papers

Achenbaum, Andrew. "Delineating Old Age: From Functional Status to Bureaucratic Criteria." In *The Politics of Age in America: Colonial Era to the Present*, edited by Corinne T. Field and Nicholas L. Syrett. New York: New York University Press, forthcoming.

Banner, Lois W. "The Meaning of Menopause: Aging and Its Historical Contexts in the Twentieth Century." Working paper no. 3, Center for Twentieth-Century Studies (Fall/Winter 1990).

Berthoff, Rowland. "Conventional Mentality: Free Blacks, Women, and Business Corporations, 1820–1870." *Journal of American History* 76 (December 1989): 753–84.

Bewell, Alan. "'Jacobean Plants': Botany as Social Theory in the 1790s." *Wordsworth Circle* 20 (1989): 132–39.

Blassingame, John. Introduction to *Narrative*, by Frederick Douglass. In *The Frederick Douglass Papers*, ser. 2. *Autobiographical Writings*, vol. 1. Edited by John Blassingame, John McKivigan, and Peter Hinks, xvii–xlix. New Haven: Yale University Press, 1999.

Bogin, Ruth, and Jean Fagan Yellin. Introduction to *The Abolitionist Sisterhood: Women's Political Culture in Antebellum America*, edited by Jean Fagan Yellin and John C. Van Horne, 1–19. Ithaca: Cornell University Press, 1994.

Botting, Eileen Hunt, and Christine Carey. "Wollstonecraft's Philosophical Impact on Nineteenth-Century Women's Rights Advocates." *American Journal of Political Science* 48 (October 2004): 707–22.

Bouwsma, William J. "Christian Adulthood." *Daedalus* 105 (Spring 1976): 77–92.

Bowles, Paul. "John Millar, the Four-Stages Theory, and Women's Position in Society." *History of Political Economy* 16 (1984): 619–68.

Boydston, Jeanne. "Making Gender in the Early Republic: Judith Sargent Murray and the Revolution of 1800." In *The Revolution of 1800: Democracy, Race, and the New Republic*, edited by James Horn, Jan Ellen Lewis, and Peter S. Onuf, 240–66. Charlottesville: University of Virginia Press, 2002.

Brewer, Holly. "The Transformation of Domestic Law." In *The Cambridge History of Law in America*, edited by Michael Grossberg and Christopher Tomlins, 1:288–323. Cambridge: Cambridge University Press, 2008.

Brown, Elsa Barkley. "Negotiating and Transforming the Public Sphere: African American Political Life in the Transition from Slavery to Freedom." *Public Culture* 7 (Fall 1994): 107–46.

———. "To Catch the Vision of Freedom: Reconstructing Southern Black Women's Political History, 1865–1880." In *African American Women and the Vote, 1837–1965*, edited by Ann D. Gordon and Bettye Collier-Thomas, 66–99. Amherst: University of Massachusetts Press, 1997.

Caine, Barbara. "Elizabeth Cady Stanton, John Stuart Mill, and the Nature of Feminist Thought." In *Elizabeth Cady Stanton, Feminist as Thinker: A Reader in Documents and Essays*, edited by Ellen Carol DuBois and Richard Candida Smith, 50–65. New York: New York University Press, 2007.

Carretta, Vincent. Introduction to *Complete Writings*, by Phillis Wheatley. Edited by Vincent Carretta, xiii–xxxviii. New York: Penguin Books, 2001.

Clarke, Norma. "'The Cursed Barbauld Crew': Women Writers and Writing for Children in the Late Eighteenth-Century." In *Opening the Nursery Door: Reading, Writing and Childhood, 1600–1900*, edited by Mary Hilton, Morag Styles and Victor Watson, 91–103. New York: Routledge, 1997.

Cogan, Jacob Katz. "The Look Within: Property, Capacity, and Suffrage in Nineteenth-Century America." *Yale Law Journal* 7 (November 1997): 473–98.

Coleman, Willi. "Architects of a Vision: Black Women and Their Antebellum Quest for Political and Social Equality." In *African American Women and the Vote, 1837–1965*, edited by Ann D. Gordon and Bettye Collier-Thomas, 24–40. Amherst: University of Massachusetts Press, 1997.

Collier-Thomas, Bettye. "Frances Ellen Watkins Harper: Abolitionist and Feminist Reformer, 1825–1911." In *African American Women and the Vote, 1837–1965*, edited by Ann D. Gordon and Bettye Collier-Thomas, 41–65. Amherst: University of Massachusetts Press, 1997.

Cox, Caroline. "Boy Soldiers of the American Revolution: The Effects of War on Society." In *Children and Youth in a New Nation*, edited by James Marten, 13–28. New York: New York University Press, 2009.

Crane, Elaine Forman. "Political Dialogue and the Spring of Abigail's Discontent." *William and Mary Quarterly* 56 (October 1999): 745–74.

Day, Barbara Ann. "Representing Aging and Death in French Culture." *French Historical Studies* 17 (Spring 1992): 688–724.

de Schweinitz, Rebecca. "'The Proper Age for Suffrage.'" In *The Politics of Age in America: Colonial Era to the Present,* edited by Corinne T. Field and Nicholas L. Syrett. New York: New York University Press, forthcoming.

DuBois, Ellen Carol. "Outgrowing the Compact of the Fathers: Equal Rights, Woman Suffrage and Women's Rights." In *Woman Suffrage and Women's Rights,* edited by Ellen Carol DuBois, 81–113. New York: New York University Press, 1998.

———. "Taking the Law into Our Own Hands: Bradwell, Minor, and Suffrage Militance in the 1870s." In *Woman Suffrage and Women's Rights,* edited by Ellen Carol DuBois, 114–38. New York: New York University Press, 1998.

Elder, Glen. "Life Course." In *Encyclopedia of Sociology,* edited by Edgar F. Borgatta and Marie L. Borgatta, 3:1121–26. New York: Macmillan, 1992.

Eyben, Emile. "Roman Notes on the Course of Life." *Ancient Society* 4 (1973): 213–38.

Fahs, Alice. Introduction to *Hospital Sketches,* by Louisa May Alcott, 1–49. New York: Bedford, 2004.

Fee, Elizabeth. "The Sexual Politics of Victorian Social Anthropology." In *Clio's Consciousness Raised: New Perspectives on the History of Women,* edited by Mary Hartman and Lois W. Banner, 86–102. New York: Harper, 1974.

Feinson, Marjorie. "Where Are the Women in the History of Aging?" *Social Science History* 9 (Fall 1985): 430–52.

Field, Corinne T. "'Are Women . . . All Minors?': Woman's Rights and the Politics of Aging in the Antebellum United States." *Journal of Women's History* 12 (2001): 113–37.

———. "Breast-Feeding, Sexual Pleasure, and Women's Rights: Mary Wollstonecraft's Vindication." *Critical Matrix: The Princeton Journal of Women, Gender, and Culture* 9 (1995): 25–44.

———. "'Made Women of When They Are Mere Children': Mary Wollstonecraft's Critique of Eighteenth-Century Girlhood." *Journal of the History of Childhood and Youth* 4 (Spring 2011): 197–222.

———. "'Male Citizens Twenty-One Years of Age': The Intersection of Gender, Race, and Age in Nineteenth-Century Citizenship." In *The Politics of Age in America: Colonial Era to the Present,* edited by Corinne T. Field and Nicholas L. Syrett. New York: New York University Press, forthcoming.

Formanek, Ruth. "Continuity and Change and the 'Change of Life': Premodern Views of the Menopause." In *The Meanings of Menopause: Historical, Medical and Clinical Perspectives,* edited by Ruth Formanek, 22–34. Hillsdale, N.J.: Analytic Press, 1990.

Foster, Frances Smith. "Frances Ellen Watkins Harper." In *Black Women in America,* edited by Darlene Clark Hine, Elsa Barkley Brown, and Rosalyn Terborg-Penn, 532–37. Bloomington: Indiana University Press, 1993.

———. Introduction to *A Brighter Coming Day: A Frances Ellen Watkins Harper Reader,* edited by Frances Smith Foster, 3–40. New York: Feminist Press at the City University of New York, 1990.

Franchot, Jenny. "The Punishment of Esther: Frederick Douglass and the Construction of the Feminine." In *Frederick Douglass: New Literary and Historical Essays,* edited by Eric J. Sundquist, 141–65. New York: Cambridge University Press, 1990.

Fraser, Nancy, and Linda Gordon. "A Genealogy of Dependency: Tracing a Key Word of the U.S. Welfare State." *Signs* 19 (Winter 1994): 309–36.

Frederickson, Barbara, and Tomi-Ann Roberts. "Objectification Theory: Toward Understanding Women's Lived Experiences and Mental Health Risks." *Psychology of Women Quarterly* 21 (1997): 173–206.

Frund, Arlette. "Phillis Wheatley, a Public Intellectual." Paper presented at the Black Women's Intellectual and Cultural History Collective, New York, N.Y., April 2010.

Fulton, DoVeanna. "Sowing Seeds in an Untilled Field: Temperance and Race, Indeterminacy and Recovery in Frances W. W. Harper's Sowing and Reaping." *Legacy: A Journal of American Women Writers* 24 (2007): 207–24.

Furniss, Tom. "Mary Wollstonecraft's French Revolution." In *The Cambridge Companion to Mary Wollstonecraft,* edited by Claudia Johnson, 59–81. New York: Cambridge University Press, 2002.

Furstenberg, François. "Beyond Freedom and Slavery: Autonomy, Virtue, and Resistance in Early American Political Discourse." *Journal of American History* 89 (March 2002): 1295–1330.

George, Sam. "The Cultivation of the Female Mind: Enlightened Growth, Luxuriant Decay and Botanical Analogy in Eighteenth-Century Texts." *History of European Ideas* 31 (2005): 209–23.

Gergen, Mary M. "Finished at 40: Women's Development within the Patriarchy." *Psychology of Women Quarterly* 14 (December 1990): 471–93.

Gibson, Donald. "Christianity and Individualism: (Re-)Creation and Reality in Frederick Douglass's Representation of Self." *African American Review* 26 (Winter 1992): 591–603.

Gordon, Ann D. Introduction to *African American Women and the Vote, 1837–1965,* edited by Ann D. Gordon and Bettye Collier-Thomas, 1–9. Amherst: University of Massachusetts Press, 1997.

———. "Stanton on the Right to Vote: On Account of Race or Sex." In *Elizabeth Cady Stanton, Feminist as Thinker: A Reader in Documents and Essays,* edited by Ellen Carol DuBois and Richard Candida Smith, 111–28. New York: New York University Press, 2007.

Graebner, William. "Age and Retirement: Major Issues in the American Experience." In *The Politics of Age in America: Colonial Era to the Present,* edited by Corinne T. Field and Nicholas L. Syrett. New York: New York University Press, forthcoming.

Graham, Maryemma. Introduction to *Complete Poems,* by Frances E. W. Harper. Edited by Maryemma Graham, xxxiii–lvii. New York: Oxford University Press, 1988.

Grimsted, David. "Anglo-American Racism and Phillis Wheatley's 'Sable Veil,' 'Length'nd Chain,' and 'Knitted Heart.'" In *Women in the Age of the American Revolution,* edited by Ronald Hoffman and Peter J. Albert, 338–444. Charlottesville: University of Virginia Press, 1989.

Grohsmeyer, Janeen. "Frances Harper." In *Dictionary of Unitarian and Universalist Biography.* http://www25.uua.org/uuha/duub/articles/francesharper.html/. 16 February 2008.

Gubar, Susan. "Feminist Misogyny: Mary Wollstonecraft and the Paradox of 'It Takes One to Know One.'" *Feminist Studies* 20 (Autumn 1994): 452–73.

Gundersen, Joan. "Independence, Citizenship, and the American Revolution." *Signs: Journal of Women in Culture and Society* 13 (Autumn 1987): 59–77.

Gutman, Robert. "Birth and Death Registration in Massachusetts, I, The Colonial Background, 1639–1800." *Millbank Memorial Fund Quarterly* 36 (January 1958): 58–74.

———. "Birth and Death Registration in Massachusetts, II, The Inauguration of a Modern System, 1800–1849." *Millbank Memorial Fund Quarterly* 36 (October 1958): 373–402.

Hayes, Edmund. "Mercy Otis Warren versus Lord Chesterfield 1779." *William and Mary Quarterly* 40 (October 1983): 616–21.

Heineman, Elizabeth. "Whose Mothers? Generational Difference, War, and the Nazi Cult of Motherhood." *Journal of Women's History* 12 (Winter 2001): 139–63.

Hewitt, Nancy. "From Seneca Falls to Suffrage? Reimagining a 'Master' Narrative in U.S. Women's History." In *No Permanent Waves: Recasting Histories of U.S. Feminism,* edited by Nancy A. Hewitt, 15–38. New Brunswick, N.J.: Rutgers University Press, 2010.

———. "Taking the True Woman Hostage." *Journal of Women's History* 14 (Spring 2002): 156–62.

Hinks, Peter P. Introduction to *David Walker's Appeal to the Colored Citizens of the World, but in particular and very expressly, to those of the United States of America,* by David Walker, xi–xliv. Edited by Peter Hinks. University Park: Pennsylvania State University Press, 2000.

Hunt, Eileen. "The Family as Cave, Platoon and Prison: The Three Stages of Wollstonecraft's Philosophy of the Family." *Review of Politics* 64 (Winter 2002): 81–119.

Jensen, Richard. "Family, Career, and Reform: Women Leaders of the Progressive Era." In *The American Family in Social Historical Record,* edited by Michael Gordon, 267–80. New York: St. Martin's Press, 1978.

Jones, Vivien. "Advice and Enlightenment: Mary Wollstonecraft and Sex Education." In *Women, Gender, and Enlightenment,* edited by Sarah Knott and Barbara Taylor, 140–55. London: Palgrave Macmillan, 2005.

Kaplan, Cora. "Wild Nights: Pleasure/Sexuality/Feminism." In *Sea Changes: Essays on Culture and Feminism.* New York: Verso, 1986.

Kasson, Joy S. "The Voyage of Life: Thomas Cole and Romantic Disillusionment." *American Quarterly* 27 (March 1975): 42–56.

Kelley, Mary. "'The Need of Their Genius': Women's Readings and Writing Practices in Early America." *Journal of the Early Republic* 28 (Spring 2008): 1–22.

Kerber, Linda. "The Paradox of Women's Citizenship in the Early Republic: The Case of Martin vs. Martin." *American Historical Review* 97 (April 1992): 349–78.

———. "Separate Spheres, Female Worlds, Woman's Place: The Rhetoric of Women's History." *Journal of American History* 75 (June 1988): 9–39.

Klinghoffer, Judith Apter, and Lois Elkis. "'The Petticoat Electors': Women's Suffrage in New Jersey, 1776-1807." *Journal of the Early Republic* 12 (Summer 1992): 159–93.

Lerner, Gerda. "The Lady and the Mill Girl: Changes in the Status of Women in the Age of Jackson." In *The Majority Finds Its Past: Placing Women in History,* 15–30. New York: Oxford University Press, 1979.

Lewis, Jan. "'Of Every Age Sex & Condition': The Representation of Women in the Constitution." *Journal of the Early Republic* 15 (Autumn 1995): 359–87.

Lorde, Audre. "Age, Race, Class, and Sex: Women Redefining Difference." In *Sister Outsider,* 114–23. Trumansburg, N.Y.: Crossing Press, 1984.

Marshall, Leni. "Aging: A Feminist Issue." *NWSA Journal* 18 (Spring 2006): vii–xiii.

Maynes, Mary Jo. "Age as a Category of Historical Analysis: History, Agency, and Narratives of Childhood." *Journal of the History of Childhood and Youth* 1 (Winter 2008): 114–24.

McDowell, Deborah. "In the First Place: Making Frederick Douglass and the Afro-American Narrative Tradition." In *Critical Essays on Frederick Douglass,* edited by William Andrews, 192–214. Boston: G. K. Hall, 1991.

Mintz, Steven. "Life Stages." In *Encyclopedia of American Social History,* edited by Mary Kupiec Cayton, Elliot J. Gorn, and Peter W. Williams, 2011–17. New York: Charles Scribner's Sons, 1993.

———. "Reflections on Age as a Category of Historical Analysis." *Journal of the History of Childhood and Youth* 1 (Winter 2008): 91–94.

Mitchell, Michele. "'Lower Orders,' Racial Hierarchies, and Rights Rhetoric: Evolutionary Echoes in Elizabeth Cady Stanton's Thought during the Late 1860s." In *Elizabeth Cady Stanton, Feminist as Thinker: A Reader in Documents and Essays,* edited by Ellen Carol DuBois and Richard Candida Smith, 128–54. New York: New York University Press, 2007.

Modell, John, Frank Furstenberg, and Theodore Hershberg. "Social Change and Transitions to Adulthood in Historical Perspective." *Journal of Family History* 1 (Autumn 1976): 7–33.

Moran, Mary Catherine. "Between the Savage and the Civil: Dr. John Gregory's Natural History of Femininity." In *Women, Gender, and Enlightenment,* edited by Sarah Knott and Barbara Taylor, 8–29. London: Palgrave Macmillan, 2005.

Myers, Mitzi. "Impeccable Governesses, Rational Dames, and Moral Mothers: Mary Wollstonecraft and the Female Tradition in Georgian Children's Books." In *Children's Literature,* edited by Margaret Higonnet and Barbara Rosen, 31–59. New Haven: Yale University Press, 1986.

———. "Reform or Ruin: A Revolution in Female Manners." *Studies in Eighteenth-Century Culture* 11 (1982): 199–216.

Neugarten, Bernice, and Nancy Datan. "The Middle Years." In *The Meanings of Age: Selected Papers of Bernice L. Neugarten,* edited by Dail A. Neugarten, 135–59. Chicago: University of Chicago Press, 1996.

Olson, Richard. "Sex and Status in Scottish Enlightenment Social Science: John Millar and the Sociology of Gender Roles." *History of the Human Sciences* 11 (February 1998): 73–100.

O'Neale, Sondra. "A Slave's Subtle War: Phillis Wheatley's Use of Biblical Myth and Symbol." *Early American Literature* 21 (September 1986): 144–65.

O'Neill, Daniel I. "John Adams versus Mary Wollstonecraft on the French Revolution and Democracy." *Journal of the History of Ideas* 6 (July 2007): 451–76.

———. "Shifting the Scottish Paradigm: The Discourse of Morals and Manners in Mary Wollstonecraft's French Revolution." *History of Political Thought* 23 (Spring 2002): 90–116.

Onuf, Peter. "Every Generation Is an 'Independent Nation': Colonization, Miscegenation, and the Fate of Jefferson's Children." *William and Mary Quarterly* 57 (January 2000): 153–70.

Perlmutter, Ellen, and Pauline Bart. "Changing Views of 'The Change': A Critical Review and Suggestions for an Attributional Approach." In *Changing Perspectives on Menopause*, edited by Ann Voda, Myra Dinnerstein, and Sheryl R. O'Donnell, 187–99. Austin: University of Texas Press, 1982.

Petrino, Elizabeth A. "'We are Rising as a People': Frances Harper's Radical Views on Class and Racial Equality in Sketches of Southern Life." *ATQ* 19 (June 2005): 133–53.

Pole, J. R. "Suffrage and Representation in Massachusetts: A Statistical Note." *William and Mary Quarterly* 14 (October 1957): 560–92.

Rael, Patrick. "A Common Nature, a United Destiny: African American Responses to Racial Science from the Revolution to the Civil War." In *Prophets of Protest: Reconsidering the History of American Abolitionism*, edited by Timothy Patrick McCarthy and John Stauffer, 183–99. New York: New Press, 2006.

Richardson, Alan. "Mary Wollstonecraft on Education." In *The Cambridge Companion to Mary Wollstonecraft*, edited by Claudia Johnson, 24–41. New York: Cambridge University Press, 2002.

Richardson, Marilyn. Introduction to *Maria Stewart: America's First Black Woman Political Writer*, edited by Marilyn Richardson, 3–27. Bloomington: Indiana University Press, 1987.

Richey, William. "'A More Godlike Portion': Mary Wollstonecraft's Feminist Rereadings of the Fall." *English Language Notes* 32 (December 1994): 28–37.

Riggs, Marcia Y. "African American Children, 'The Hope of the Race': Mary Church Terrell, the Social Gospel, and the Work of the Black Women's Club Movement." In *The Child in Christian Thought*, edited by Marcia J. Bunge, 365–85. Grand Rapids, Mich.: William B. Eerdmans, 2001.

Robinson, Daniel. "Theodicy versus Feminist Strategy in Mary Wollstonecraft's Fiction." *Eighteenth-Century Fiction* 9 (January 1997): 187–99.

Rupp, Leila J. "Is Feminism the Province of Old (or Middle-Aged) Women?" *Journal of Women's History* 12 (Winter 2001): 164–73.

Ryan, Patrick J. "The Competency Within: Liberalism and the History of Modern Childhood." Paper presented at the annual meeting of the American Historical Association, Washington, D.C., 9 January 2004.

Saillant, John. "'Some Thoughts on the Subject of Freeing the Negro Slaves in the Colony of Connecticut, Humbly Offered to the Consideration of All Friends to Liberty and Justice,' by Levie Hart." *New England Quarterly* 75 (March 2002): 107–28.

Schmidt, James D. "'Restless Movements Characteristic of Childhood': The Legal Construction of Child Labor in Nineteenth-Century Massachusetts." *Law and History Review* 23 (Summer 2005): 315–50.

Scott, Anne Firor. "Making the Invisible Woman Visible: A Review Essay." *Journal of Southern History* 38 (November 1972): 629–38.

Shapiro, Sam. "Development of Birth Registration and Birth Statistics in the United States." *Population Studies* 4 (June 1950): 86–111.

Shuffelton, Frank. "On Her Own Footing: Phillis Wheatley in Freedom." In *Genius in Bondage: Literature of the Early Black Atlantic*, edited by Vincent Carretta and Philip Gould, 175–89. Lexington: University of Kentucky Press, 2001.

Siegel, Reva B. "Home as Work: The First Woman's Rights Claims Concerning Wives' Household Labor, 1850–1880." *Yale Law Journal* 103 (March 1994): 1075–1217.

Smith, Hilda L. "'Age': A Problematic Concept for Women." *Journal of Women's History* 12 (Winter 2001): 164–73.

Smith-Rosenberg, Caroll. "Puberty to Menopause: The Cycle of Femininity in Nineteenth-Century America." In *Disorderly Conduct: Visions of Gender in Victorian America*, 167–81. New York: Oxford, 1985.

Sontag, Susan. "The Double Standard of Aging." *Saturday Review*, 23 September 1972, 29–38.

Stansell, Christine. "Missed Connections: Abolitionist Feminism in the Nineteenth Century." In *Elizabeth Cady Stanton, Feminist as Thinker: A Reader in Documents and Essays*, edited by Ellen Carol DuBois and Richard Candida Smith, 32–49. New York: New York University Press, 2007.

Syrett, Nicholas L. "'I Did and I Don't Regret It': Child Marriage and the Contestation of Childhood in the United States, 1880–1925." *Journal of the History of Childhood and Youth* 6 (Spring 2013): 314–31.

Taylor, Barbara. "Feminists versus Gallants: Manners and Morals in Enlightenment Britain." *Representations* 87 (Summer 2004): 125–48.

———. "The Religious Foundations of Mary Wollstonecraft's Feminism." In *The Cambridge Companion to Mary Wollstonecraft*, edited by Claudia Johnson, 99–118. New York: Cambridge University Press, 2002.

Tetrault, Lisa. "The Incorporation of American Feminism: Suffragists in the Post-bellum Lyceum." *Journal of American History* 96 (March 2010): 1027–56.

Thiebaux, Marcelle. "Mary Wollstonecraft in Federalist America: 1791–1802." In *The Evidence of the Imagination: Studies of Interactions between Life and Art in English Romantic Literature*, edited by Donald H. Reiman, Michael C. Jaye, and Ricki B. Herzfeld, 195–235. New York: New York University Press, 1978.

Treas, Judith. "Age in Standards and Standards for Age: Institutionalizing Chronological Age as Biographical Necessity." In *Standards and Their Stories: How Quantifying, Classifying, and Formalizing Practices Shape Everyday Life*, edited by Martha Lampland and Susan Leigh Sar, 65–87. Ithaca: Cornell University Press, 2009.

Tyler, Alice Felt. "Paulina Kellogg Wright Davis." In *Notable American Women: A Biographical Dictionary,* edited by Edward T. James, Janet Wilson James, and Paul S. Boyer, 1:444–45. Cambridge, Mass.: Harvard University Press, 1971.

Wach, Howard M. "A Boston Vindication: Margaret Fuller and Caroline Dall Read Mary Wollstonecraft." *Massachusetts Historical Review* 7 (January 2005): 3–35.

Wallach, Alan. "The Voyage of Life as Popular Art." *Art Bulletin* 59 (June 1977): 234–41.

Wellman, Judith. "The Seneca Falls Women's Rights Convention: A Study of Social Networks." *Journal of Women's History* 3 (Spring 1991): 9–37.

———. "Women's Rights, Republicanism, and Revolutionary Rhetoric in Antebellum New York State." *New York History* 69 (July 1988): 378–81.

Welter, Barbara. "The Cult of True Womanhood, 1820–1860." In *Dimity Convictions: The American Woman in the Nineteenth Century,* 21–41. Athens: Ohio University Press, 1976.

Winsborough, Halliman H. "Changes in the Transition to Adulthood." In *Aging from Birth to Death: Interdisciplinary Perspectives,* edited by Matilda White Riley, 137–52. Boulder: Westview, 1979.

Zagarri, Rosemarie. "Morals, Manners, and the Republican Mother." *American Quarterly* 44 (June 1992): 192–215.

———. "The Rights of Man and Woman in Post-Revolutionary America." *William and Mary Quarterly* 55 (April 1998): 203–30.

Zebrowski, Martha K. "Richard Price: British Platonist of the Eighteenth Century." *Journal of the History of Ideas* 55 (January 1994): 17–35.

Zuckerman, Michael. "The Social Context of Democracy in Massachusetts." *William and Mary Quarterly* 25 (October 1968): 530–33.

INDEX

Figures are indicated by italicized page numbers.

Made in the USA
Middletown, DE
15 November 2019